New Dimensions in Ecological Economics

New Dimensions in Ecological Economics

Integrated Approaches to People and Nature

Edited by

Stephen Dovers

*Centre for Resource and Environmental Studies,
Australian National University*

David I. Stern

Department of Economics, Rensselaer Polytechnic Institute, USA

Michael D. Young

*Policy and Economic Research Unit, Land and Water,
Commonwealth Scientific and Industrial Research
Organisation, Australia*

Edward Elgar

Cheltenham,UK • Northampton, MA, USA

Published by
Edward Elgar Publishing Limited
Glensanda House
Montpellier Parade
Cheltenham
Glos GL50 1UA
UK

Edward Elgar Publishing, Inc.
136 West Street
MIC Suite 202
Northampton
Massachusetts 01060
USA

A catalogue record for this book
is available from the British Library

Library of Congress Cataloguing in Publication Data

New dimensions in ecological economics: integrated approaches to people and nature/
    edited by Stephen Dovers, David I. Stern, Mike Young.
      p. cm.
    Includes index.
    1. Environmental economics. I. Dovers, Stephen II. Stern, David L., 1964–
III. Young, M. D. (Michael Denis), 1952–
HD75.6 N498 2003
333.7—dc21

                                 2003044097

ISBN 1 84376 079 7

Typeset by Cambrian Typesetters, Frimley, Surrey
Printed and bound in Great Britain by MPG Books Ltd, Bodmin, Cornwall

Contents

v

Figures

Tables

Contributors

Jon Barnett is a lecturer with the School of Anthropology, Geography and Environmental Studies at the University of Melbourne, Australia.

Sasha Courville is a Research Fellow with the Regulatory Institutions Network based at the Research School of Social Sciences, The Australian National University, Canberra.

Stephen Dovers is a Senior Fellow in the Centre for Resource and Environmental Studies, The Australian National University, Canberra.

Heidi Ellemor is a post-doctoral fellow with RMIT University in Melbourne, working in the Centre for Risk and Community Safety, a collaborative venture with The Australian National University and Emergency Management Australia.

Jack Knetsch is Professor Emeritus of Economics and Resource and Environmental Management at Simon Fraser University, Canada.

Stephen Lea is an economic psychologist, and is currently Deputy Vice-Chancellor of the University of Exeter, UK.

Richard Norgaard is professor of Energy and Resources and of Agricultural and Resource Economics at the University of California, Berkeley.

John Proops is Professor of Ecological Economics in the School of Politics, International Relations and the Environment at Keele University, UK.

David Stern is Associate Professor in the Department of Economics at Rensselaer Polytechnic Institute in Troy, New York.

Jeroen van den Bergh is Professor of Environmental Economics in the Faculty of Economics and Business Administration, and Professor of 'Water, Nature and Space' in the Institute for Environmental Studies, both at the Free University in Amsterdam.

Martijn van der Heide is a PhD student at the Department of Spatial Economics at the Free University and the Tinbergen Institute, both in Amsterdam.

Ekko van Ierland is Professor of Environmental Economics at Wageningen University, The Netherlands, and Chair of the Environmental Economics and Natural Resources Group.

Lorrae van Kerkhoff is a post-doctoral fellow with the National Centre for Epidemiology and Population Health, The Australian National University, Canberra.

Robert Wasson is Director of the Centre for Resource and Environmental Studies, The Australian National University, with interests in river catchment management.

Michael Young is Director of the Adelaide-based Policy and Economic Research Unit of Australia's Commonwealth Scientific and Industrial Research Organisation (CSIRO).

Preface

This book aims to inform an extended discussion of what ecological economics is, and what it could be. It does so by exploring avenues for integrative and interdisciplinary research within ecological economics as presently practised, and by considering possible links and overlaps with a range of other 'interdisciplines' that focus on sustainability problems. If it does spark discussion and even unsettle views of ecological economics, expands the catchment of ideas and methods available and connects the enterprise more to other interdisciplinary endeavours, then it will have performed a useful role.

Most of the chapters arise from papers delivered to special symposia on integrative approaches run within the International Society for Ecological Economics biennial conference held during July 2000 in Canberra. The editors thank all those who sponsored the event and assisted with its organization, the authors who have contributed to the volume, reviewers of chapters and the staff at Edward Elgar Publishing.

1. Ecological economics: prospects for integration and interdisciplinarity

Stephen Dovers, David I. Stern and Michael D. Young

This book sets out to pursue three aims as presented in the three 'dimensions' of the volume. The first presents a selection of works that review and challenge the nature of ecological economics as an interdisciplinary or integrative field, probing into what ecological economics is and could be. The second aim is to present methods and approaches for integration, to suggest what could be done. Finally, more specific applications are presented in the third dimension to further ground the discussion. In each case, we aim to push outside the normal square of ecological economics by including perspectives from elsewhere than economics and ecology (loosely defined), including from other integrative fields – *interdisciplines* – that deal with sustainability problems. In dealing with ecological economics in this way, broader issues of integration and interdisciplinarity inevitably arise. In this chapter we look forward to see how these insights can be integrated into a better and more interdisciplinary ecological economics.

For many, it is axiomatic that sustainability – the broad subject matter of ecological economics – requires non-traditional modes of research and analysis; that is, integrative or interdisciplinary approaches. The principle of policy integration – ecological, social and economic – is central to all expressions of sustainability before and after the 1992 Rio Declaration formally set out that challenge. Along with pervasive uncertainty, complexity, difficult temporal scales and the increasingly realized criticality of ecological processes, policy integration has proved hugely difficult for existing, individual disciplines wielding their specialized tool kits. In addition to its scientific aims of understanding the human-environment system, ecological economics was constructed as a response on the policy level, as set out in a foundation definition:

> *Ecological Economics* addresses the relationships between ecosystems and economic systems in the broadest sense. These relationships are the locus of many of our most pressing current problems (i.e. sustainability, acid rain, global warming,

1

species extinction, wealth distribution) but they are not well covered by any existing discipline. Environmental and resource economics, as it is currently practiced,
covers only the application of neo-classical economics to environmental and
resource problems. Ecology, as it is currently practiced, sometimes deals with
human impacts on ecosystems, but the more common tendency is to stick to
'natural' systems. *Ecological Economics* aims to extend these modest areas of overlap. It will include neo-classical environmental economics and ecological impact
studies as subsets, but will also encourage new ways to think about the linkages
between ecological and economic systems (Costanza 1989).

There are other definitions, but this one captures the overall flavour and
intent of most others and contains themes with which this book is concerned.
Integration or interdisciplinarity is a central aim of ecological economics,
given the claimed failure of single discipline approaches. So is the relevance
of the enterprise to significant policy problems such as those cited. The inclusiveness of the terms 'economics' and 'ecology' is vague and remains unclear
– probably intentionally so. The most generous use of these two terms is as
shorthand for a whole range of relevant social and natural sciences, which
invites the question of what other disciplines have purchase on sustainability
problems. If read more specifically as referring to those two disciplines alone,
the question of the role of other disciplines arises.

With that in mind, we can briefly consider the direction ecological economics has taken since then. While only a partial indicator of a discipline (or interdiscipline), what gets published can give some guide, and so the content of
ecological economics can be reflected in that of its main journal. Costanza and
King (1999) reviewed the first 10 years of *Ecological Economics*, and reminded
us of the intended characteristics of the journal: transdisciplinarity; discussion
rather than confrontation; conceptual pluralism; and a focus on problems. The
first observation from their review is the growth of the field, as represented by a
1989–99 increase in papers published from less than 20 to over 100 per year. The
journal publishes articles in sections entitled: 'Commentary, Methods (formerly
Ideological and Methodological Options), and Analysis'. The vast bulk of
papers in more recent years were classified as 'analysis' or 'commentary'.
Interestingly for this book, papers on 'methods' have remained static in numbers
over time, but proportionally now represent a very small fraction. As to who
publishes in *Ecological Economics*, economists dominate strongly, with biologists and ecologists the next largest, but relatively small, disciplinary group.
Among the smaller groups of contributors are social sciences other than
economics and natural sciences other than biology/ecology. The humanities do
not feature in this breakdown. The source of papers is, with very minor excep-
tions, the rich, developed world, and in particular North America. Papers with
multiple authors representing different disciplines – used in the review as a
surrogate for interdisciplinarity – make up one-fifth of the total.

There are a great many positive features to the growth and nature of ecological economics over the past decade; indeed, the world would be intellectually poorer in its understanding of sustainability in its absence. But taking a critical view of the indicators just cited, we can highlight the shortcomings in the ecological economics enterprise relative to its stated aims – insufficient interdisciplinarity, domination by economists from the rich world, not enough ecology and certainly little of other disciplines, and little theory or method. That may seem overly harsh, but the value of constructive criticism is to identify where things can be moved forward. The contributions in this book present strategies to address such shortcomings and this chapter distils some broader points from those contributions.

However, before turning to the themes that emerge from this book, we should return to an important starting assumption – is interdisciplinarity and integrative scholarship universally accepted as required for progressing sustainability, even if not well understood operationally? Most ecological economists think so, but it is not clear that others do as well. Perusal of a few key documents and reviews from the time of the 1992 Earth Summit in Rio de Janeiro and more recently in the lead up to the 2002 World Summit on Sustainable Development in Johannesburg suggests that interdisciplinarity is not so firmly on the agenda (OECD 2001; see UN 1992; UN Economic and Social Council 2001, 2002; UN Environment Programme 2002). Agenda 21 at chapter 35.9(a) issues a minimal instruction (UN 1992), but none of the other documents cited above explicitly state such a need even when discussing science, information and education, although to those so inclined there are some strong implicit suggestions. Most of what is said about research and education is either recognizably disciplinary, or about the better application and distribution of existing skills and capacities rather than the development of new foundational perspectives. So perhaps the integrative imperative is not as widely recognized as we might think. On top of that, integrative enterprises – interdisciplines – like ecological economics are still tiny, apostate even, and not highly influential against traditional disciplinary trajectories. Not only do the theory and practice of integration require development; the very need for it requires selling. In fact, the two tasks are linked, as nothing is more convincing of an approach or method than a solution offered.

This perusal of recent documents reveals a significant issue for those promoting integration. On the eve of the World Summit, *Nature* discussed the role of 'science' in sustainable development (Clarke 2002). This emphasized that the main game was better use of existing knowledge and, especially, delivery of existing disciplinary capabilities to poorer countries. The argument that much could be achieved in this way is convincing. When integration was mentioned, the need for local scale projects was highlighted, and the meta-issue of interdisciplinary research and integrative methods hardly rated. Such views suggest that broader integrative work in ecological economics – and in the other interdisciplines discussed below – has not made a great impact. This invites clarity as to the claims of the need for integrative relative to disciplinary research and applications.

Obviously enough, integration and interdisciplinarity are needed when other (disciplinary) approaches fail. Yet it is not evident that the demarcation between when interdisciplinarity might or might not be needed is always well understood. However, it must be if scarce resources are to be targeted well in the face of the need for more disciplinary efforts and the existence of norms and incentives in research institutions that still overwhelmingly favour traditional disciplines. Otherwise, being 'interdisciplinary' becomes only a fashionable password at workshops or, worse still, diversion therapy for failures to apply existing disciplinary knowledge. Establishing the justification for integrative approaches in specific contexts – extending the general admonishment – is necessary.

Clarity as to what 'interdisciplinary' means is needed to support that justification. Often, the distinction is made between multi- and interdisciplinary, with the former being purely *additive* and containing no potential for transformation of the contributing discipline. An environmental assessment with separate segments on different aspects typifies such an approach. Multidisciplinary approaches are often claimed to be insufficient for some sustainability problems, as the inadequacies of existing disciplines are not addressed. Simply putting together techniques without questioning their basis may be and probably will be insufficient.

Interdisciplinarity hence has the defining feature of *transformative potential*, where the particular theoretical assumptions and 'epistemological commitments' of participating disciplines are explicitly open to questioning (for a discussion, see Schoenberger 2001). Ecological economics certainly has the aim of transforming the operating assumptions of neoclassical economics, although whether an agenda exists to fundamentally alter the ecological sciences is less clear. A further characteristic of interdisciplinarity for sustainability should be, given the human-natural system interaction that defines the problem, that integration across the natural and social science divide (and arguably the humanities as well) will be especially sought after. Taking that and transformative potential as the hallmarks, interdisciplinary endeavours may consist of two or more disciplines, one or more people, a practical, theoretical or methodological problem, and an endless variety of styles of inquiry.

In this context, to contribute to the broader debate of what ecological economics is or what it might/should be and to indicate some new and emerging methodological approaches, this book presents a selection of contributions that range across disciplinary standpoints and from the general to the more specific. The intent is not to be prescriptive or comprehensive or even representative. A diverse range of perspectives is gathered, to engender debate as much to suggest particular ways forward, although individual chapters do serve the latter end. The following discussion identifies some of the themes that emerge in the book, organized through the three 'dimensions' of challenges, reorientations and approaches.

DIMENSIONS OF INTEGRATION AND INTERDISCIPLINARITY

In the first dimension of the book some big challenges are presented. It would seem that the criticisms of key features of neoclassical economics are sharper and deeper than ever. Proops opens the book in Chapter 2 with six arenas of inquiry for ecological economics in the twenty-first century, and it is not a modest menu. The stress is on the conceptual and the theoretical, on the basis that there is too much reliance still in ecological economics on theoretical underpinnings from neoclassical economics that are, he says, inadequate in many ways. Proops' recommendations would take ecological economics into the realms of the teleological, epistemological and phenomenological, where conceptualization and argument loom larger than numbers – an unfamiliar terrain for many practitioners. In Chapter 3 Norgaard emphasizes the normative element in all intellectual endeavours, and the henceforth necessary recognition of 'preanalytic visions' that structure the discourse and practice of knowledge-based (epistemic) communities. Familiarity with terminology and methods of another discipline is not sufficient for sustained engagement, which requires a deeper conceptual and theoretical understanding as well.

The normative element, or even simply recognition of the subjectivity inherent in choice of topic and research path, goes beyond *what* we seek to do and questions more deeply *why and how* we do it. The exploratory frame of inquiry discussed by van Kerkhoff in Chapter 4 places the position of the researcher-as-agent more prominently in the enterprise than would be familiar (or perhaps comfortable) to either economists or ecologists. Later in the book, Barnett et al. (Chapter 5) focus on the 'critical element' introduced to thinking about sustainability by some social sciences other than economics, and the largely (but not only) positive potential to sharpen reflexivity in interdisciplinary interactions. Exploratory and critical approaches offer an alternative to more traditional and deterministic modes of inquiry with attractive potential in the face of the complexity and uncertainty that characterizes sustainability problems. The multiple strategies recommended by an exploratory approach invite the mix-and-match of new and existing approaches and methods, some of which are reviewed and presented in the third dimension of the book.

The first dimension opens ecological economics to more than just economics and ecology, even if those are broadly construed, with some strong suggestions of new pathways. The second dimension of the book takes us further down that path, offering reorientations and openings to other disciplines and interdisciplinary endeavours. Barnett et al. review the genealogies and current features of some other, notable interdisciplines that engage with sustainability, some of which predate and overlap with ecological economics. Indeed, the comment has been made that 'ecological economics is, in my view, another name for human ecology' (Martinez-Alier 1999: 112). Alongside these mostly recent integrative fields, Barnett et al. review the potential contribution of the longest standing 'interdisciplinary discipline' – geography, reminding us that existing capacities may be overlooked in the rush to construct new approaches. Negotiating overlaps and possibilities for mutual learning across the increasing array of interdisciplines hovering about sustainability should occur more than it does. Barnett et al.'s 'essential elements of interdisciplinarity' at the very least make good discussion points. They cite a pithy definition of ecological economics by Common (1996: 7, emphasis added) as:

> an economics that takes what we think we know about our biophysical circumstances, and about *human psychology*, seriously – which standard neoclassical economics, including the sub-disciplines of environmental and resource economics, does not do.

This potential contribution of psychology is addressed in the following Chapters 6 and 7 by Knetsch and Lea, respectively. Whether understood as analogues or quite distinct enterprises, economic psychology and behavioural economics provide fresh insights into how individuals and groups behave in relation to sustainability dilemmas, and can inform policy interventions that seek to change unsustainable behaviours. Such insights are important, as public policy is one of many disciplines that have yet to comprehend and respond adequately to sustainability. Dovers in Chapter 8 describes the policy processes in a manner relevant to sustainability, showing the large range of potential contributing disciplines required to make sense of the complex, multiple and connected stages of the policy process. A policy orientation, it is argued, provides one entry into problem framing for integrative approaches to sustainability. Given that 'economics', seemingly narrowly defined, dominates the social science side of ecological economics, and that ecology, in its nature, has little purchase on policy, the contribution of other policy-oriented disciplines and their very different insights is an important question.

The policy orientation invites the third, more operational dimension of the book – frameworks, methods and applications capable of providing better purchase on at least aspects of the challenge of integration for sustainability. Within boundaries recognizable to most ecological *economists*, van der Heide et al. in Chapter 9 offer a sophisticated review of methods and approaches in view of their suitability for nature (that is sustainability) policy as opposed to narrower environmental policy. Some of these are familiar, others less so – cost–benefit analysis (CBA), safe minimum standards (SMS), integrated spatial modelling and Weitzman's ranking criterion for biodiversity. They discuss the strengths and weaknesses of each. They note that the SMS approach presents a lower barrier to resource exploitation than the much more widely expressed precautionary principle. That raises an interesting question of hierarchies and choice among approaches. Is SMS better viewed as one way of applying the more generic policy principle, the precautionary principle, or as an alternative? This begs the question of the array of other approaches that can inform policy- and decision-making in the face of uncertainty – quantitative or qualitative risk assessment, deliberative methods, performance assurance bonds, adaptive management and so on (for a discussion, see Dovers et al. 2001). If multiple theoretical approaches, methods and policy instruments are required for sustainability, as is generally proposed, then the question of filling the 'tool-kit' of diverse approaches, and of the choice of approach in specific contexts, will arise often. Choice and combination demand an understanding of the nature of different theoretical, methodological and policy options.

In Chapter 10, Stern takes an empirical approach to modelling relationships between technological change, economic production and the environment. This is a stochastic implementation of the insight that, from an ecological economic perspective, change in the quality of the environment and resources is the same as change in technologies created by humans. It can be contrasted to many extant approaches that treat technologies in theoretical, or deterministic and linear ways. We must clearly take stochasticity in human and environmental systems seriously in order to say useful things about sustainability. Wasson in Chapter 11 draws on systems thinking and associated ideas of stocks and flows from both economics (that is materials balance) and from non-ecological natural sciences to propose a general style of inquiry with interdisciplinary potential. The discussion of just how widely congruent concepts and methods dealing with stocks and flows recur across seemingly distant disciplines and professional domains is striking. This suggests we might do well to seek other conceptual common grounds to advance interdisciplinary communication, and perhaps lay the ground for further development of integrative methods.

Finally, in Chapter 12, Courville sets out two approaches to exploring trade and sustainability that take us further in applying a systems' perspective. As she notes, traditional approaches are weak on the social and ecological aspects of trade, and the integrative report card and integrative flows analysis evidence an ability to both describe complex systems and to support policy deliberation. This kind of conceptualization and detailed analysis certainly goes a long way in addressing the vision of ecological economics set out at the start of this chapter, whether that particular work is seen to fall under the rubric of ecological economics, political or economic geography, development studies or human ecology.

PROSPECTS AND OPPORTUNITIES

So to future prospects, which remain delightfully open. The future of ecological economics seems strong, with the subject matter – sustainability – hardly about to go away and the interdiscipline not lacking in participants and material for study. However, the contributions in this book illustrate that, against the chosen problem set of sustainability, ecological economics has shortcomings, many of them inevitable or understandable. How important these shortcomings are depends on our view of what ecological economics is now and should be in future.

There are disciplines not well represented in ecological economics currently, but clearly relevant to the problems being tackled: some are more obvious, like psychology, others less so but just as critical, like law and natural sciences other than ecology. Connections with other interdisciplines are less than they might be, and the fault for that lies with the others as well. In particular, some useful contributions might be made through connection with environmental history, an equally active and rapidly growing field, and from the critical perspective of fields such as political ecology. Such connections could enhance ecological economics' time depth and understanding of human agency. Finally, an apparent lack of methodological development in ecological economics, and elsewhere, is an issue, but the contributions here suggest that there is a range of viable options in addition to the many others not surveyed here. Yet methodological development between disciplines arguably needs to be preceded by greater conceptual understanding of other perspectives, even between economists and ecologists.

That brings us to two points not explored here, but key to such common conceptual understanding. The first is the position of ecology in ecological economics, where it exists as a junior partner. Ecology is a diverse, young discipline where theory and method are constantly contested (for example Dovers et al. 2001; Peters 1991). The ecology represented in ecological economics is a partial subset of the discipline – mainly various brands of ecosystem theory. For an economist to connect with one individual or a like-minded group of ecologists and assume that they have achieved coverage of that discipline is as mistaken as an ecologist presuming that all economists think the same. It is a common error to presume homogeneity in other disciplines, even while recognizing the multiple fractures in an individual's own.

The choice of interdisciplinary collaborator is a crucial one, as that will influence, if not determine, the framing of the research problem, the theory, methods and data used, and ultimately the findings of research or the content of eduction.

The second is the matter of where researchers and practitioners gain such conceptual understanding. To date most have been introduced to ecological economics after completion of their formal education. Neither undergraduate nor postgraduate education in ecological economics has received much attention, but can be argued as a most crucial activity for determining the future of the enterprise. The theory and practice of *interdisciplinary* education, postgraduate research and research supervision for sustainability requires ongoing attention to make it the art and craft, and key area of professional practice, that it should be. What ecological economics becomes in the longer term will be determined by the thinking of present and future students.

Should ecological economics be understood as the emerging big 'science of sustainability', as a more narrowly defined interdiscipline, or, as viewed by non-mainstream economists, as a new paradigm within economics, or finally, as viewed by most mainstream economists, as just another field within neoclassical economics? It is apparent that there is support for and belief in all four options within the ecological economics 'community'. At this stage, just over a decade on, to make that choice would be premature – ecological economics should not have to decide now, or even soon, what it wants to be when it grows up. Though we would certainly argue against the fourth alternative. Economics and ecology took much longer to crystallize, and ecology in particular is not yet stable even after a century. We think that single-discipline approaches are inadequate but have no guarantee that still-emerging interdsiciplinary ones will work either, or which ones will prove the most effective. Ecological economics is at present only one of a number of integrative enterprises attending sustainability problems, and the nature and scale of those problems justify and demand a diversity of approaches. For now, ecological economics would do best to remain diverse and evolving, and to seek additional perspective outside of its existing catchment.

BIBLIOGRAPHY

Clarke, T. 2002. Sustainable development: Wanted: scientists for sustainability. *Nature*. 418: 812–14.

Common, M.S. 1996. What is ecological economics? In: Gill, R. (ed). *R&D priorities for ecological economics*. Canberra: Land and Water R&D Corporation, pp. 6–20.

Costanza, R. 1989. What is ecological economics? *Ecological Economics*. 1: 1–7.

Costanza, R. and King, J. 1999. The first decade of ecological economics. *Ecological Economics*. 28: 1–9.

Dovers, S., Norton, T. and Handmer, J. 2001. Ignorance, uncertainty and ecology: key themes. In: Handmer, J., Norton, T. and Dovers, S. (eds). *Ecology, uncertainty and policy: managing ecosystems for sustainability*. Harlow: Prentice Hall, pp. 1–25.

Martinez-Alier, J. 1999. The socio-ecological embeddedness of ecological activity: the emergence of a transdisciplinary field. In: Becker, E. and Jahn, T. (eds). *Sustainability and the social sciences: a cross-disciplinary approach to integrating environmental considerations into theoretical reorientation*. London: Zed Books, pp. 112–39.

Peters, R.H. 1991. *A critique for ecology*. Cambridge: Cambridge University Press.

OECD. 2001. *OECD environmental strategy for the first decade of the 21st century*. Paris: OECD.

Schoenberger, E. 2001. Interdisciplinarity and social power. *Progress in Human Geography*. 25: 365–82.

United Nations. 1992. *Agenda 21: the UN programme of action from Rio*. New York: UN.

UN Economic and Social Council. 2001. *Implementing Agenda 21: report to the Secretary-General*. Document E/CN.17/2002/PC.2/7.

UN Economic and Social Council. 2002. *Secretary-General's note for the multi-stake holders dialogue segment of the Second Prepatory Committee, Addendum no. 8: Dialogue paper by Scientific and Technological Communities*. Document E/CN.17/2002/PC.2/6.Add.8.

UN Environment Programme. 2002. *Global environmental outlook 3: past, present and future perspectives*. London: Earthscan.

FIRST DIMENSION

Challenges and Reviews

QS7   QS8

2. Research challenges in the twenty-first century

John Proops

At the beginning of the twenty-first century, the new (inter)discipline of ecological economics seems to be flourishing. In little more than a decade it has expanded from bare beginnings to being an acknowledged arena for discussion and publication, with a steadily increasing recognition in both academic and policy circles.

As ecological economics has developed it has begun to establish both a theoretical and empirical literature, as well as a concern with environmental policy. The range of issues ecological economists have addressed is vast, ranging from ethics of the environment, through attitudinal research, valuation, to modelling and statistical analysis. However, I feel that there are some areas of ecological economics ripe for further development, and some of these are discussed in this chapter.

In 1900, the mathematician David Hilbert offered a range of challenges for twentieth-century mathematics, in the hope that these would stimulate fruitful research in what he considered to be then crucial areas. While ecological economics is radically different from Hilbert's pure mathematics (and I am certainly no Hilbert!), I also offer some research challenges for the twenty-first century, in the hope that they may stimulate discussion and research. I have six areas of challenge, as follows:

- ecosystem pricing independent of human agency;
- integrating entropy with production theory;
- teleology and sustainability;
- evolutionary principles and environmental policy;
- epistemology and environmental policy;
- phenomenology for conceptualizing human-nature interactions.

These are addressed individually in the succeeding sections of the chapter. The reader will notice that these challenges are largely theoretical/conceptual in nature. So, for example, under the first challenge, ecosystem pricing, I am not immediately seeking empirical answers to practical problems. Rather, I am

challenging the standard approach to valuing nature, and suggesting an alternative method. There are two reasons for this stress on the theoretical and conceptual. First, I am at heart a theorist, so naturally the sort of research I see as
needing work is of this nature. Second, and less related to my personal research
tastes, I am concerned that environmental theory is still largely an *ad hoc* practice. The only area where it can be said to have well-established theoretical
underpinnings is when it uses neoclassical economics, and I find this very unsat-
isfactory. This is principally because I do not believe that neoclassical economics is suited to problems with such long time horizons, or with the high levels of
uncertainty and ignorance that are typically found in human-nature interactions.
Therefore, I believe ecological economics needs to construct firm conceptual
foundations for environmental policy, which are not reliant on the standard
neoclassical paradigm. The areas that I have identified are those I believe have
much to offer the construction of these conceptual foundations.

A final word on the ordering of the following sections. I begin with areas
that are more easily related to current methods, and move steadily towards
challenges that are successively less well supported by extant methods and
literature. This progression is also reflected by the steadily diminishing
amount I have to say on each area. So the valuation issue I first raise is well
founded in the current (very extensive) literature (for example on contingent
valuation), and also derives from the long-established general equilibrium
theory, and consequently I dwell on it at some length. Later topics are less well
supported in the literature, and the limits of my own understanding of these
challenges is also more rapidly reached, so these topics are necessarily treated
at less length. However, in some sense this indicates that these areas are more
deserving of work, and probably this work would be challenging. To quote the
old saw of economic (and mathematical) analysis, 'Problems worthy of attack,
show their worth by fighting back'.

ECOSYSTEM PRICING INDEPENDENT OF HUMAN AGENCY

The first area of challenge is environmental valuation. Looking at the number
of papers and monographs published on this topic, it could probably be said that
it is the most heavily researched area of environmental economics. It might also
be felt that it is one of the most contested areas. The principal reasons for valuation methods to be contested seem to fall into three categories:

- Practical problems, such as issues of 'framing', or the way willingness-
  to-accept estimates consistently exceed willingness-to-pay estimates (cf.
  Pearce and Barde 1994; Knetsch, Chapter 6 this volume).

- Ethical concerns, arguing that certain things (for example human life, species extinction) are inappropriate for valuation. (See the special issue of *Ecological Economics*, 1995.)
- Measurement concerns, noting that the accuracy of such valuation estimates cannot be externally tested, as there is no benchmark against which to judge them. (If there were, there would be no need to estimate these values. This largely relates to the well-known problem of public goods not generating markets, so there can be no market prices for them; cf. Common et al. 1993; Knetsch 1994).

I should like to note another problem with current approaches to valuation. This relates to the fact that these methods are strictly anthropocentric, being based on welfare economics (for example contingent valuation). However, in ecological economics we might seek a broader perspective on value.

One approach is to abandon valuation altogether and rely instead on ethics as a means of bypassing the need for valuation. While I have some sympathy with this idea, I am intrigued by the notion that the interconnected nature of an ecosystem might be modelled within, effectively, a general equilibrium framework. This notion depends on the well-established general equilibrium theory from standard economics. There the prices observed in interconnected markets can be viewed, mathematically, as the 'dual' variables of the corresponding quantities of sales/purchases that occur in these markets. The theory derives from the standard method of constrained optimization, with the 'co-state' variables (or Lagrange multipliers) being interpretable as the system's opportunity costs (that is prices) (for a clear introduction to the theory, see Baumol 1977, chapter 4).

Some work has already been done in this area (cf. Hannon 2001; Klauer 2000). However, in both cases they have made some simplifying assumptions that could perhaps be eliminated. The general model I have in mind would run something like this. We generally think of prices in material terms – what we pay for a good. Economic theory tells us that there is an alternative interpretation of price – the opportunity cost of that good; that is, what we would have to forego (in some general measure) to obtain one extra marginal unit of the good. If we focus on this notion of opportunity cost, we begin to see that nature itself may have 'prices' implicit within its very operation. To measure these (immaterial and non-realized) prices we would need to have two sorts of information:

- A notion of the 'objectives' of the various parts of nature (just as in neoclassical economics, we assume that humans have the objective of maximizing utility of profit). One candidate here for species' objectives is 'evolutionary fitness'.

- An understanding of how the various parts of nature 'constrain' each other. For example, foxes constrain rabbits by eating them; rabbits constrain grass by eating it and so on.

   This information could then be cast as a constrained optimization problem, which would give rise to a 'primal' solution of the activities and relative species abundances. It would also, and more significantly, give a 'dual' solution of the corresponding shadow prices (that is opportunity costs) of each species *for the ecosystem as a whole*. The modelling of ecosystems as inter-connected systems is widely practiced in ecology, but rarely are notions of 'objectives' introduced. Thus the method I suggest can be seen as an extension of present approaches.

   There remain three theoretical problems that have yet to be addressed for this analysis, but which have been widely studied in neoclassical economics, in general equilibrium theory (cf. Arrow and Hahn 1970). The first is exis-tence; does the theory actually give rise to such prices? Second, there is uniqueness. If we could identify the opportunity cost/price of a rabbit for a fox, and of a rabbit for a wolf, would they be the same? The third problem is that of stability. If there is a unique set of natural 'prices' defined by such a system, is it one that a dynamic system would generally converge towards? At present I have no idea whether nature would be so 'well behaved' as to allow such relatively simple modelling, with the existence of unique and stable prices. But if this area of theory *could* be solved, then I believe it would hold rich promise for environmental policy.

   In particular, if we could identify these *natural* shadow prices (at least in relative terms), we might gain insights into the mismatch of these 'natural' prices compared with our 'economic' prices. I would suggest that harmony in economy-environment interactions would require that the two sets of (relative) prices be the same.

THE INTEGRATION OF THE ENTROPY PRINCIPLE WITH PRODUCTION THEORY

The entropy principle seems to be one of the foundational notions in ecologi-cal economics, with Nicholas Georgescu-Roegen as one of ecological economics 'patron saints' (to quote Herman Daly). However, from experience I know how hard it is to use the entropy principle as more than a heuristic device. (For an excellent discussion of the uses and problems of entropy analy-sis, deriving from Georgescu-Roegen's work, see the special issue of *Ecological Economics*, 1997.)

   Though the entropy concept is extremely useful for such heuristic arguments,

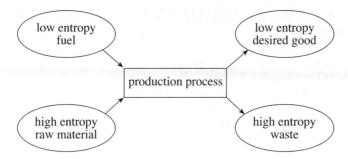

Source: Adapted from Bäumgartner et al. (2001: 366).

Figure 2.1   The thermodynamic structure of industrial production

some have argued that it offers almost nothing in the way of analytical or modelling usefulness (though for an example of such an application, see Faber et al. 1987). However, it is clear that the distance from entropy to economic theory is very great, and it would be useful if we could find a means of making a more direct link. I believe the theory of joint production could be that link.

Why joint production? Because the entropy law tells us that to produce wanted low-entropy goods we *must* produce high-entropy wastes (Faber et al. 1998; Baumgärtner et al. 2001). This is illustrated in Figure 2.1. On the left-hand side the material inputs to production are shown, while the corresponding material outputs are shown on the right-hand side.

The second law of thermodynamics tells us that the outputs from such a production process must have greater entropy than the inputs. Also, if we note that most produced goods have relatively low specific (that is per unit mass) entropy, then it becomes clear that *some* output must carry away the high entropy. Therefore, with any produced low specific entropy good, there *must* be a jointly produced high specific entropy waste.

Perhaps this offers some opportunities for ecological economics. First, it gives an access from standard production theory, especially those approaches that are easily adapted to joint production (for example activity analysis, cf. Koopmans 1951; neo-Austrian capital theory, cf. Faber et al. 1999). Second, it offers a way that the insights into the role of entropy of Georgescu-Roegen and other scholars can be given some purchase on actual production processes, and thence on policy formulation. Finally, this approach may be able to act as one of the foundations of a theory of 'waste', which is so far lacking in ecological economics (though see Baumgärtner 2002).

In summary, if we recast the second law as joint production, perhaps we have a bridge to economic theory, and also a language for policy analysis, which is firmly rooted in physical reality.

A TELEOLOGICAL APPROACH TO SUSTAINABILITY THEORY

'Sustainability' is a concept that has gone down a storm (for an excellent overview of the concept, see Pezzey 1992). But how do we achieve sustainability? The usual approach is to set up 'indicators of sustainability', which tell us if things are getting better or worse (for example Neumayer 2001; Ekins and Simon 2001). However, they do not tell us whether things are *becoming sustainable*. In particular, sustainability must be about the *overall* pattern of human production and consumption, not just about any one piece of the picture. I suggest that a way forward, in making sustainability a *practical* concept, is to start not with the present state of the world, but rather with the state of the world we hope to achieve. That is I think we need to be oriented to a goal or *telos*; we need to be 'teleological' (cf. Faber and Proops 1998, chapter 8; Faber et al. 1995).

Being teleological or goal-oriented need not mean being inflexible. So if we take a certain state of the world as the goal to be pursued, it would be foolish in the extreme to be bound by this goal, despite the emergence of new knowledge. Rather, the goal or telos will need to evolve as experience is gained. However, *without* a notion of a goal, I find it hard to see that sustainability is either a practical concept or an achievable end.

How might teleology be used in environmental policy? Following Proops et al. (1996), I think that an 'overall goal of sustainability' could be defined (which may be rather abstract); this could give rise to an 'operational goal of sustainability' in the long term, which would be much more practical in its nature. In the shorter term, there would need to be a 'goal towards an intermediate target', which would take society along the path towards the 'operational goal'. The role of decision-makers would be to attempt to 'steer' society and its effects on nature, using the 'overall goal' as akin to a constitutional requirement. The 'operational goal' would define the broad outline of an agreed target (provisionally sustainable) outcome. The practicalities of policy would be based on the 'intermediate target', and this would evolve over time, as the success (or failure) of current policies towards sustainability became apparent. However, so far the implementation of sustainability into policy has not even begun. Perhaps such a teleological approach could be used to 'kick-start' policy in a sustainable direction.

THE INTEGRATION OF EVOLUTIONARY PRINCIPLES INTO ENVIRONMENTAL POLICY ANALYSIS

A major challenge facing ecological economics is change. In particular, technical change is causing economy-environment interactions to alter rapidly. For example, over the last 100 years (a very short time historically and geologically), humans have come to rely on oil as a principal fuel. In even more recent times, the demand for timber has been one of the causes of extensive global deforestation.

One way of approaching these changes in technology is to adopt an evolutionary perspective and terminology (Faber and Proops 1998; Norgaard 1984). The nature of the underlying economic and social system can be thought of as being the 'genotype' or potentialities of the system. This genotype gives rise to an observable set of phenomena, deriving from these potentialities; that is the 'phenotype'.

While the notions of genotype and phenotype were originally developed for biological systems, they clearly have a wider interpretation. For economic systems, we can think of the techniques available, the natural resources, consumer tastes, the legal system, and so on, as constituting the genotype. The phenotype is the outcome of this genotype; that is the quantities and prices of produced goods, resource depletion and pollution, income distribution and so on.

I consider this approach potentially fruitful for two reasons. First, it explicitly allows for the emergence of novelty in human-nature systems, through the (unpredictable) changes that occur in the genotype. For biological systems, in the long run, this would be the emergence of new species. For economic systems, in the much shorter run, it could be because of the invention of new techniques, or because of changing consumer tastes. A wider appreciation of the importance of novelty (and other forms of unpredictability) would therefore be brought to the fore, indicating the limits to modelling and prediction (discussed further in the next section).

The second reason I favour the use of an evolutionary perspective is that employing these notions for ecological economics and policy analysis opens up two potential lines of communication: to the biological sciences, where evolutionary concepts originated, and to evolutionary economics, which is developing some of these notions, though not from an environmental perspective.

EPISTEMOLOGY AND ENVIRONMENTAL POLICY-MAKING

The role of knowledge seems to me to be very problematic for many environmental issues. Indeed, it could even be said that the one thing we can be sure about is how little we know – we are most knowledgeable about our ignorance! (For a preliminary analysis of some of these issues, see Faber et al. 1992.) However, so far these problems of knowledge, or epistemology, have been addressed in a rather piecemeal fashion, which means that while we may recognize that there are epistemological limits to environmental policy analysis, we have no clear notion of where these limits lie, or what they imply for the conceptual foundations of environmental policy-making.

For example, the above brief discussion of an evolutionary perspective shows that the process of invention is a source of irreducible 'ignorance'; there is no way that we can predict the invention of new techniques (as an accurate prediction would be to make the invention!). Another area of modern research that illustrates irreducible ignorance is the existence of 'chaotic' systems. These are dynamic systems that have *infinite* sensitivity to their initial conditions. If there is even the slightest deviation from an initial starting point, the later dynamics of the system produce a time path that is *completely uncorrelated* with the original path. That is, approximate knowledge of the system allows no prediction of the system's behaviour.

Given this sure knowledge of our ignorance, how can we use it rationally, in formulating environmental policies? Clearly, problems of knowledge reflect back on the teleological approach discussed earlier, and I suggest that combining a teleological approach with an explicit recognition of our ignorance may go some way to setting sustainability policy on firm epistemological foundations.

PHENOMENOLOGY AS A NEW APPROACH TO CONCEPTUALIZING HUMAN-NATURE INTERACTIONS

Here I start to get on shaky ground. On the other five challenges I have done some preliminary work myself, and from my background in physics and economics, I see at least some potential directions for travel. For these areas, I have some preliminary 'mental maps'.

However, in the branch of philosophy known as phenomenology, I am very much an amateur (the fundamental texts are Heidegger 1962; Husserl 1999; Merleau-Ponty 1962). What I have read, though, has made me very excited. In this I have been mainly stimulated by the wonderful work of Jane Howarth (for example Howarth 1995). Briefly, phenomenology starts from the 'phenomena', not 'theories'. While in ecological economics we usually start with a notion of 'nature', as distinct from 'us', phenomenology would reject this dichotomy. Indeed, it would even reject the distinction between 'subject' and 'object'. As Howarth (1995: 24) puts it:

> Phenomenology rejects the distinction between inner and outer. For the phenomenologist, phenomena are not contents of the mind. Phenomena have to do with ways of being-in-the-world, prior to distinguishing between the being and the world. The characters of the beings and the world are as they are because of their connectedness.

It seems to me that this approach could give us new ways of conceptualizing the world, which would allow us to move away from the ecocentric/anthropocentric debate, and by dissolving current distinctions, allow us to find a new way of thinking about nature and our 'natures'. For example, Howarth discusses Heidegger's notion of 'dwelling' and Merleau-Ponty's term 'body-subject' to illustrate that phenomenology offers a very fresh way of addressing humans and nature (though space here does not permit any further discussion of these terms; see Howarth, 1995: 25–8). What could phenomenology offer to ecological economics? As a newcomer to the area, let me give the final word on this to Howarth (1995: 29–30):

> [T]he phenomenological understanding would not be geared to manipulation and control, that is, to the pernicious and avoidable kind of anthropocentrism. It would be geared to recognizing what is of value and significance in our lives. If we were more explicitly aware of this, we might be more able to detect comparable value and significance in the lives of all living things.

CONCLUDING REMARKS

While I have offered six challenges, I was keenly aware that they represent only a small fraction of the theoretical and practical issues confronting ecological economics. However, at least from my perspective, these problems have the merit of being identifiable and potentially useful, so I hope they provide some stimulus and food for thought.

REFERENCES

Arrow, K. and Hahn, F. 1970. *Competitive general equilibrium analysis*. San Francisco: Holden Day.

Baumgärtner, S. 2002. Thermodynamics of waste generation. In: Bisson, K. and Proops, J. (eds). *Waste in ecological economics*. Cheltenham: Edward Elgar, pp. 13–37.

Baumgärtner, S., Dyckhoff, H., Faber, M., Proops, J. and Schiller, J. 2001. The concept of joint production and ecological economics. *Ecological Economics*. 36: 365–72.

Baumol, W. 1977. *Economic theory and operational analysis*. 4th edn. Englewood Cliffs: Prentice Hall.

Common, M., Blamey, R. and Norton, T. 1993. Sustainability and environmental valuation. *Environmental Values*. 2: 299–334.

Ekins, P. and Simon, S. 2001. Estimating sustainability gaps: methods and preliminary applications for the UK and the Netherlands. *Ecological Economics*. 37: 5–22.

Faber, M., Niemes, H. and Stephan, G. 1987. *Entropy, environment and resources: an essay in physico-economics*. Heidelberg: Springer-Verlag.

Faber, M., Manstetten, R. and Proops, J. 1992. Humankind and the environment: an anatomy of surprise and ignorance. *Environmental Values*. 1: 217–41.

Faber, M., Manstetten, R. and Proops, J. 1995. On the conceptual foundations of ecological economics: a teleological approach. *Ecological Economics.* 12: 41–54.

Faber, M. and Proops, J. 1998. *Evolution, time, production and the environment.* 3rd edn. Heidelberg: Springer-Verlag.

Faber, M., Proops, J. and Baumgärtner, S. 1998. All production is joint production. In: Faucheux, S., Gowdy, J. and Nicolaï, I. (eds). *Sustainability and firms.* Cheltenham: Edward Elgar, pp. 131–58.

Faber, M., Proops, J. and Speck, S. 1999. *Capital and time in ecological economics: neo-Austrian modelling.* Cheltenham: Edward Elgar.

Hannon, B. 2001. Ecological pricing and ecological efficiency. *Ecological Economics.* 36: 19–30.

Heidegger, M. 1962. *Being and time.* (Trans. Macquarrie, J. and Robinson, E.) Oxford: Basil Blackwell.

Howarth, J. 1995. The crisis of ecology: a phenomenological perspective. *Environmental Values.* 4: 17–30.

Husserl, E. 1999. *The idea of phenomenology.* (Trans. Hardy, L.) Dordrecht: Kluwer.

Klauer, B. 2000. Ecosystem prices: activity analysis applied to ecosystems. *Ecological Economics.* 33: 473–86.

Knetsch, J. 1994. Environmental valuation: some problems of wrong questions and misleading answers. *Environmental Values.* 3: 351–68.

Koopmans, T. (ed). 1951. *Activity analysis of production and allocation.* New York: Wiley.

Merleau-Ponty, M. 1962. *Phenomenology of perception.* (Trans. Carr, D.) Evanston, IL: Northwestern University Press.

Neumayer, E. 2001. The human development index and sustainability – a constructive proposal. *Ecological Economics.* 39: 101–14.

Norgaard, R. 1984. Coevolutionary development potential. *Land Economics.* 60: 160–73.

Pearce, D. and Barde, J.-P. (eds). 1994. *Valuing the environment.* London: Earthscan.

Pezzey, J. 1992. Sustainability: an interdisciplinary guide. *Environmental Values.* 1: 321–62.

Proops, J., Faber, M., Manstetten, R. and Jöst, F. 1996. Achieving a sustainable world. *Ecological Economics.* 17: 133–5.

Special Issue. 1995. *Ecological Economics.* 14: 67–159.

Special Issue. 1997. *Ecological Economics.* 22: 171–312.

QS7

3. Passion and ecological economics: towards a richer coevolution of value systems and environmental systems

Richard B. Norgaard

Environmental economists are 'dispassionate' and 'focus on matters of fact,' and 'some aspects of ecological economics do not fit this mold (Trudy Ann Cameron, in a Letter to *Science* 1997).

The models of environmental economists 'do not inform us of the consequences of exercising our passions, should we wish to do so' (Richard B. Norgaard, Letter in Reply to *Science* 1997).

Ecological economists think it is important to sustain functioning social and ecological systems for the future of humankind. We accept that systems have thresholds before they transform and limits before they crash. In a world of great and increasing inequity, we think justice is a central issue. And, yes, we are passionate about these shared working tenets. Different academic communities stress different issues, and these are inevitably intertwined with their shared passions. Entomology attracts people who think insects are interesting and important; engineering attracts people who like to build. For the last few decades, economics has attracted people who are fascinated by market solutions. Ecological economics attracts people who think natural and social systems are complex and justice is important. Our 'problem' is that we are 'a new kid in the academic neighbourhood' and a little different, even self-consciously so, and thus we stand out. The more established academic communities are taking notice because we start from different premises. Some, ignoring their own culture of embedded beliefs, are crying 'passion, passion', warning all that we do not gaze out on reality objectively from some god-like position. Their response is a normal part of the sociology of modern science. Nevertheless, it is important that we consciously respond to such cries of 'passion' when they arise.

New endeavours such as ecological economics provide highly visible examples of scholars grappling with the long-standing complexities between knowledge and values. It is important to note that we have always made our values explicit. The introductory chapter to the book that followed from the first biennial meeting of the International Society for Ecological Economics was titled 'Goals, agenda, and policy recommendations for ecological economics' (Costanza et al. 1991). After more than a decade since the founding of the International Society for Ecological Economics, I would like to provide one perspective on how we are doing (see also Costanza, 2001).

Herman Daly (1996) tells a wonderful story of his efforts to have a small correction made in a diagram of the macroeconomy in the draft of the 1992 World Bank Report on sustainable development. The macroeconomy, he argued, works within and is constrained by the larger natural system, the availability of ecological services providing material and energy inputs and pollution control and sinks. The World Bank economists made various efforts to respond to his arguments without also forsaking their own beliefs. To admit at the outset that the economy was a subsystem of a larger system raised a whole series of questions about economies and their growth that the Bank economists did not want to consider. No compromise proved possible, and in the end they simply eliminated the diagram from the report. Four decades ago, I received a grade of 'C' in my first macroeconomic course for asking quite similar questions about the 'real' basis of economic growth. Daly, building on Schumpeter's argument about the importance of one's preanalytic vision when thinking about business cycles, argues that making progress towards sustainable development is largely a matter of changing our preanalytic vision. In my opening paragraph I used the term 'shared working tenets'; others have referred to 'worldview', but for this address I pay homage to Schumpeter and Daly while perhaps stretching the term 'preanalytic vision'.

In the following sections, I briefly comment on: (1) the necessity of preanalytic visions and their relation to values; (2) the nature and source of the preanalytic visions of ecological economics; (3) the implications of our preanalytic visions to how we think about value; and (4) the possibilities for moving towards a richer coevolution of value systems and environmental systems.

THE NECESSITY OF PREANALYTIC VISIONS AND THEIR RELATIONS TO VALUES

Preanalytic visions are necessary simply because we cannot know all of reality. We cannot incorporate its complete complexity into our thinking. Each analytical model starts from a vantage point and focuses on some aspect of reality. Assumptions must be made about how that aspect, or vision, relates to the whole and about how the whole functions in relation to the particular aspect, or vision, under study. Thus, to some extent, scientists have different preanalytic visions because they use different models with different foci and have to account for different things that are not in their models through their preanalytic vision. Even given a focus, however, whether one preanalytic vision is correct, or even better than another, cannot be determined by reasoning alone, for reasoning itself depends on adapting a preanalytic vision. Nevertheless, we can update our preanalytic vision as knowledge develops in the disciplines around us, and ecological economists are challenging the larger profession to do just this. We find the preanalytic vision of economists to be pre-ecology; to a large extent it is simply out of date. Furthermore, new information and good reasoning can help us better compare and ponder the implications of alternative starting visions. So, preanalytic visions are not purely relative. We do have information to go on.

It is also important, however, to realize that the relation between models and preanalytic visions are not simply matters of fact. The choice of an analytic model and its corresponding preanalytic vision entails the value judgement that the model selected focuses on the most important, that is most valuable, things. How things are represented in a model also entails value judgements. Macroeconomic models may aggregate labourers as the total number of individuals employed or as the total wages paid. Each approach entails putting weight on, or valuing, people differently. Preanalytic visions are further enriched in order to go from analytical findings to policy recommendations. Policy analyses incorporate the preanalytic vision used in the determination of what 'is', or 'could be', but taking the next step to recommending what 'should be' requires additional assumptions. Economists, for example, share preanalytic visions with respect to how values are aggregated and whether winners and losers net out across policy recommendations or whether compensation between winners and losers is really necessary or not. Again, these assumptions made in the process of going from what 'is' or 'could be' to 'ought' entail value judgements.

Scholars and practitioners – professors of silviculture and professional foresters, physicists and engineers, biologists and wildlife managers, economists and policy analysts – work largely in separate epistemic communities. Each epistemic community's efforts to 'focus on matters of fact' are built on the preanalytic visions necessarily associated with the formal models they share. By looking at communities of scholars, however, we also see the role of culture and history, not simply formal models, in the evolution of preanalytic visions. Epistemic communities learn together, practise together, and reinforce and pass on to the next generation their preanalytic visions. As economists assumed greater roles in government in the later half of the twentieth century, the preanalytic visions supporting policy analysis arose and gained greater importance.

Few, however, are aware that they have preanlaytic visions because most spend nearly all of their time within or close to their discipline working with people who share the same visions. This lack of awareness makes it very difficult for those in one epistemic community to work in another. They soon realize that something is 'wrong' with the way the other community reasons. The preanalytic visions clash, but only a few realize that their reasoning too is predicated on a preanalytic vision.

In this respect, ecological economists are unusual. Those with stronger training in economics are consciously aware of its dominant preanalytic visions of economics, have rejected them and have chosen to work from start-ing points more familiar to environmental scientists. Those with stronger train-ing in the environmental sciences and their associated preanalytic visions have chosen to work with economic models. And, in these choices, both are more conscious of their preanalytic visions and likely to realize they have made value judgements.

As we develop educational programmes in ecological economics itself, fewer ecological economists will be making transitions between epistemic communities and be so conscious of the preanalytic visions of their new group. Yet, another feature of what binds us together provides hope that we will continue to be more aware than other epistemic communities. Ecological economics is consciously methodologically pluralistic (Norgaard, 1989a). So long as this is perpetuated in the training of future ecological economists, they too will have to grapple with the explanatory and value incongruities implicit between the structure and preanalytic visions of different ecological and economic models.

I have made an implicit parallel argument that the 'fact-value dichotomy' on which positivist analysis supposedly rests is largely false. Positivism, the belief that science can and should be value-free, dominates modern under-standings. Let me discuss how we contradict this understanding more explic-itly. I would not deny that gravity, or even our understanding of it, exists apart from human values. I am, however, arguing that we cannot extend our under-standing of the concept of facts derived from studying physical systems to studying highly complex and evolving systems, especially those containing people acting on their values.

Let me tell another story. I attended a late twentieth-century workshop of economists and ecologists on how to integrate socioeconomic and ecological systems. Early in the meeting, a well-established economist spoke out that we needed to keep the scientific aspects of our work free of value judgements, saving the normative analysis, the parts dealing with values, until the end of research projects. No one questioned this statement even though the workshop was about the interaction of socioeconomic and ecological systems. Surely, values are integral, indeed driving forces, of socioeconomic systems and thereby of how they interact with ecological systems. As such, values are not something that can be considered after the facts. And indeed participants in the workshop did discuss quite openly how values interact and coevolve with other factors affecting the environment. Equally importantly, the participants shared each other's values and were quite conscious of this. We were able to come together and work effectively with each other because we all valued biological diversity and functioning ecosystems and wanted to pass a naturally rich and complex world on to our children. Nevertheless, as scientifically trained people, we shared a heritage of 'positivism', a strain of philosophy that argues, among other things, that science is about facts that stand apart from values. The contradictions between our positivist heritage and the systemic thinking about social and environmental systems that our interdisciplinary group espoused to do occasionally impeded our advance, but only a few participants seemed to sense a glimmer of the contradictions.

Different academic communities have different ways of rationalizing how they fit within a positivist tradition. Those who work across epistemic communities are more likely to be conscious of how different communities have different rationales as to how their work fits the fact-value dichotomy. I acknowledge the concern of many within ecological economics that we need to develop these rationales also, that we cannot challenge so many scientific beliefs and also hope to be effective in a world still largely framed by such beliefs. This makes even talking about values in a fundamental way difficult for many of us. Philosophical and pragmatic realism are clearly not in harmony here. I find myself operating in different modes – positivist and non-positivist – for different audiences, and I suspect that this will be necessary for some time to come.

THE NATURE AND SOURCE OF OUR PREANALYTIC VISION

We are a diverse group using different formal models, with different histories, working in different cultures. Thus, I run some risk in trying to identify the preanalytic vision for all of us. I am, however, less concerned with being 'right' than with keeping a critical conversation going. With that caveat, let me foolishly rush in and argue that though any one of us may not put great emphasis on each of the following starting positions, collectively our preanalytic vision holds that:

- Economies and the global economy overall require energy, materials and diverse genetic/species/ecosystem patterns and reproductive capacities provided by a healthy biogeophysical system, and
  - current levels of energy use, material flows, and genetic/species/ecosystem loss are both unnecessary to a good life and a threat to the health of the biogeophysical system.

- Economies and the global economy overall require healthy social systems, and
  - current levels of material inequity are both immoral and a threat to healthy social systems, and
  - current rates of economic change, especially 'globalization,' are outpacing our abilities to socially adapt and thereby threaten healthy ecosystems.

With respect to the main points, I have consciously used the term 'healthy system' deliberately, relying on our understanding of health as humans and stretching the metaphor to cover a great number of characteristics of larger systems that are difficult, indeed ultimately impossible, to specify (for a critique of the use of the term 'ecosystem health' see Lackey, 2001). Faced with this difficulty, some ecological economists argue that specific indicators such as energy use or material flows or pollution thresholds, or biodiversity are adequate indicators of ecosystem health. Presumed relationships between such specific indicators and the complexity of reality are critical aspects of their preanalytic vision. My effort to provide a more encompassing, albeit more vague, preanalytic vision acknowledges that no single formal model provides an aggregate vision for ecological economics as a whole.

The preanalytic vision of economists, as Daly (1996) points out, does not include our central two points with respect to biogeophysical and social systems. The fact that ecological economists are explicit about biogeophysical and social systems reflects that we inherently value natural and social communities. Ecological economists are concerned when there are changes in these systems. Economists, on the other hand, view the material and social worlds at worst as parts with no systemic nature and dynamics of their own or, at best, as mechanical systems where no parts are ever lost and all changes in configuration are reversible. Again, by not putting the economy within larger natural and social systems, economists are implicitly not valuing natural and social systems *per se* and can discuss their transformation passion free.

When challenged, economists have addressed biogeophysical systems, or simply the loss of their parts, by amending their preanalytic vision with the assumption that capital produced through the economic system can substitute, without limit, for what might be viewed as similar to such capital in biogeophysical systems. Our response to their position has been twofold, one explicit, the other implicit and both deserve elaboration.

First, economists and other technological optimists may prove to be correct with respect to the possibilities for continual substitution between produced and natural 'capital'. We contend, however, that, on the one hand, the burden of proof should be on them, and, on the other, that with only one planet suitable for people that we know of, the experiment should not be run. This, of course, is a value judgement, but one we freely make. Second, and more implicit and more clearly a value judgement, ecological economists prefer a people-in-nature world over a people-above-nature world. Similarly, we prefer a people-in-society world over an individuals-above-society world. We value healthy social and biogeophysical systems *per se* (realizing again that 'healthy' hides many contentious issues). Note that I have included 'sub-points' that are even more clearly value judgements under the main points of our preanalytic vision with respect to both biogeophysical systems and social systems. I think it is correct to include them as prior beliefs and as integral to our preanalytic vision. There are corresponding values integral to the preanalytic vision of mainstream economists that stem from historic beliefs in how science allows us to 'rise above' nature and how material progress helps all live a better life. Whether we see people as in nature or rising above it is not simply an issue of fact but of preference as well. Similarly, I find my moral concern with inequity and strategic concern that inequity threatens the health of social systems are difficult to separate. In any case, these value judgements help us select and frame the research efforts that contribute to the ecological economics literature just as surely as historic beliefs that change is progress and therefore good affect the research and literature of mainstream economists.

Let me now elaborate on how ecological economists have come to a different preanalytical vision. I see three interrelated paths. First, many of us have personal reasons, special attachments to nature or community or experience with inequity, that motivate us to question the worldview of most economists. Second, ecological economics is new and we have not inherited the visions of many ancestors and our history as 'inside actors' is still very thin. Third, and closely related to the first two, it is easier for us to incorporate new empirical evidence that contradicts dominant beliefs about nature and society directly into a new preanalytic vision rather than simply respond to new information from historic positions.

Much of our preanalytic vision is rooted in the ecological and environmental sciences more broadly, hence the appropriateness of 'ecological' as a modifier to 'economics'. Our concern with human communities and how these are threatened by inequity and the speed and nature of current economic change, however, are nurtured by our broader roots in the social sciences. To my knowledge, the intertwining of these two roots into one preanalytic vision is nearly unique to participants in ecological economics and owes much of its richness to the combination of scholars interacting through the International Society for Ecological Economics over the last decade. It is difficult to define ecological economics by approaches we take, for we take so many. Since ecological economists use many of the models of neoclassical economics, it is not the models that distinguish us. But I think we can find a defining coherence forming around a common preanalytic vision that is distinctive.

Let me emphasize again that ecological economists have been relatively free to choose from diverse historical roots. The preanalytical vision of economists of most other persuasions, on the other hand, has been closely tied to their longer histories, largely dating to the nineteenth century. The preanalytic vision of economics became well established before ecology arose as a serious science in the middle of the twentieth century. On the other hand, there are also moderately recent historical reasons why so many economists pay so little attention to equity. In the middle of the twentieth century, welfare economics was adapted to provide theoretical justification for ignoring equity issues as economists assumed a greater role in public policy analysis. At about the same time, economists became significant players in the rise of international development efforts that assumed that the best way to reduce poverty was through growth. We should acknowledge that as ecological economists age and perhaps become more involved in framing and implementing new institutions, we too will have a history to defend. This process is like growing old in that it is better than the alternative.

IMPLICATIONS OF OUR PREANALYTIC VISION TO VALUES AND VALUATION

Given the preanalytic vision I have suggested ecological economists cohere around, it is clear why our understanding of values is setting us off on a new course, a new adventure.

First, we recognize that different values are embedded in our different frameworks of analysis and that each allows us to see some types of values better than others. Thus, we understand that multiple approaches will give us a richer understanding of values than a single approach. This does not mean that each ecological economics research project should use multiple approaches, though this can be very insightful. It does mean that we are respectful of different approaches and the information they provide. It also means that perfecting a single approach will still only lead to a perfect, partial understanding.

Second, one of the most pernicious but absolutely inevitable ways that values are embedded in analyses is through the aggregation of data. Aggregation is a necessary part of simplification. Economists are accustomed to aggregating labourers according to the wages they earn, capital by its value in the market at current interest rates and resource flows by their current prices. We accept current market indicators as measures of value, and we find this necessary even when undertaking a study of market imperfection or inequity. Nor is the dilemma limited to economic studies. Epidemiologists when presenting health data for policy analysis, for example, might differentiate how an air pollutant affects the mortality of children from that of adults, or how one pollutant interacts with another in different populations. However, only a bare minimum of the details of the different environments and lives of people actually affected can be presented for public understanding before the information overwhelms the public, or even policy-makers. There is no way around what I have referred to as the values-aggregation dilemma (Norgaard, 1989b), but being aware of it can certainly help us discuss what might be hidden by particular aggregation decisions.

Third, for ecological economists, sustainability is a 'prior', in essence a 'higher', value than those indicated by the prices that equilibrate the market. We have shown with purely neoclassical models that sustainability is a matter of the rights of future generations. I find it amusing that the overlapping generations model of sustainability that Richard Howarth and I (1992) have espoused over the last decade has been labelled by an environmental economist as an 'ecological economics approach' (Krautkraemer, 1998). By arguing that sustainability is a distributive question requiring a form of moral reasoning beyond economics, we have crossed an epistemic cultural line. Yet every time economists introduce a social welfare function, which is less common than it used to be, values beyond those of economics are implicit. Economists simply choose not to discuss them.

Fourth, we take equity seriously, and not simply the intergenerational equity necessary for sustainability. Had Larry Summers (1991) been an ecological economist, he would not have written his infamous memo while he was in the World Bank suggesting that polluting industries 'should' move to developing countries. Taking equity seriously means we recognize the contradictions between accepting the 'polluters-pay-principle' for policy purposes and accepting 'willingness-to-pay' in contingent valuation analyses. It means we should initiate what neoclassical economists should have been doing all along, developing ways of modelling alternative efficient economies under different asset distributions for use in policy analysis. This is proving to be much more work than simply taking the existing income distribution as given and doing cost–benefit analysis. This is a very important path to continue to pursue because we do not think marginal adjustments are sufficient for addressing environmental and social problems. We are not simply a little out of adjustment and should not undertake analyses using assumptions that presume we are.

Fifth, by accepting the systemic nature of social and ecological systems, that they cannot simply be represented as the sum of their parts, means that we cannot always accept the approach that social values are simply the sum of individual values. Some values are collective in nature because they can only be understood and experienced collectively. What does it mean for an individual to value biodiversity when our understanding of biodiversity indicates it is largely a public good? How can a typical individual understand biodiversity adequately to value it when so much of our understanding is concentrated in the hands of field biologists, indigenous peoples and genetic researchers? As that knowledge has been shared more widely over the last 25 years, individuals have begun to value it. We need, however, to recognize that we value biodiversity because of a particular historical social process of shared learning about the importance of biodiversity to all of us that occurred in the last 25 years alone. On what basis can we assume that our understanding of the importance of biodiversity, or other subjects, is now complete?

TOWARDS A RICHER COEVOLUTION OF VALUE AND ENVIRONMENTAL SYSTEMS

By emphasizing the importance of social and environmental systems, I think we are also acknowledging that values coevolve and reproduce in the context of social and environmental systems. In my own work, I have represented this as a specific aspect of the coevolution between social and environmental systems (Figure 3.1). The important point is that we do not take values as simply stemming from individual preferences that are independent of how we interact in society and nature.

Now let me make a critical argument using a coevolutionary preanalytic vision. The positivist, utilitarian approach to values dominant in economics (knowledge) has favoured the selection of the market over other types of social organization. This in turn has favoured the use of individual, materialist values, which in turn has favoured markets and utilitarian explanations

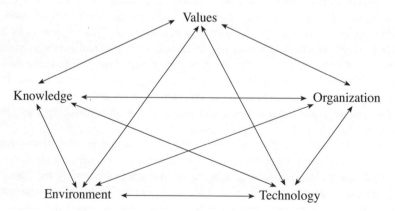

Figure 3.1   The coevolutionary development process

of values. In other words, how economists think about values has been coevolving with individualism, materialism and markets, all reinforcing how economists think about values, materialism and markets. Each has been making the other more dominant in their respective areas represented in Figure 3.1. And in positive analysis, the better the description fits 'reality', the more 'correct' it is. And from here many further conflate what 'is' with what 'ought' to be.

Indeed, economists argue that it is people choosing, acting on preferences, that expands choice through markets and diminishes the role of other forms of social organization. Because people's values are driving this outcome, how could economists possibly prescribe another direction? Certainly, in their mind the burden of proof that something is wrong must be borne by those who are concerned about the status quo. Positive analysis has not become prescriptive by some magical process on its own. The values were there in the first place. And thus we see how the values inherent in ignoring larger social and environmental systems in the first place also reinforce themselves.

Ecological economics offers the possibility of a richer understanding of values into our knowledge system that may help sustain the remaining richness of our social organization and the ways it supports value richness. We may also facilitate new developments that could help diversify social organization itself. Our theorizing supports the further development and use of juries to deliberate values, risk and the appropriateness of new technologies. It provides rationales for integrating people without western scientific credentials into learning and valuing processes. These new ways of making choices will never fully substitute for markets, but they could complement them and support coevolution towards social and environmental system richness rather instead of the sterility of shopping mall culture.

CONCLUSION

Ecological economists should retain their passions and openly defend them. They should also stand ready to adjust them as new concepts and information arise. We had neither sufficient conceptual nor empirical bases to have a passion for biodiversity 25 years ago. At that time, many of us still hoped that equity would trickle down. Few defended cultural diversity. Our understanding and values have coevolved with each other along with how history has unfolded, which itself has coevolved with our understanding and values. Surely being conscious of the relationships between the systems of understanding, value systems, systems of social organization, technological systems and environmental systems is better than not being conscious.

BIBLIOGRAPHY

Cameron, T.A. 1997. Environmental economics and ecological economics. Letter to the Editor. *Science*. 277 (18 July): 300.

Costanza, R. 2001. Visions, values, and valuation, and the need for an ecological economics. *BioScience*. 51: 459–68.

Costanza, R., Daly, H.E. and Bartholomew, J.A. 1991. Goals, agenda, and policy recommendations for ecological economics. In: Costanza, R. (ed). *Ecological economics: the science and management of sustainability*. New York: Columbia University Press, pp. 1–20.

Daly, H.E. 1996. Introduction. *Beyond growth: the economics of sustainable development*. Boston: Beacon.

Howarth, R.B. and Norgaard, R.B. 1992. Environmental valuation under sustainable development. *American Economic Review*. 82: 473–7.

Krautkraemer, J.A. 1998. Nonrenewable resource scarcity. *Journal of Economic Literature*. XXXVI: 2065–107.

Lackey, R.T. 2001. Values, policy, and ecosystem health. *BioScience*. 51: 437–43.

Norgaard, R.B. 1989a. The case for methodological pluralism. *Ecological Economics*. 1: 37–57.

Norgaard, R.B. 1989b. Three dilemmas of environmental accounting. *Ecological Economics*. 1: 303–14.

Norgaard, R.B. 1997. Economics and informed passions. Letter. *Science*. 277 (29 August): 1186.

Summers, L. 1991. Memo to economists within the World Bank dated 21 December.

FURTHER READING

This chapter was prepared for delivery as an opening plenary address to the International Society for Ecological Economics Conference, Canberra, July 2000, without references. While specific references have been added for this publication, the following publications elaborate some of the general points in greater detail.

Norgaard, R.B. 1994. *Development betrayed: the end of progress and a coevolutionary revisioning of the future*. London: Routledge.

Norgaard, R.B. 2002. Optimists, pessimists, and science. *BioScience*. 52: 287–92.

Norgaard, R.B., Scholz, A. and Fleisher Trainor, S. 2001. Values, valuing processes, and valuation. In: Ekko C. van Ierland, Jan van der Straaten, Herman R. J. Vollebergh (eds). *Economic growth and valuation of the environment*. Cheltenham, UK: Edward Elgar, pp. 151–69.

Various Authors. 2001. Special Issue: Scientific objectivity, value systems, and policy-making. *BioScience*. 51 (6): 433–95.

Q 57

4. Beyond disciplines: exploring exploratory research as a framework for integration

Lorrae van Kerkhoff

Calls for research to become more 'integrated' are now commonplace in Australia, following a global trend. In recent years growing numbers of authors have commented on the changing nature of research, as relationships both among scientists, and between scientists and 'end-users', 'stakeholders', 'clients' or 'customers' have become characterized by closer and closer engagement. However, while boundaries are arguably getting blurrier and barriers to greater cooperation are getting smaller, the impact of these changes on research methodologies, methods and processes – how you actually *do* integrative research – are lagging. Integrating research in such a way that the potential benefits of collaboration and cooperation can be reaped is a conceptual and methodological challenge as well as an institutional one.

This chapter is concerned with the conceptual, methodological challenge, and draws heavily on my own research. In particular it is based on my experiences of doing a qualitative study centred on exploring the concept of integrated research, and how it was being applied in two hybrid, quasi-virtual research organizations, both Australian Cooperative Research Centres (CRCs). These Centres were good examples of integrated research in practice. Indeed, they operated under a formal mandate to do integrated research (Commonwealth of Australia, 2000), although it was not clearly defined what that was. They were quasi-virtual, in that they had a 'core' office and several core staff who were employed by the Centres, but the research was carried out by various partner organizations: universities, government research agencies, industry partners and so forth. The CRC Program had operated for almost 10 years when my research started, and was a well-established and highly respected part of the Australian research community, not least for its efforts to bridge the gaps between academia and research users. As such, they were prime examples of a much broader, worldwide trend: integrated research in action.

Yet, it is not the outcomes of that study that are focused on in this chapter, but rather my own reflections on the research process *I* undertook in attempting to do integrated research about integrated research. As such this chapter is not about CRCs (although they were undoubtedly influential in shaping my thinking) but about the basis of my own research design, the methodological proposition that exploratory research can be a highly integrative process. To do this I draw a contrast between interdisciplinary research and exploratory research, and illustrate that each are integrative in different ways. Drawing on my own research, I then focus on exploratory research as a possible framework for integration that is often overlooked or downplayed, but one as yet insufficiently articulated to serve as a reliable guide to research design. The aim of this chapter is to make some progress towards that articulation.

A 'TYPICAL' RESEARCH APPROACH?

The implication of the calls for integrated research methods and methodologies is clearly that integrative research is somehow different from conventional research. Consequently, to draw an effective contrast, it may be useful to start with a brief overview of a conventional research process, and then indicate how integrated approaches may differ. A 'normal science' research process is often described as some variation of Figure 4.1.

First, the researcher establishes their philosophical stance towards the nature of the world and how we come to know and understand it. This forms

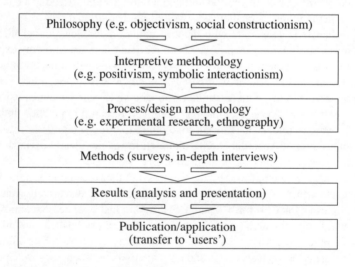

Source: Adapted from Crotty (1998) with permission.

Figure 4.1   A common process of research decision-making and design

a preliminary set of assumptions about what legitimate research is, and what it is trying to achieve. In disciplinary research this is often a decision made elsewhere and by others – researchers must be consistent with the philosophical stance of their discipline. (For example, biophyiscal scientists often go to great lengths to establish the objectivity of their research, where social researchers often deny that objectivity is possible.)

Next, these assumptions are refined or formalized via interpretive methodologies. Methodologies serve two purposes in research that are often conflated in discussion and reporting, but may be quite distinct in practice. Methodologies can act as guidelines to appropriate ways of gathering data ('process' or 'design' methodologies) or as guidelines on interpreting it (interpretive methodologies), or both. Crotty refers to the latter as 'theoretical perspectives' (p. 7), formalizations of assumptions about the world that underpin research. These underpinnings are taught early, as the fundamental bases on which the disciplines stand, and are often simply assumed (or perhaps forgotten). Few economists, for example, need to specify that their work is based on a characterization of people as rational, utility-maximizing human beings when writing a paper or presenting to peers. These assumptions are more specific than (but must be consistent with) the preceding philosophical assumptions. In other words, the choice of interpretive methodologies is restricted by the philosophies that went before it, although it need not be determined by them. As shown in Figure 4.1, examples of theoretical perspectives include symbolic interactionism and positivism.

Research process or design methodologies places the methods – actual data collection techniques – within a framework considered appropriate given the assumptions already built in. Again, these are nested within the larger categories: a positivist/objectivist could choose to carry out experimental research with a control group to establish causality, or carry out statistically based research to work out probabilities. Again, decisions of research design will be made according to the assumptions the researcher wishes to make about the subject, and the relative importance or relevance of different issues within the general subject area.

In other words, conventional research processes can be described as the progressive accumulation of simplifying assumptions about the topic being investigated. As noted earlier, the 'higher level' assumptions about philosophy and interpretive methodologies are often implicit, forming parts of the disciplinary infrastructures being both used and adhered to. These disciplinary infrastructures direct attention towards some issues and hide others, and shape the ways we understand which issues or aspects of real-world complexity are most relevant. The results of this approach tend to be fragments of detailed understanding, delineated by the sets of assumptions that have been made. It is through these assumptions that the messiness of the real world gets progressively pared back to simpler units of analysis until the research question or problem is 'do-able'.

This approach is usually referred to as 'reductionist' (Capra 1982). The shortcomings of reductionism in natural resource management have become increasingly apparent as natural resource managers struggle to shape those fragments into something relevant to the complex world in which they must act. As Kinzig et al. (2000) have recently noted in a report to the National Science Foundation, 'to reach a comprehensive understanding of crucial human-environment interactions, disciplinary analysis must be complemented by interdisciplinary research – spanning the natural, social, behavioural and engineering sciences' (p. 1). The need for research that deals with the bigger picture has supported many calls for research beyond the disciplines, and several responses to this have emerged. At a generic level, these can be differentiated in terms of issues and approaches.

Issues and Approaches

As the assumptions built in to disciplines highlight some aspects of the world and render others invisible (or at least irrelevant), they are often closely allied to particular issues or dimensions of day-to-day life. Indeed, it is possible to view research as a combination of *approaches* as they are applied to certain *issues*. For example, economics as a research *approach* is about understanding and predicting the behaviour of utility-maximizing human beings under conditions of resource scarcity. It can be directed towards *issues* such as market analysis, economic growth forecasts and business management – issues that are concerned with the flow of resources throughout society. Breaking research down into issues (subject matter, topics) and approaches to investigating those issues (disciplinary views of the world) yields the four categories illustrated in Figure 4.2.

| | | Approaches | |
		One	Many
Issues	One	Disciplinary research	Multi-, inter- transdisciplinary research
	Many	Disciplinary exploratory research	Transdisciplinary exploratory research

Figure 4.2   Issues and approaches in research

A researcher or research team can choose to apply a single approach to a single issue, which most commonly describes disciplinary research. They could apply a single approach but attempt to remain open to many possible issues that may emerge from its application – applying a sociological approach to the broad subject area of technological innovation may be an example of this. This could be categorized as disciplinary *exploratory* research.

Alternatively, researchers could combine more than one approach towards a single issue, stepping into the realm of inter-, multi- or transdisciplinary research. Research that has been classified as 'problem-solving' or 'problem-oriented' often takes this form. In Australia, the development of the National Carbon Accounting System (NCAS) is an example of this. The issue of carbon accounting was relatively clearly understood in terms of what was needed (a system for measuring biomass-based carbon sinks and fluctuations), and a range of scientists from many relevant disciplines each contributed to its development.

Finally, when the 'problem' is not clear, and there are many potential issues of concern with complex or largely unknown interrelations, researchers can deal with this uncertainty and complexity by being open to adopting several disciplinary approaches. This type of research falls in the fourth quarter, one that is not as easily labelled as the others. As it is exploratory in its aim to investigate across 'issue' boundaries, and transdisciplinary in that it attempts to cross disciplinary boundaries, I have called it transdisciplinary exploratory (TDE) research. TDE research may be used where problems are only vaguely identified, but can also be used when problems are unknown. In my research, which I discuss in more detail below, it was not clear that there were 'problems' to be solved – rather there were processes to be investigated that may or may not have been problematic.

In the right-hand column of Figure 4.2 the methodological assumption-setting questions of Figure 4.1 are no longer built in as invisible disciplinary infrastructure, but are open for change. By stepping out of the purely disciplinary realm, the research process can no longer be assumed, but needs to be made explicit and justified on some basis other than disciplinary convention. In terms of countering the fragmentation of conventional disciplinary research, at a broad level two different integrative processes can be readily identified. These are illustrated in Figures 4.3 and 4.4.

In Figure 4.3, the additive approach, integration is achieved when the bits of information that are already known about the subject area are juxtaposed and perhaps actively reworked to achieve a more complete understanding. For this to be possible, the box that all the pieces fit into (representing the topic area or problem) must already be fairly well identified. In other words, the problem itself sets the boundaries within which multi- or interdisciplinary

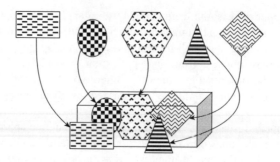

Figure 4.3   An additive approach to integrated research

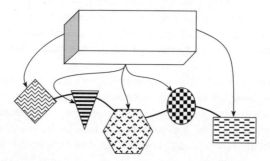

Figure 4.4   An exploratory approach to integrated research

research can identify gaps or overlaps, seek synergies and perhaps model some broader processes than would have been possible before.

In Figure 4.4, the exploratory approach, the whole situation (as far as possible) is investigated first, to see which information bits emerge as significant. These bits may then be developed more fully using disciplinary or inter-, multi- and trans-disciplinary tools. Little needs to be known about the box beforehand, and links between separate topics that emerge may be preserved.

While there has been considerable investigation and writing on the former model, Figure 4.3, in the context of multi-, inter- and transdisciplinary science (for a recent summary, see Bradshaw and Bekoff 2001) there has been little written on exploratory research in general, and even less on transdisciplinary exploratory research in particular. Given the potential advantages in developing research frameworks that allow for rigorous scoping of broad issues rather than detailed pursuit of particular issues, as well as the risks of sliding into a personal, 'unscientific' quest, there is a strong need to reflect and learn from efforts to do this less common type of research.

Consequently the remainder of this chapter will draw heavily on my own attempts to do 'transdisciplinary exploratory' research. Using my experiences as a point of reflection and illustration, I focus on the early steps of exploratory research design. Beyond these first steps it becomes difficult to generalize, as the later steps are ultimately dependent on the first three.

EXPLORATORY RESEARCH: A CASE AND SOME PRINCIPLES

Researching What? Early Boundaries

As mentioned earlier, my area of research interest was driven by informal observations of a trend in environmental research funding away from single discipline or even interdisciplinary work towards research that actively 'integrates' scientists with various non-science communities. While still nascent in some arenas (such as coastal research) and more widely used in others (the agricultural sector, for example), the extent of these changes was growing rapidly. Yet their consequences had not been examined in any systematic way. In general, it appeared that the benefits of this type of research were largely assumed, and potential (or actual) problems were often overlooked.

Yet, despite many examples of scientific organizations, including CRCs, trying to implement research structures that actively and cooperatively attempt to cross 'scientific' and 'non-scientific' boundaries, the literature about this topic (more specifically, the lack thereof) suggested that practice was outstripping theoretical understandings of the processes involved and their outcomes. Consequently, the area appeared ripe for investigation, as greater empirical study and theoretical understanding could be used to help inform this rapidly growing area.

Which Discipline? Which Issues?

In the initial stages of my research, I tried to establish which disciplinary approach would best suit my research topic. It was clear that the disciplinary approaches that had been used to study science and scientific research were many and varied, including:

- sociology of science/scientific knowledge;
- anthropology;
- organization studies;
- natural resource management;
- agricultural extension;
- economics;

- political science;
- philosophy of science;
- psychology and so on.

To return to an earlier point, in attempting to decide which approach was best suited to my research area, I was essentially trying to decide which issues within my general topic were most important, as each discipline prioritized one issue over others. The issues included:

- relationships;
- culture;
- management;
- outcomes;
- science communication;
- power;
- efficiency;
- competing ontologies and epistemologies;
- coping with complexity and so on.

In light of the newness of this research area, I had no way of telling which issue was most important – it was not at all clear to me that the assumptions entailed in selecting one disciplinary approach over any other were justified. There was a need to carry out some preliminary, exploratory research as a scoping study, to form an empirical base from which assumptions about disciplines and further methods and methodologies could be drawn. As such this study fell into the transdisciplinary exploratory quarter of Figure 4.2.

A TRANSDISCIPLINARY EXPLORATORY RESEARCH PROCESS

Having conceptualized this research as transdisciplinary and exploratory, I then needed to work out how this impacted on the research process itself – what constitutes a transdisciplinary exploratory approach? It should be stressed here that this is an *approach* or a framework for research design, rather than an actual research methodology. Like 'interdisciplinary' research, the TDE approach outlined here is an overarching research structure within which appropriate methodologies can be situated.

To understand my own starting position in the study, I asked myself a series of key questions. These are summarized in Figure 4.5, and approximate to the first steps of Figure 4.1. They are given here as questions and decisions about rationale and boundary-setting, operationalisation, and implementation.

Step 1: Rationale

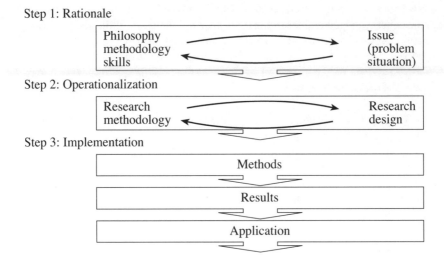

Step 2: Operationalization

Step 3: Implementation

Figure 4.5   An exploratory research process

Step 1: Rationale and Boundary Setting

In the absence of discipline- or problem-based assumptions to limit the study, boundaries were still needed to be set to ensure the work was 'do-able'. At the same time the researcher needs to come to some (perhaps vague) understanding of their own preconceptions, to sensitize them to how they might affect the research. In my study, the first step was to ask 'What do I perceive needs greater understanding?' and 'How can I best contribute to that understanding?' While these questions in themselves are quite straightforward, and are commonly confronted by all researchers, they seldom figure prominently in the documentation of research methodologies. Explicitly including them as methodological decisions reflects the more personalized dimension of TDE research.

Asking these two questions simultaneously creates a balance and counterbalance between the researcher's preconceived notions of the issue to explore, and the skills, philosophies and techniques they can bring to explore it, each of which narrow the field of methodologies that could be used in operationalization and implementation. It also acknowledges that these two traditionally academically separate categories (research 'content' and research 'process') are often closely intertwined and can jointly influence how a project is framed. In my case, as a researcher trained in qualitative methods, I tend to see areas in terms of their qualitative research potential ('Who can be interviewed here?

Where are the rich sources of data?' and so on). The interactions between researchers' understandings of the topic area and their own skills and preferred methodologies need to be actively incorporated into the research design process, rather than leaving these interactions unexamined.

Step 2: Operationalization

Operationalization is about designing the research in an academically rigorous way. It is this step that primarily distinguishes TDE from other types of research. Given the boundaries set in the first step, a broad topic and a methodological starting point, operationalization draws on both of these in the development of a research plan. In this instance, I looked towards how a qualitative approach could inform my chosen research area. My questions at this point were 'How can I best achieve that understanding?' and 'How can my contribution to understanding be formalized?'. This echoed the first step in that it once again generated a tension between personal, perhaps intuitive but certainly informal, understandings and the need to step away from the purely personal towards formal processes that test the researcher's own assumptions.

At this stage, five principles were used to shape my research design while attempting to capture the integrity of being exploratory and transdisciplinary (whatever that integrity might be). While these principles were developed from my own social research, and hence have a 'sociological flavour', the broad themes presented here are not necessarily restricted to social research but can be applied to a range of TDE contexts.

Start Broad and Narrow Down: Iterative Research Design

The breadth and uncertainty of a TDE research area indicates that the researcher needs to start by looking at a wide range of issues that can be progressively narrowed down to more specific topics of particular relevance. Effectively, this means building empirically justified assumptions – not empirical in the sense of statistical validity, but in the sense that they are based on investigation of practical experiences rather than theoretical abstraction or, worse, guesswork.

An iterative research design allows wide-ranging exploration of broad areas that are then focused in an iterative cycle as relevant issues are identified and pursued in more detail. Iteration allows a researcher to justify the issues they decide to focus on. These issues may not necessarily be the most 'important' or pervasive. In my research, for example, significant issues that fell into established research domains such as economics or organizational studies could be bracketed aside as issues that could be fruitfully pursued in a disciplinary framework. Other issues that did not fall neatly within such boundaries but were nonetheless significant could also be targets of iterative processes.

Prioritize practice, not theory

As extant academic theory (like the disciplines it springs from) highlights certain issues and topics at the expense of others, in TDE research it needs to be treated cautiously. By initially focusing on practice, what is happening in the field, so to speak, rather than theory-coloured views on how that practice can be explained, the researcher can limit the temptation of plausible theories to provide a ready-made interpretation. While it is not possible for researchers to be 'theory-neutral' they can, at least, try to avoid being 'theory-driven'. This gives a certain amount of freedom to pursue the most interesting, least understood phenomena, rather than focusing on those that 'fit' existing theories.

In the context of social research, it is also important to note that the people who participated in my study had their own theories about what they were doing and why. These 'folk' theories also needed to be understood with respect to my own developing theoretical understandings. By prioritizing practice (what people do) over theory (what they say they do, and why), it was possible to continually check my own interpretation, to some extent.

In sociological research, this approach is akin to 'grounded theory' (Glaser and Strauss 1967; Strauss and Corbin 1998), and 'adaptive theory' (Layder 1998), as well as techniques such as convergent interviewing (Dick 1986). Readers familiar with these methodologies will recognize similar principles here. Certainly these methodologies and methods offer valuable guidance *if* the researcher wishes to use sociological methods, particularly qualitative ones (although they may offer useful advice to other methods, too). However, again, TDE research is not restricted to sociological methods and approaches – nor even to human-focused phenomena. The philosophical assumptions embedded in each of those methodologies are not necessary here; in terms of broad principles it is just as possible to develop a positivistic, biophysically based TDE research project as it is to develop a sociological one. It might be argued, for example, that bio-prospecting for pharmaceuticals from natural ecosystems such as rainforests and coral reefs adopts a TDE approach, where new research frameworks are being applied.

Theory-generating, not hypothesis-confirming

To say that practice is prioritized over theory is not to say that theory can or should be fully set aside. Indeed, the research process could be described as one of theory creation, articulation, modification and refinement. The boundary-setting of Step 1 lays out a rough-and-ready theory derived from informal observation. This theory is provisional, constantly modified and increasingly

targeted in certain directions, challenged through the focus on action and practice, and gradually developed into a more robust form.

However, there is no formal 'hypothesis' to be tested, unless it is of such a
vague and general form as 'There's something interesting going on here'!
While it may be useful to think of the research development process in terms
of hypotheses, the work is not finished when a hypothesis is disproved. Rather
hypotheses need to be constantly revised, changed and developed – indeed, a
set of robust hypotheses may well be the end point of TDE research rather than
the starting point. Again, this iterative and developmental process is similar to
the process described within the social research context as 'adaptive theory'
(Layder 1998).

Look for diversity, as well as sameness
To have rough-and-ready theories or understandings develop into more robust
ones requires careful investigation of contradictions and challenges. In TDE
research it is more important to encompass the diversity of possibilities, rather
than excluding statistical outliers or aberrant views. Difference is valuable, and
needs to be sought and pursued as consistently as sameness. In my study, for
example, understanding why two people disagreed with my perception of a situation could offer far more insight into the shortcomings of my perception (or the
complexity of the context around it) than of the 10 who do agree. Designing
research to capture diversity as well as sameness has a particularly strong influence on the methods selected for data collection, which is discussed in Step 3.

Reflecting on purpose
Other authors have written on the need for the interdisciplinary researcher to
be reflective, or reflexive, as an acknowledgement of the deeply personal
nature of research. This is perhaps even more important in TDE research,
where it is easy to generate vast amounts of tenuously connected data. Purpose
can serve as an 'anchor' in this sea of data.

In my study I found it useful to periodically revisit and reflect on what I
wished to achieve by undertaking this study. That I wanted to develop theoretical tools that were useful both academically and practically shaped the
issues I saw in my data as having potential for further investigation. Perhaps
transdisciplinary research is, if not problem- or theory-driven, purpose-driven.
Being clear about what those purposes are can help deal with the uncertainties
inherent in this type of research.

Step 3: Methods

These guiding principles, in turn, shaped the selection of my actual methods.
While there is nothing inherent in the principles to dictate 'you should use

these methods' – that is, after all, the whole point – they do point out some issues in terms of selecting appropriate techniques and tools.

Start with complementary methods
To cover the diverse range of possible issues, it is unlikely that a single method will cover all potentially relevant aspects of a situation. Choosing complementary methods can increase the coverage of the data collected. This is not triangulation in the classical sense of using different methods to confirm a single result, but using multiple methods to explore different dimensions.

In my research I used three different methods in the initial iteration to try to cover three different aspects of personal relationships: qualitative interviews, participant observation and document analysis. These three data collection methods open doors to different (but connected) dimensions to life in a work setting. They complement each other in providing a more complete picture from which to develop theoretical understandings.

Sampling for difference
Data sample methods need to allow the researcher to generate pictures of diversity as well as patterns of sameness. However, most data collection and analysis techniques focus on identifying sameness – representative sampling techniques, for example. Specific techniques and methods may be needed to counteract the tendency to exclude the outlying statistics.

For example, within the methods I chose I used purposive sampling techniques to ensure that my data were as inclusive as possible, maximizing the likelihood of different voices being heard. While purposive sampling can sometimes be accused of being a 'biased' sampling technique, sampling purposively to maximize diversity can reduce the researcher's bias toward scertain 'mainstream' people or issues at the expense of others.

Maintain interconnections
There are few established methods available to counter the tradition of scientific fragmentation. Consequently, it is very easy for researchers to compartmentalize their subject areas – after all, that is what the bulk of research training encourages researchers to do. To maintain a sense of interconnectedness between issues may require specific methods or analytical tools; social research examples include actor networks; others may be integrated assessment, or integrated modelling. Even if some (or most) of the connections are bracketed aside from the main development of the research project, acknowledging these links may help future research, or perhaps existing research, see new explanations for difficult, cross-disciplinary issues.

'Test' and refine theory

Once they have begun to take shape, the researcher's theories can then be 'tested', or investigated in more detail to see whether they hold up to closer scrutiny. In social research this may mean taking theories back to the field to get responses from people who contributed data earlier in the process, or to new participants. This is not to say that research participants necessarily have any 'right of veto' over theories, although in some methodologies this may be appropriate. In biophysical research, testing may be incorporated through fairly standard research procedures such as replication. Regardless, tests that can balance the researcher's original theoretical constructs need to be included in the research design.

WIDER IMPLICATIONS OF TRANSDISCIPLINARY EXPLORATORY RESEARCH

Needless to say, these brief points probably raise many more questions about the implementation of transdisciplinary exploratory research than they answer. Certainly there is a long way to go before TDE can become an 'off-the-shelf' research framework if, indeed, that is ever possible. In this final section I turn to brief consideration of some of the wider implications of this research.

Justification

How can a researcher justify that this approach was to be preferred over more conventional types of research? Conventional justifications for taking an 'exploratory' research approach may apply – examining new issues, for example. Important for my study, however, was the presence of theoretical confusion, where the prevailing view of the relationship between science and non-science stakeholders and publics had collapsed, and there were many competing perspectives vying to take its place. In this case, adopting a single-discipline approach – even an exploratory one – would have meant aligning my research project with one of those competing perspectives, and would have limited my results.

Academic Rigour

Implicit throughout this chapter has been the question of academic rigour. One of the largest challenges with transdisciplinary exploratory research is doing the research in a way that conforms to general standards of academic rigour. From the perspective of the researcher, it is a relatively simple exercise to go and talk to a few people and get some ideas about what is going on, but much more complex when any outcomes need to meet criteria that are, at this general level, poorly defined. In the absence of clear disciplinary criteria, how do you assess the quality of this research?

Inevitably, compromises have to be made in carrying out different types of research. The freedom and flexibility provided by an exploratory approach is often described by critics as weak methodology and poor design. While in many cases they may be correct, the potential benefits of this approach to research suggest that it deserves further development. Better understanding of what is lost and what is gained in undertaking transdisciplinary exploratory research may help. Ultimately, though, the question of how to assess when a satisfactory level of academic rigour has been achieved is open.

WHERE FROM HERE?

Exploratory research is currently a greatly underutilized, but potentially highly productive integrative research approach. To date, lack of clarity as to what this style of research is designed to achieve, as well as a general suspicion of work that runs counter to (still popular) reductionist science, have rendered it a risky and largely unrewarded process. Further development of a TDE framework may help to diminish the stigma and increase the application of such integrative research. In this chapter I have attempted to delineate a platform from which this further development can take place.

BIBLIOGRAPHY

Bradshaw, G.A. and Bekoff, M. 2001. Ecology and social responsibility: the re-embodiment of science. *TRENDS in Ecology & Evolution*. 16: 460–65.

Capra, F. 1982. *The turning point: science, society and the rising culture*. London: Wildwood House.

Commonwealth of Australia 2000. *Cooperative Research Centres Program: guidelines for applicants – 2000 Selection Round and general principles for Centres*, Canberra: Department of Industry, Science and Tourism.

Crotty, M. 1998. *The foundations of social research: meaning and perspective in the research process*. St. Leonards: Allen & Unwin.

Dick, R. 1986. *Convergent interviewing: a systematic approach to open-ended interviews*. Chapel Hill: Interchange.

Gibbons, M., Limoges, C., Nowotny, H., Scott, P., Schwartzman, S. and Trow, M. 1994. *The new production of knowledge: the dynamics of science and research in contemporary societies*. London: Sage.

Glaser, B.G. and Strauss, A.L. 1967. *The discovery of grounded theory: strategies for qualitative research*. Chicago: Aldine Press.

Ison, R. and Russell, D. 2000. *Agricultural extension and rural development: breaking out of traditions*. Cambridge and New York: Cambridge University Press.

Kinzig, A.P., Carpenter, S., Dove, M., Heal, G., Levin, S., Lubchenco, J., Schneider, S.H. and Starrett, D. 2000. *Nature and society: an imperative for integrated environmental research* (executive summary). Arizona: National Science Foundation.

Layder, D. 1998. *Sociological practice: linking theory and social research*. London: Sage Publications.

Quelin, B. 2000. Core competencies, R&D management and partnerships. *European Management Journal*, 18: 476–87.

Romm, N. 1998. Interdisciplinary practice as reflexivity. *Systemic practice and action research*. 11: 63–77.

Strauss, A. and Corbin, J. 1998. *Basics of qualitative research: techniques and procedures for developing grounded theory*. Thousand Oaks, London, New Delhi: Sage Publications.

SECOND DIMENSION

Reorientations and Openings

Q56

Q57

5. Sustainability and interdisciplinarity

Jon Barnett, Heidi Ellemor and
Stephen Dovers

Since the World Commission on Environment and Development's landmark report *Our Common Future* (WCED 1987), the concept of sustainability has become widespread in application and powerful in influence. Harrison's (1992: 350) claim that it is universally accepted as the prime goal of human progress may be overstated, but given that sustainability figures in the policies of almost all international organizations, national governments and non-governmental organizations, it is near universal at least in policy terms. Thus, sustainability, however defined, is an important object of study. Nevertheless, relative to the importance of the concept, the response of academia, including the discipline of geography, has been slow and *ad hoc* (Eden 2000; Gober 2000; Liverman 1999). Sustainability is a multi-scale, cross-spatial and multi-sectoral problem that inhabits an 'unexplored borderland that cannot be appropriately investigated either by the social or natural sciences alone' (Becker et al. 1999: 3). Thus sustainability requires interdisciplinary research, a point now well established by the United Nations Conference on Environment and Development in policy since Agenda 21, which called for:

> Supporting new scientific research programmes, including their socio-economic and human aspects, at the community, national, subregional, regional and global levels, to complement and encourage synergies between traditional and conventional scientific knowledge and practices and strengthening interdisciplinary research related to environmental degradation and rehabilitation (Article 35.9[a], UNCED 1992).

This need for interdisciplinary research was formally and multilaterally recognized by the Organization for Economic Cooperation and Development (OECD) as long ago as 1972 (Apostel 1972). In the contemporary era, it is stressed in prominent global-change research programmes such as UNESCO's Management of Social Transformations (MOST) project, the International Geosphere–Biosphere Programme (IGBP), and the International Human Dimensions Programme on Global Environmental Change (IHDP) (Ehlers 1999).

The intellectual challenge of interdisciplinarity is substantial, involving negotiation of epistemological differences between the physical, biological and social sciences and humanities (Jones et al. 1999). Ecological economics is, in intent if not achievement, a recent interdisciplinary venture. Geography is unique in that it has a long history of disciplinary introspection, including a substantial corpus of work which addresses the synthesis of physical and social systems. Despite this, geography has (arguably) not fully capitalized on this capacity in terms of the growing importance of sustainability (Gober 2000; Sneddon 2000; Wilbanks 1994). Further, geography and ecological economics are not the only locations of interdisciplinary sustainability research.

This chapter highlights key issues involved in undertaking interdisciplinary research, from a geographic as well as an ecological economic perspective, focusing on sustainability. The concept of sustainability is a powerful lens into the nature of doing interdisciplinary research, for the causes of sustainability problems are systemic to modern economies, have certainly non-trivial if not immense implications for society, are pervaded by uncertainty, are complex, and cut across multiple spatial and temporal scales (Dovers 1997). We begin by briefly defining sustainability and then discuss the need for, and key problems associated with, interdisciplinary research. To gain insight into the nature of interdisciplinary research on sustainability, we briefly discuss major integrative approaches to sustainability – ecological economics, but also development studies, environmental history, human ecology, political ecology and social ecology – to elicit their interdisciplinary character. Although an academic 'discipline' in its own right, we argue that the interdisciplinary nature of much geographical research and teaching situates it well to address sustainability problems. The problem of scale in sustainability research and policy, and the dilemmas posed by the necessary application of critical theories to sustainability, are discussed. We then explore in a little more detail the bases on which geography can act as an (inter)disciplinary meeting ground of sustainability research. The chapter does not provide a comprehensive review of ecological economics, geography or the other interdisciplinary fields, but rather focuses on key issues involved in undertaking interdisciplinary research.

SUSTAINABILITY AND SUSTAINABLE DEVELOPMENT

It is commonplace to consider sustainability a contested concept, open to appropriation by vested interests in society, and indeed by various disciplines. The dimensions of the concept's ambiguity and the nature of its appropriation are already well known through the work of Becker and Jahn (1999), Redclift

(1987), Sachs (1993) and Sneddon (2000). For clarity, a statement of this chapter's understanding of sustainability is necessary.

The current concept of sustainability has evolved from sustainable development, and is now the preferred term of many because it (at least semantically) avoids the problematic word 'development'. The classic definition of sustainable development comes from the WCED (1987: 87) which defined it as 'development that meets the needs of the present without compromising the ability of future generations to meet their own needs'. This is different from sustainability that is, according to Dovers, 'the ability of a natural, human, or mixed system to withstand or adapt to, over an indefinite time scale, endogenous or exogenous changes' (Dovers 1997: 304). The distinction is that sustainability is the system *property* and *goal*, and sustainable development is the *policy activity* aimed at achieving that goal (Dovers 1997). In terms of research, then, sustainability is a 'generator of problems' to which many disciplines can and should contribute (Becker et al. 1999: 3). This chapter regards global changes, such as climate change or economic globalization, as being part of the broad sustainability problematique, as processes to which systems must withstand or adapt.

(UN)DISCIPLINING SUSTAINABILITY

As a problem caused by and impacting on virtually all aspects of modern society, unsustainability challenges all institutions. The 'institutional challenge' to which *Our Common Future* referred applies to academia as well. Thus Bennett and Dahlberg (1990: 78) write of 'the narrowness of functionally specialized agencies and scholarly disciplines', which 'further blocks out large areas of awareness and understanding, a process reinforced by the vested interests and ideologies growing up around them'. Recognition of this problem of specialization predates the ascension of sustainability, as evident in the work of Collingwood (1945) and Toynbee, the latter of whom writes that academic specialization 'is foolish, perverse, and inimical to true knowledge and understanding' (Toynbee 1966: 89). Aristotle's observation that the sum of the parts does not equal the whole is germane, for the reductionist understanding of parts that attends disciplinary-rootedness cannot in totality deliver understanding of the whole. But the meaning of 'interdisciplinary' is less than clear, and it should not infer research of higher purpose or superior quality. It is common to distinguish between multidisciplinarity and interdisciplinarity. The former refers to autonomous disciplinary perspectives working contiguously on a joint problem; the latter to integration of different perspectives through common terminology, mutual understanding of problems and concepts, and common or at least compatible methodologies (after McNeill 1999; see also

Klein 1990). To qualify the following discussion, the place for multi- and single-discipline research and teaching is recognized; the approach should match the problem at hand. Yet, it is widely acknowledged that significant sustainability problems require 'interdisciplinary' approaches, and hence that is our focus.

A frequent problem with discussions of interdisciplinarity is handling the way knowledge and its generation is categorized. Discussion tends to focus on the demarcation of knowledge production (the disciplining of knowledge) rather than the knowledge itself. This is evident, for example, in many chapters in Becker and Jahn's volume on *Sustainability and the social sciences* (1999). It is perhaps instructive that of all the disciplines and study areas which have contributed, the fields of development studies and ecological economics have most informed the concept of sustainability. These approaches pay little heed to disciplinary divides and focus instead on problems. That they are interdisciplinary adds credence to the idea that to restrict people to one discipline is to limit explanatory capacity. Interdisciplinary approaches are therefore necessary and tend to yield greater understanding of sustainability problems. However, there are risks of interdisciplinary scholarship, one of which is the danger of crudely treating the deeper insights arising from a singular perspective. Rose is particularly succinct on this subject:

> I know when I draw on ideas from a discipline not my own I worry if I've got that discipline right, if there aren't certain assumptions it makes that I'm breaking which invalidates my account, if there isn't something really important I just don't know about. In one sense that worry is quite groundless, of course; interdisciplinary work is all about risk, about juxtaposing the unexpected, about two different discourses brushing unevenly against each other's grain. On the other hand, that worry is also a part of the pleasurable dangers of transgression which come from saying something quite new and disruptive (Rose 1994: 117).

Conducting such transgressive research also risks offending specialists, runs up against time constraints and tends not to be conducive to career development (Redclift 1998). There are no simple answers to these problems; nevertheless, much useful scholarship on sustainability takes these risks, and the most impressive mitigates against them by extensive and intensive reading across disciplines. Conversely, those who wish to address unavoidably interdisciplinary subjects such as sustainability without making the effort to understand the breadth of knowledge that informs it can make gross errors, sometimes with serious consequences. For example, biophysical scientist Norman Myers (1996) writes about environmental conflict without understanding the complex causes of conflict or the implications of his writing. The result is a Malthusian and realist analysis justifying militarized environmental security policies (Barnett 2001). In the final analysis, interdisciplinary research requires not just hard work, but also the humility to proceed with caution. That humility requires also the recognition of multiple interdisciplinary projects, some of which we now survey, in a necessarily staccato fashion, to search for key issues.

INTERDISCIPLINES: INTEGRATIVE APPROACHES TO SUSTAINABILITY

There are a number of integrative approaches to sustainability issues, including development studies, environmental history, ecological economics, human ecology, political ecology and social ecology. Some of these have emerged, at least in part, in response to the challenge of sustainability problems, while for others sustainability has provided a new or reworked focus and direction. All are relatively successful because they make the considerable effort to understand and combine a diverse range of ideas and concepts from a range of disciplines.

Development Studies

The concept of sustainable development is a response to ecologically destructive aspects of development, so learning from 'development studies' can enhance the study of sustainability. Above all else, development studies seeks to 'understand and make policy suggestions for the elimination of poverty and exploitation at a global level' (Toye 1987: 512). As such, it is not a discipline *per se*, but rather an area or 'field' of study that involves various social sciences (Faber 1987). Development itself is a contested concept, but is seen here as a process of intentional, self-guided change towards an improved quality of life, with the content of this improvement determined by different societies themselves (after Sachs 1999: 29). 'Whose' development, determined by whom, by what means and at what cost all remain key questions in development research and policy.

Development studies is characterized by an interdisciplinary approach with strong and direct links to policy. According to Drabek (1987), development studies is a 'problem-oriented approach' to change and development with a strong 'pragmatic content' (p. 501). Toye (1987) goes so far as to say that development studies has a 'zeal' to connect with policy (p. 501). McNeill (1999) identifies such policy relevance (and hence research funding) as a key rationale behind the push for interdisciplinary research. This is certainly true in the development studies context, but Apthorne and Krahl (1986) and van Benthem van den Bergh (1986) argue that this close coupling of research to policy is to the detriment of a critically self-aware and morally appropriate scholarship. Harrod is most damning:

Development Studies . . . follows rather than leads: it justifies, rationalizes, excuses and pacifies the conscience-stricken. It is a court discipline and bleats the similar sycophantism as do those who have traditionally bleated accolades to decisions taken by the kings of world power. For such kings, development studies is sometimes a useful instrument of world governance ... (Harrod 1986: 204).

Harrod's critique is perhaps unfair when applied to all development research, but is an appropriate formulation of the dangers of scholarship becoming captive to a singular policy objective, be it development or sustainable development. It follows, then, that if policy relevance is a key engine of the push for interdisciplinary research, then interdisciplinarity offers no automatic claim to higher moral ground.

Contemporary development theory did not emerge until the post World War II period. Economists and to a lesser extent political scientists were central to this first wave of development theory, the content, contestation and subsequent waves of which are ably described elsewhere (Harrod 1986; Leys 1996). It was in the 1970s that the distinct field of development studies emerged (Faber 1987). Thereafter rural economists, anthropologists, geographers, rural sociologists and ethnographers became involved (Harrod 1986). Since the 1980s field research in development studies has addressed issues of cultural meaning, ethnicity, gender, migration and religion. In the late 1980s, two seemingly unconnected and potentially contradictory new strands of development research emerged. The first strand is sustainability, whose strong local-level empirical orientation (Eden 2000) is perhaps a reflection of the empirical nature of development research. The second strand is the nationally oriented, economistic and managerial 'governance' agenda that focuses on state formation and the performance of the state sector as a means to ensure development. This neo-liberal governance agenda potentially undermines the capacity of government to tackle sustainability problems.

In his review of trends in development studies over time, van Benthem van den Bergh (1986) argues that it is an increasingly specialized field, and advocates a move away from policy relevance to the broader theoretical synthesis of the kind originally advanced by Hegel and Marx. This theoretical synthesis, he argues, is the 'only possible road to interdisciplinarity' in development studies (p. 133). Leys (1996) also argues for a theoretical reinvigoration and a shift back from the strong emphasis on policy relevance. Theoretical formulation, it seems, is integral to a consistent and coordinated interdisciplinary research programme.

Given the fluxes in development research in the last 50 years, and its seeming inability to fully negotiate its own path, Harrod's (1986) claim that development studies is a 'court jester' to power has some truth, and Apthorne and Krahl's (1986) explanation that this is due to strong ties to policy and a lack of sufficient (inter)disciplinary self-examination seems valid. Interdisciplinarity, then, may be pragmatic to the point of appropriation, and fragmented to the point of myopia. The tentative lesson is that to be successful a large-scale inter-disciplinary research enterprise requires a degree of distance from policy imperatives, a balance between theory and empirical research across all relevant scales, and a commitment to critical introspection, pluralism and honest exchange.

Environmental History

The industrial revolution was enabled by the development of scientific reason in the European Enlightenment and the later rise of an instrumental, largely economic rationality where means (the market) are more important than ends (social well-being), thus emptying political discourse of substantive issues to do with the common good (Adorno and Horkheimer 1979). This has under-mined the basic preconditions necessary for society to collectively resolve its social and ecological problems. These underlying historical-philosophical problems are not sufficiently recognized in the sustainability literature, save for the pre-sustainability writings of Bookchin (1982), Leiss (1972) and Merchant (1982). This is partly the domain of environmental history (and philosophy), which is notable for its interdisciplinary character. A historical approach to environmental problems is important, for without an appreciation of history we address present and impending problems without the benefit of accumulated knowledge. In addition, history offers a source of optimism; it helps us to know that the world was once different and might be so again (Frank 1985). Thus, environmental history is:

> the investigation and description of previous states of the biophysical environment, and the study of the history of human impacts on and relationships with the non-human setting. Environmental history seeks to explain the landscapes and issues of today and their evolving and dynamic nature, and from this to elucidate the problems and opportunities of tomorrow (Dovers 1994: 3).

Environmental histories vary in temporal and spatial scale. The bulk of environmental history published to date focuses on changes in the biosphere from a local and biophysical perspective (for example Hurley 1997; Isenberg 2000). There is less material available that is global in scope and focuses on the interaction between human culture and the biosphere, although Boyden (1987), Diamond (1991, 1997) and Ponting (1991) discuss the relationship between environmental and social change over time – what Bailes calls 'the dialectic between nature and culture' (1986: 5).

In that 'society' is the study of many social sciences, just as 'environment' is the study of many biological sciences, then environmental history is a highly interdisciplinary endeavour. Dovers describes environmental history as 'loosely defined and bounded, eclectic, fluid', calling on a range of social and natural sciences 'in constantly shifting and invigorating combinations according to the inquiry at hand' (2000: p. 132). There is recognition from practitioners of environmental history that it is an interdisciplinary endeavour, a foundation that allows for experimentation and innovation which, in turn leads to new insights. That most environmental historians give short shrift to the issue of disciplinary boundaries is beneficial for their field and for the advancement of our understanding of sustainability problems and solutions.

Ecological Economics

The problem of unsustainable development can be in large part attributed to industrialization, harnessed in both centrally planned and capitalist political systems, with the latter overwhelmingly dominant in the contemporary world. This heralded massive increases in fossil energy use and primary resources, and subsequent pollution of the atmosphere, soils and water. Intertwined with this system of production today is the ideology of the free market, which holds that the maximum public good is to be achieved by the unregulated efforts of private, autonomous, rational and self-seeking individuals and capital. Environmental sources and ecological sinks are free goods, or at best externalities, in this market system, and 'free' often implies that the State should not intervene to maintain environmental quality. In response to this neoclassical economic paradigm, *ecological* economics has come to dominate the study of sustainability. The juxtaposition with the neoclassical paradigm is highlighted in Common's definition of ecological economics as:

> An economics that takes what we think we know about our biophysical circumstances, and about human psychology, seriously – which standard neoclassical economics, including the sub-disciplines of environmental and resource economics, does not do (Common 1996: 7).

Ecological economics is a systems-oriented field that considers the interdependence of biophysical and economic systems (broadly defined) (Martinez-Alier 1999). Issues that concern ecological economics, and its relationship to geography, are detailed elsewhere (Sneddon 2000), so we are limiting ourselves to a short discussion of its interdisciplinary nature, recognizing that the field is little more than a decade old and thus still more prospective than defined. The fundamentally interdisciplinary character of ecological economics arises from its focus on the dynamic interactions of ecological and economic systems. This allows for diverse, competing ideas to be exchanged and reconciled in productive ways. Indeed, it is the honest character of this exchange of diverse ideas and approaches – as evident in the journal *Ecological Economics* – that makes ecological economics work as an interdisciplinary project, albeit one still under construction. This communicative and tolerant character is exemplary of the *software* needed for interdisciplinary research. In general, ecological economists acquire and employ knowledge not just of their own field but of some other social sciences (for example Martinez-Alier 1999; Norgaard 1989; Pezzey 1992). On the subject of interdisciplinarity they can be thoughtful; Martinez-Alier identifies the need for an 'orchestration of the sciences', where 'contradictions and incompatibilities would be addressed, instead of dismembered into the different departments of the universities' (1999: 136). As we argue later, geography is ideally situated to act as this meta-directory and meeting ground, for sustainability research and policy.

Human Ecology

The oldest of the 'ecologies' is human ecology which, like ecology itself, tends to mean different things to different people and disciplines. Human Ecology can be broadly defined as the study of the relations between people and their immediate surroundings (Lawrence 1993: 213), with recent developments sharing the 'common denominator' of awareness of serious large-scale environmental degradation (Steiner and Nauser 1993: 6). It is a field of study long associated with, but not exclusive to geography (for example White and Renner 1936). Indeed, it has been to the detriment of geography, the discipline seemingly most able to study human interactions, that it has not sufficiently utilized its tradition in human ecology to speak to sustainability (Gober 2000). There are also sociological and anthropological approaches to human ecology (see Young 1983), and there are strong linkages between human ecology and environmental history – for example Boyden was a key figure in UNESCO's human-ecology 'Man and the Biosphere' programme, and later went to develop 'biohistory' (Boyden 1987, Boyden et al. 1981). Human ecology in these manifestations is quite applied, focusing on the flow of material and energy through societies, often cities, and can be seen as a precursor to Wackernagel and Rees' (1996) work on ecological footprints. According to Martinez-Alier (1999) human ecology is a precursor to ecological economics.

Given its long history human ecology has extensive experience with the need for, and means of, interdisciplinary approaches to human-environment problems. In terms of means, Boyden (1993) Feachem (1977) and Steiner (1993) all stress the problem of different disciplines having different languages to speak of common problems. From their respective experiences in applied human-ecology research, all argue that there is a need for 'a certain degree of interdisciplinarity in person, or personal transdisciplinarity', which involves 'venturing from the familiar grounds of the home discipline on to the neighbouring grounds of other relevant disciplines' (Steiner, 1993: 55). This is necessary for any individual wishing to do research of a transdisciplinary nature; however, all three stress that this personal involvement is crucial for successful multi-person interdisciplinary research as well. Steiner identifies a 'strong' variant of interdisciplinary research relying on at least one person who has this 'intrapersonal integration' and so can act as a communicative generalist and coordinator (Steiner 1993: 55). According to Feachem, 'it always depends on one or two people with the ability and strength of character to direct the team and then to sit down and write the synthesis of complex data' (1977: 8). The lesson for interdisciplinary research projects is that adaptable generalist *people* with communication skills are vital.

Political Ecology

A more recent interdisciplinary approach is political ecology, concerned with political economy-oriented explanations of ecological issues (Greenberg and Park 1994). It is, according to Bryant, 'an inquiry into the political sources, conditions and ramifications of environmental change' (Bryant 1997: 4). Political ecology research is largely of a local-level and empirical-investigative kind, as made popular by Blaikie and Brookfield's *Land degradation and society* (1987). However, it need not necessarily have this emphasis because it has its roots in the rich theoretical domain of political economy. Political ecology need not be oriented to the local level either; as Bryant (1997) argues, international forces and interstate relations drive ecological change and so should be considered part of the domain of political ecology. This is consistent with Greenberg and Park's (1994) recognition of the importance of Wallerstein's world-systems theory to political ecology. Thus political ecology can contribute to the study of global environmental politics and environmental security (Barnett 2001).

Consistent with its intellectual heritage, political ecology has a concern for justice dimensions of environmental problems. Indeed, political ecology can speak directly to the concept of *environmental justice* from Marxist, feminist and local-level perspectives (Loker 1996; Low and Gleeson 1998; Rocheleau et al. 1996). This concern for justice makes political ecology 'normative', understood here as a mode of theorizing that incorporates the inescapable beliefs and values of the theorist into the theory in explicit ways. While such theorizing is seen to be suspicious by some, normative critique can be powerful in enabling the present to be assessed relative to a set of ideals; thus 'we continuously uphold normative or value propositions that are entirely unproblematic and without doubt rational in every sense: children should not play with fire; fraud is unjust' (Morrow 1994: 239). Morrow calls this 'normative argumentation' and points out that rather than being irrational or irregular, it actually occurs in everyday practice and is a very rational technique of critique and persuasion.

In so far as it rests on a foundation of geographic, historical, legal and ecological research, political ecology is interdisciplinary (Pezzoli 1997). However, its interdisciplinary capacity is furthered given that, not unlike development studies, it stems from the dialectical political economy approach of Marx and Engels (and before them Hegel) (at least as Greenberg and Park 1994 see it). The dialectical approach emphasizes the (social) *system* rather than its parts, and looks to history, processes and connections to understand the system. This dialectical Marxist political economy predates and is the foundation of the modern social sciences, and in that political ecology draws on this synthetic tradition as well as on threads of contemporary ecological thought, it is potentially profoundly interdisciplinary.

Social Ecology

A less well-defined approach to sustainability is social ecology, with two main variants. One is as 'an environmentally oriented sociology', studying the relations between the ecological infrastructure and culture, the polity, social structure and the economy (Guha 1994: 5). This is an approach comfortable with terms like 'class', 'power' and 'justice', overlapping with political ecology. This variant is exemplified in the work of Guha who, writing of the need to 'pick up and apply the necessary scientific knowledge yourself' (1999: 109), is clearly one of Steiner's (1993) 'intrapersonal integrators'. This school combines abstract concepts with grounded experience to produce understanding and solutions that take account of scale-varied processes from local to global.

There is a more philosophical version of social ecology developed by Murray Bookchin. Zimmerman (1993) calls this a 'radical ecophilosophy' as it is concerned with hierarchies of power and the way in which these oppress people and degrade nature (see Bookchin 1982, 1986). This social ecology is based on a dialectical naturalism that views humans as a part of – not separate from – nature; a dialectics which, like its Marxist (and in Bookchin's case critical theory) origins is inherently interdisciplinary in character, at least to some degree. Clark understands this dialectical naturalism to mean that the relations that transpire among humans are continuous with the human relationship to nature (Clark 1993). Bookchin sees humans as 'nature rendered self-conscious', the first part of nature to become aware of itself (Bookchin 1986). However, Bookchin sees this self-consciousness as an incomplete project, and argues that it can come to fruition through a deepening of social-ecological sensibility, with the result that the 'modern crisis' can be overcome. Hence the modern crisis is not merely institutional, but ideological, psychological and cultural (Bookchin 1986). Understanding this deeper and broader setting helps to contextualize the goal of sustainability.

Guha and Bookchin's social ecologies are complementary and could be more integrated. Although Guha does not mention Bookchin in his work, he acknowledges the need to bridge what he calls 'the wide chasm' between utopian visions (such as Bookchin's) and the 'focused, nose to the ground studies of social scientists on the management of water, pasture, forests and fisheries' (Guha 1999: 104). This is a key disjuncture in the spectrum of literatures on sustainability; the problem of linking the likes of Bookchin's broader and abstract ecologically oriented explanation of the *The modern crisis* with the applied and generally local nature of sustainability problems, where the latter is 'bounded by region or resource' and the former is 'free and unconstrained, seeking to turn the nations (and nature) upside down' (Guha 1999: 104). Gadgil's and Guha's (1995) model of omnivore and ecosystem people goes a long way in this regard. Akin to a world systems theory of ecological consumption, Gadgil and Guha's model loosens what is otherwise a cognitive difficulty with sustainability, that is the problem of scale.

THE SLIDING SCALES OF SUSTAINABILITY

For most of history, human impact on the environment was small-scale and fragmented. However, as a result of the industrial revolution and the large-scale use of fossil fuels and resources there are now truly *global* environmental problems, the most obvious being climate change. Thus, a comprehensive approach to sustainability now requires understanding systems at the widest possible range of scales; this underlies the slogans 'think global, act local', and 'everything is connected to everything else', which embody a perspective on scale, systems and structuration. Few would doubt that the global economy affects environmental change at all scales, including transnational corporations siting polluting industries according to the comparative advantages offered by the different development and regulatory contexts in southern countries; cumulative carbon emissions of automobile manufacturing and the urban air pollution effects of automobile use; and soil degrading and biodiversity depleting agricultural practices necessitated by the need to repay debt in underdeveloped countries. These are multi-scale problems traditionally studied within disciplinary and scale-bounded contexts where 'each [disciplinary] perspective has its corresponding scale, a relation between the real size of things and the virtual size employed for analysis' (Reboratti, 1999: 219). Such multi-scale processes run against disjunct jurisdictions and policy responses as much as they do against discrete disciplines. For example, while the chemist studies the problem of lead pollution in Mexico City and the economist designs solutions aimed at local control, deeper issues of global reform of the automobile and oil industries are ignored because there is insufficient connection between the affected thousands and the broader political and economic determinants of the problem. Or, while the ecologist sees damage to New Zealand's freshwater aquatic ecosystems from increased dairying, this is not related to the political anthropologist's observation of changes in the culture of the national trade policy community, which is not understood in terms of the development scholar's awareness of trade liberalization. The incomplete understanding that results from the disaggregation of disciplines is compounded by the structuring of knowledge according to imagined hierarchies of scale.

The predominantly local-scale focus of many human-environment studies, including much of that by the 'ecologies', runs the risk of what Reboratti calls 'the trap of localism' (1999: 221), where there is a risk of losing sight of the big picture, rendering solutions incomplete and *ad hoc* (Eden 2000). This is compounded by the trend of interpreting sustainability as 'sustainable management', as is the case in New Zealand through the mechanism of its widely known *Resource Management Act* 1991 (Buhrs and Bartlett 1993). Compared to sustainable development, sustainable management is more narrowly concerned with the use of renewable natural resources in locales rather than the overall ecological effects of development. Thus, although sustainability needs to be operationalized in specific places in detailed ways, these actions need to be consistent with broader systemic imperatives.

Different scale and disciplinary-based approaches could at least be made contiguous simply by communication in common forums – a possibility mitigated against by the channelling of publications into disciplinary journals, arrangement of conferences by disciplinary themes rather than common subjects, antipathy of the disciplines towards each other and discipline-defined processes of review and career enhancement. Thus, even a superficially scale-varied mosaic of sustainability issues is difficult to obtain. This is not a call for a superscholar or a meta-discipline, but rather the identification of the problem of scale and the possibility of deeper understanding of the nested nature of social and ecological systems where changes in one have cascading (and often non-linear) implications in many others. Advancing this understanding requires a new outlook, disciplined but undisciplinary research, and people who proceed with humility and communicate with clarity and honesty. Such communication requires, in turn, a reflexive and critical capacity capable of exposing and questioning disciplinary (and other) claims to knowing.

THE 'CRITICAL' PROBLEM

The call for increasing involvement of the social sciences in sustainability was always likely to increase the complexity of research (Miller 1998). The social sciences have brought with them not just those positivist epistemologies that are compatible with natural science, but also theories and insights that ask questions of theory, research and policy. As a result, one of the tensions within the social sciences – the challenge of social constructionism – now also lurks at the margins of the study of sustainability. Social constructionism sheds light on 'the social and cultural elements involved in producing environmental knowledge . . . to foster a deeper understanding of how scientific knowledge assumes authority in the public domain' (Jasanoff and Wynne 1998: 4–5). It suggests that what science reveals is less the 'truth' of the object of study and more a reflection of the nature of the subject doing the study. In sustainability terms – and taken to its extreme – this means that the problem of environmental change itself is unknowable, but the formulation of the problem reveals insights into the condition of society and the way it produces knowledge. This presents a profound challenge to sustainability by exposing the epistemological question – 'how do we know?' – on which so much policy ('what do we do?') is premised.

Unsurprisingly, social constructionism is the source of acrimony. It has been called 'a new environmental villain' (Proctor 1998: 352). Redclift identifies McNaughton and Urry's paper (1995) 'Towards a sociology of nature' and Hannigan's *Environmental sociology* (1995) as examples of 'the limitations which social constructionism places on the explanatory possibilities of environmental social science' (Redclift 1999: 66–7). Nevertheless, in the wake of social constructionism, environmental science can no longer claim to be purely objective or the sole conveyor of truth to power (Blaikie 1996; Jasanoff and Wynne 1998).

The potential dangers of deconstructing knowledge of environmental change are that it can be seen to relativize all claims to knowing, granting alternative and more destructive agendas equal legitimacy (see Gleeson 1996; Soule and Lease 1995). Representations of sustainability problems then become endlessly contestable, with no possibility of a truth on which judgements can be made. However, this is more a possibility than an observed outcome of social constructionism; it does not necessarily lead to relativism. There are few if any pure relativists to be found, and so the danger of social constructionism should not be overstated.

The value of social constructionism is that it checks for the possibility that we are wrong. Redclift writes that 'we need to acknowledge the provisional nature of our models and be prepared to accept that they may not provide a good reflection of what "reality" is actually like' (1999: 68). Various discourses on sustainability communicate competing emphases and solutions to common problems; consider for example Dryzek's (1997) unpacking of survivalist, Promethean, administrative rationalist, democratic pragmatist and economic rationalist discourses, all leading to different policy platforms. So, questioning science is only part of the critical programme: it also questions policy in similar ways (Jasanoff and Wynne 1998). To offer another example, there is a need, as Dalby (1996) does, to deconstruct politically realist and Malthusian tracts such as Kaplan's influential *The coming anarchy* (1994), which understands sustainability problems as ethnically aligned security threats, thereby countenancing reactive military responses to underdevelopment in other (non-western) places. Deconstructions of such extreme accounts are necessary if there is to be even a broad zone of consensus about the causes and importance of environmental degradation, and a forward-looking debate about sustainable development. Further, understanding the way knowledge is socially constructed also helps to illuminate the origins of controversy and scientific uncertainty (Jasanoff and Wynne 1998).

Beyond this paradigmatic introspective function, the broader spectrum of critical approaches – of which social constructionism is part – are more frequently deployed to expose the broader modernity-situated processes that generate *un*sustainable development. This is the most important contribution of critical theory to sustainability; indeed, it is a contribution that came well before contemporary recognition of a sustainability problem, and is a contribution that warrants more frequent inclusion in discussions of sustainability. Some of the 'interdisciplines' above are inherently critical, such as political and social ecology, whereas others are less so, such as ecological economics and environmental history (although the latter has strongly critical elements emerging, for example Maddox 2002). Common to most critical approaches is a concern for theorizing in ways that seek to question established orders of knowledge and praxis and how they shape the world. Thus the critical theory of the Frankfurt School exposes the way in which society organizes itself to provide for its material needs, arguing that it is imperfect in as much as these needs could be supplied without repression of nature both internal and external (Leiss 1972; Marcuse 1969).

The critical project of ecofeminism understands the domination of nature, rationalized and expressed through the dualism 'man/nature', to be consistent with the underlying dualism 'man/woman' that rationalizes the domination of woman (Merchant 1982; Seager 1993). Post-structuralists ask how knowledge, truth and meaning are determined, viewing knowledge and power as being mutually constitutive such that claims to 'know' have the power to make the world in their image, thereby oppressing alternative possibilities that may be less damaging (and presumably more sustainable) (Foucault 1977). For the post-structuralist the uprooting of truth merely demands an awareness that each author constructs her own discourse and her own subjective theory; thus the post-structuralist 'must be persistently, openly, blatantly politicizing in the theory she does . . . she must understand that theoretical practice is inescapably as much a political practice as any other practice she might care to name' (Ashley 1989: 280). Most forms of feminist, critical theory and post-structuralist critique appreciate this point – to do theory is to do politics. Thus, critical approaches tend to demand recognition of the murky and political nature of knowledge production and deployment so that the possibility of alternative ways of knowing and doing are not suppressed, and decisions socially negotiated in a more honest and discursively pluralistic context. This is as true for sustainability as any other science policy discourse, and represents a major nexus of, alternatively, creative engagement or misunderstanding and conflict between disciplines.

Having considered a range of interdisciplines and the additional issues of scale and critical capacity, we now propose that ecological economists (and others) may not need to look only to newer interdisciplinary ventures and critical traditions for insights, but perhaps to a more familiar and longer-established source: geography.

SUSTAINABILITY, INTERDISCIPLINARITY AND GEOGRAPHY

Geographic research has and can continue to be highly relevant to sustainability. A review of the recent contributions of geographers to sustainability has been provided elsewhere (Sneddon 2000) and is not our focus. The aim of the following discussion is to elucidate some general characteristics of geography in terms of interdisciplinary sustainability research, although this requires recognizing the contentious nature of what defines geography. The following discussion outlines at least five principal characteristics of geographic research that render it an ideal (inter)disciplinary node for sustainability research and policy.

In the first instance, if we accept Hartshorne's (1959) definition of geography as the study of the earth's surface then this is germane to sustainability problems that are spatially complex. This capacity to comprehend spatial processes becomes even more applicable in the revitalized, larger-scale sustainability research programme envisaged by Eden (2000). Second, in addition to this *horizontal* perspective that enables the relation of different elements (Reboratti 1999), geography also has a long history of studying *vertical* relations between humans and the ecosystems in which they reside – as exemplified in human ecology. Indeed, understanding human-environment relations has been a constant theme throughout the history of geography, with an increasing emphasis on the human side of the equation and a consideration of the socio-cultural environment (Golledge 2002).

The third basis of geography as an (inter)disciplinary node of sustainability research and policy is its ability to study regions, where horizontal and vertical perspectives are fused into the study of an area. This is not to assume away ongoing debates about regional geography; however, geography of a regional kind has already played a leading role in climate change and sea-level rise impact assessments (see for example Brookfield 1989; Burton 1997; Downing et al. 1997; Easterling and Kates 1995; Liverman and O'Brien 1991; Nicholls et al. 1999). Liverman (2000) sees an enhanced role here drawing on geography's historical ability to understand regional change. However, the regional scale is but one of the many scales at which geographic research operates, and the fourth sustainability-relevant characteristic of geography is its demonstrated capacity to track through the implications of global scale processes through to regional and local-level impacts, and conversely to understand how local and regional scale processes influence global change. Thus, geographers are prominent in the 'human dimensions of global change' research programme (Ehlers 1999).

Finally, geography is a discipline that can *synthesize* knowledge derived from other natural and social sciences – although again it must be acknowledged that this does not hold for all geographic research (Stoddard et al. 1986). The overlapping venn diagrams of Fenneman (1919), Holt-Jensen (1988) and Taylor (1953) all seek to depict geography's integrative and synthesizing nature, with astronomy, biology, economics, geology, history and meteorology figuring prominently. These disciplines are key contributors to the study of environmental change as well. As Turner notes, 'geography embraces most ways of knowing, ranging from the sciences to the humanities, and for this reason, among others, claims a bridging role across the realms of understanding' (2002: 53). Turner's (2002) view is that the discipline sometimes struggles to work successfully across these competing epistemologies. However, it remains that as well as synthesizing disciplines, geography does have a unique ability to comprehend diverse epistemologies, as graduates are exposed to both social and natural sciences, and increasingly to critical and humanities-based theories. This is vitally important for genuine interdisciplinary research on sustainability, which is the product of knowledges generated by diverse underlying assumptions about what can be known and how knowledge is attained (Jones et al. 1999).

These synthesis arguments should not be taken to mean that geography has definitive answers to the problems of integrating the physical and social sciences – Smith's (1987) 'unity myth' – but there is little doubt that geography has a long history of dealing with and understanding diverse epistemologies. Gober (2000) argues that the future of geography lies in enhancing this capacity for synthesis, but is clear that this should be organized around 'ideas, concepts and theories', and involves 'discovering strategic connections, not in returning to the general, all purpose geographies of the 1940's and 1950's' (p. 8). As Liverman (2000) suggests, this new geography of sustainability should include an enhanced role for the more critical sub-fields of feminist, political and cultural geographies, whose potential is evident in, for example, Seager (1993), Dalby (1992) and Ellemor (2000) respectively.

Not all geographic research displays all, or indeed any of these characteristics; however, the discipline has the potential to enhance understanding of spatial processes, human-environment interactions, regional change and multi-scale processes, and it is also more capable than most of synthesizing knowledge derived from other natural and social sciences. These are good grounds for geography to identify itself as an (inter)discipline with substantial historical and ontological credentials in the field of sustainability. This is not to romanticize the past or inflate the future of geography, but rather to articulate the bases on which geography can maximize its contribution to interdisciplinary sustainability research and policy. Why neither geography itself or other sustainability-oriented endeavours recognize this potential often enough invites an investigation for which there is not space here.

CONCLUSION

Sustainability is a multifaceted and difficult problem set, and our cursory survey demonstrates the necessary traditions and foci that are brought to bear by the different fields identified above. Some of the essential elements of interdisciplinarity identified here are:

- a problem focus, whether the problems be applied, theoretical or methodological;
- but also wariness of the dangers of capture by singular or partial policy objectives;
- a critical capacity, including recognition of normative elements of theory and practice;
- openness to other disciplines, theory, method and arenas of inquiry;
- a 'systems' orientation, in terms of appreciating the whole rather than only selected parts (and encompassing both quantitative and qualitative constructions of systems);
- a close appreciation of multiple and dynamic spatial and temporal scales, including a capacity to account for historical determinants of modern situations;
- appreciation of the personal/group qualities required to undertake inter-disciplinary work, and the balance of risks and rewards in disciplinary boundary transgression.

However, this chapter also demonstrates that, while necessary in their contribution, none of the fields surveyed are sufficient in themselves, and interdisciplinary research on sustainability will remain a joint and widely shared topic, even if individual practitioners and endeavours do not fully realize that.

For ecological economists, engagement with a geography that realizes the potential proposed here, or at least a deeper appreciation of these issues behind this potential, some of which do not as yet feature as strongly in ecological economics, should reap good rewards, and vice versa. The same can be said for engagement with the other interdisciplines surveyed here, on the basis that all display attributes necessary but insufficient for developing strong interdisciplinary approaches to sustainability. Stronger connections and communication between the range of interdisciplines is an obvious recommendation.

BIBLIOGRAPHY

Adorno, T. and Horkheimer, M. 1979. *Dialectic of enlightenment*. (Trans. Cumming, J.) London: Verso.

Apostel, L. (ed). 1972. *Interdisciplinarity: problems of teaching and research in universities*. Paris: Organization for Economic Cooperation and Development.

Apthorne, R. and Krahl, A. 1986. Epilogue: researching for development. In: Apthorne, R. and Krahl, A. (eds). *Development studies: critique and renewal*. Leiden: E.J. Brill, pp. 250–63.

Ashley, R. 1989. Living on the border lines: Man, poststructuralism, and war. In: Der Derian, J. and Shapiro, M. (eds). *International/Intertextual relations: Postmodern readings of world politics*. Massachusetts/Toronto: Lexington Books, pp. 259–321.

Bailes, K. 1986. Critical issues in environmental history. In: Bailes, K. (ed). *Environmental history: critical issues in comparative perspective*. Lanham: University Press of America, pp. 1–21.

Barnett, J. 2001. *The meaning of environmental security: ecological politics and policy in the new security era*. London and New York: Zed Books.

Becker, E. and Jahn, T. (eds). 1999. *Sustainability and the social sciences: a cross-disciplinary approach to integrating environmental considerations into theoretical reorientation*. London and New York: Zed Books.

Becker, E., Jahn, T. and Stiess, I. 1999. Exploring uncommon ground: sustainability and the social Sciences. In: Becker, E. and Jahn, T. (eds). *Sustainability and the social sciences: a cross-disciplinary approach to integrating environmental considerations into theoretical reorientation*. London and New York: Zed Books, pp. 1–22.

Bennett, J. and Dahlberg, K. 1990. Institutions, social organization, and cultural values. In: Turner, B. (ed). *The earth as transformed by human action: global and regional changes in the biosphere over the past 300 years*. Cambridge: Cambridge University Press, pp. 69–86.

Blaikie, P. 1996. Post-modernism and global environmental change *Global Environmental Change*. 6: 81–5.

Blaikie, P. and Brookfield, H. 1987. *Land degradation and society*. London: Methuen.

Bookchin, M. 1982. *The ecology of freedom: the emergence and dissolution of hierarchy*. Palo Alto: Cheshire Books.

Bookchin, M. 1986. *The modern crisis*. Philadelphia: New Society Publishers.

Boyden, S. 1987. *Western civilisation in biological perspective: patterns in biohistory*. Oxford: Clarendon Press.

Boyden, S. 1993. Human ecology and biohistory: conceptual approaches to understanding human situations in the biosphere. In: Steiner, D. and Nauser, M. (eds). *Human ecology: fragments of anti-fragmentary views of the world*. London: Routledge, pp. 31–46.

Boyden, S., Millar, S., Newcombe, K. and O'Neill, B. 1981. *The ecology of a city and its people: the case of Hong Kong*. Canberra: Australian National University Press.

Brookfield, H. 1989. Global change and the Pacific: problems for the coming half-century. *The Contemporary Pacific*. 1–2: 1–17.

Bryant, R. 1997. *The political ecology of forestry in Burma, 1824–1994*. Honolulu: University of Hawai'i Press.

Buhrs, T. and Bartlett, R. 1993. *Environmental policy in New Zealand: the politics of clean and green?* Auckland: Oxford University Press.

Burton, I. 1997. Vulnerability and adaptive response in the context of climate and climate change. *Climatic Change*. 36: 185–96.

Clark, J. 1993. Introduction. In: Zimmerman, M. (ed). *Environmental philosophy: from animal rights to radical ecology*. New Jersey: Prentice Hall, pp. 345–53.

Collingwood, R. 1945. *The idea of nature*. London: Oxford University Press.

Common, M. 1996. What is ecological economics? In: Gill, R. (ed) *R&D priorities for ecological economics*. Canberra: Land and Water Resources Research and Development Corporation, pp. 6–20.

Dalby, S. 1992. Ecopolitical discourse: 'environmental security' and political geography. *Progress in Human Geography*. 16: 503–22.

Dalby, S. 1996. The environment as geopolitical threat: reading Robert Kaplan's 'Coming anarchy'. *Ecumene*. 3: 471–96.

Diamond, J. 1991. *The rise and fall of the third chimpanzee*. London: Vintage.

Diamond, J. 1997. *Guns, germs, and steel: the fate of human societies*. New York: W.W. Norton.

Dovers, S. (ed). 1994. *Australian environmental history: essays and cases*. Melbourne: Oxford University Press.

Dovers, S. 1997. Sustainability: demands on policy. *Journal of Public Policy*. 16: 303–18.

Dovers, S. 2000. On the contribution of environmental history to current debate and policy. *Environment and History*. 6: 131–50.

Downing, T., Ringius, L., Hulme, M. and Waughray, D. 1997. Adapting to climate change in Africa: prospects and guidelines. *Mitigation and Adaptation Strategies for Global Change*. 2: 19–44.

Drabek, A. 1987. Development studies and contemporary change in Britain. *World Development*. 15: 501–502.

Dryzek, J. 1997. *The politics of the earth: environmental discourses*. Oxford: Oxford University Press.

Easterling, W. and Kates, R. 1995. Indexes of leading climate indicators for impact assessment. *Climatic Change*. 31: 623.

Eden, S. 2000:. Environmental issues: sustainable progress? *Progress in Human Geography*. 24: 111–18.

Ehlers, E. 1999. Environment and geography: international programs on global environmental change. *International Geographical Union Bulletin*. 49: 5–18.

Ellemor, H. 2000. The cultural geography of resource management: a case study from

Australia. In: Roche, M. (ed). *Proceedings of twentieth New Zealand geography conference, Palmerston North, July 1999*, Hamilton: New Zealand Geographical Society, 2000, pp. 115–19.

Faber, M. 1987. Development studies in Britain: a look at ourselves. *World Development*. 15: 533–6.

Feachem, R. 1977. The human ecologist as superman. In: Bayliss-Smith T. and Feachem, R. (eds). *Subsistence and survival: rural ecology in the Pacific*. London: Academic Press, pp. 3–10.

Fenneman, N. 1919. The circumference of geography. *Annals of the Association of American Geographers*. 9: 3–11.

Foucault, M. 1977. *Language, counter-memory, practice: selected essays and interviews*. (Ed. Bouchard, D.) Oxford: Blackwell.

Frank, R. 1985. Comment. In: Bailes, K. (ed). *Environmental history: critical issues in comparative perspective*. Lanham: University Press of America, pp. 99–103.

Gadgil, M. and Guha, R. 1995. *Ecology and equity: the use and abuse of nature in contemporary India*. London: Routledge.

Gleeson, B. 1996. Justifying justice. *Area*. 28: 229–34.

Gober, P. 2000. In search of synthesis. *Annals of the Association of American Geographers*. 90: 1–11.

Golledge, R. 2002. The nature of geographic knowledge. *Annals of the Association of American Geographers*. 92: 1–14.

Greenberg, J. and Park, T. 1994. Political ecology. *Journal of Political Ecology*. 1: 1–12.

Guha, R. 1994. Introduction. In: Guha, R. (ed). *Social ecology*. New Delhi, Oxford University Press, pp. 1–18.

Guha, R. 1999. From experience to theory: traditions of social-ecological research in modern India. In: Becker, E. and Jahn, T. (eds). *Sustainability and the social sciences: a cross-disciplinary approach to integrating environmental considerations into theoretical reorientation*. London and New York: Zed Books, pp. 96–111.

Hannigan, J. 1995. *Environmental sociology: a social constructionist perspective*. London: Routledge.

Harrison, P. 1992. *The third revolution: population, environment and a sustainable world*. Harmondsworth: Penguin.

Harrod, J. 1986. Development studies: from change to stabilization. In: Apthorne, R. and Krahl, A. (eds). *Development studies: critique and renewal*. Leiden: E.J. Brill, pp. 204–17.

Hartshorne, R. 1959. *Perspective on the nature of geography*. Chicago: Rand McNally.

Holt-Jensen, A. 1988. *Geography: history and concepts*. London: Edward Arnold.

Hurley, A. (ed) 1997. *Common fields: an environmental history of St. Louis*. St. Louis: Missouri Historical Society Press.

Isenberg, A. 2000. *The destruction of the bison: an environmental history, 1750–1920*. New York: Cambridge University Press.

Jasanoff, S. and Wynne, B. 1998. Science and decisionmaking. In: Rayner, S. and Malone, E. (eds). *Human choice and climate change, volume one: the societal framework*. Columbus: Battelle Press, pp. 1–87.

Jones, P., Merritt, J. and Palmer, C. 1999. Critical thinking and interdisciplinarity in environmental higher education: the case for epistemological and values awareness. *Journal of Geography in Higher Education*. 23: 347–57.

Kaplan, R. 1994. The coming anarchy. *Atlantic Monthly*. 273: 44–76.

Klein, J. 1990. *Interdisciplinarity: history, theory and practice*. Detroit: Wayne State University Press.

Lawrence, R. 1993. Can human ecology provide an integrative framework? The contribution of structuration theory to the contemporary debate. In: Steiner D. and Nauser, M. (eds). *Human ecology: fragments of anti-fragmentary views of the World*. London: Routledge, pp. 213–28.

Leiss, W. 1972. *The domination of nature*. New York: George Braziller.

Leys, C. 1996. *The rise and fall of development theory*. Bloomington: Indiana University Press.

Liverman, D. 1999. Geography and the global environment. *Annals of the Association of American Geographers*. 89: 107–20.

Liverman, D. and O'Brien, K. 1991. Global warming and climate change in Mexico. *Global Environmental Change*. 1: 351–64.

Loker, W. 1996. 'Campesinos' and the crisis of modernization in Latin America. *Journal of Political Ecology*. 3: 69–88.

Low, N. and Gleeson, B. 1998. *Justice, society and nature: an exploration of political ecology*. London: Routledge.

Maddox, G. 2002. 'Degradation narratives' and 'population time bombs': myths and realities about African environments. In: Dovers, S., Edgecombe, R. and Guest, W. (eds). *South Africa's environmental history: cases and comparisons*, Cape Town and Athens: David Philip Publishers and Ohio University Press, pp. 252–60.

Marcuse, H. 1969. *Negations: essays in critical theory*. London: Allen Lane the Penguin Press.

Martinez-Alier, J. 1999. The socio-ecological embeddedness of economic activity: the emergence of a transdisciplinary field. In: Becker, E. and Jahn, T. (eds). *Sustainability and the social sciences: a cross-disciplinary approach to integrating environmental considerations into theoretical reorientation*. London and New York: Zed Books, pp. 112–39.

McNaughton, P. and Urry, J. 1995. Towards a sociology of nature. *Sociology*. 29: 203–20.

McNeill, D. 1999. On interdisciplinary research: with particular reference to the field of environment and development. *Higher Education Quarterly*. 53: 312–32.

Merchant, C. 1982. *The death of nature: women, ecology, and the scientific revolution*. London: Wildwood House.

Miller, R. 1998. Social science and the challenge of global environmental change. *International Social Science Journal*. 50: 447–54.

Morrow, R. 1994. *Critical theory and methodology*. Newbury Park: Sage.

Myers, N. 1996. *Ultimate security: the environmental basis of political stability*. Washington: Island Press.

Nicholls, R., Hoozemans, F. and Marchand, M. 1999. Increasing flood risk and wetland losses due to global sea-level rise: regional and global analyses. *Global Environmental Change*. 9: 69–87.

Norgaard, R. 1989. The case for methodological pluralism. *Ecological Economics*. 1: 37–57.

Pezzey, J. 1992. Sustainability: an interdisciplinary guide. *Environmental values*. 1: 321–62.

Pezzoli, K. 1997. Sustainable development: a transdisciplinary overview of the literature. *Journal of Environmental Planning and Management*. 40: 549–74.

Ponting, C. 1991. *A green history of the world*. London: Penguin Books.

Proctor, J. 1998. The social construction of nature: Relativist accusations, pragmatist and critical realist responses. *Annals of the Association of American Geographers*. 88: 352–76.

Reboratti, C. 1999. Territory, scale and sustainable development. In: Becker, E. and Jahn, T. (eds). *Sustainability and the social sciences: a cross-disciplinary approach to integrating environmental considerations into theoretical reorientation*. London and New York: Zed Books, pp. 207–22.

Redclift, M. 1987. *Sustainable development: exploring the contradictions*. London: Methuen.

Redclift, M. 1998. Dances with wolves? Interdisciplinary research on the global environment. *Global Environmental Change*. 8: 177–82.

Redclift, M. 1999. Sustainability and sociology: northern preoccupations. In: Becker, E. and Jahn, T. (eds). *Sustainability and the social sciences: a cross-disciplinary approach to integrating environmental considerations into theoretical reorientation*. London and New York: Zed Books, pp. 59–73.

Rocheleau, D., Thomas-Slayter, B. and Wangari, E. (eds). 1996. *Feminist political ecology: global issues and local experiences*. London: Routledge.

Rose, G. 1994. Across the disciplines: What is feminist theory? *Gender, Place and Culture*. 1: 115–117.

Sachs, I. 1999. Social sustainability and whole development: Exploring the dimensions of sustainable development. In: Becker, E. and Jahn, T. (eds). *Sustainability and the social sciences: a cross-disciplinary approach to integrating environmental considerations into theoretical reorientation*. London and New York: Zed Books, pp. 25–36.

Sachs, W. (ed). 1993. *Global ecology: a new arena of political conflict*. London and New York: Zed Books.

Seager, J. 1993. *Earth follies*. New York: Routledge.

Smith, N. 1987. Academic war over the field of geography: the elimination of geography at Harvard 1946–51. *Annals of the Association of American Geographers*. 77: 155–72.

Sneddon, C. 2000. Sustainability in ecological economics, ecology and livelihoods: a review. *Progress in Human Geography*. 24: 521–49.

Soule, M. and Lease, G. (eds). 1995. *Reinventing nature? Responses to postmodern deconstruction*. Washington: Island Press.

Steiner, D. 1993. Human ecology as a transdisciplinary science, and science as part of human ecology. In Steiner, D. and Nauser, M. (eds). *Human ecology: fragments of anti-fragmentary views of the world*. London: Routledge, pp. 47–76.

Steiner, D. and Nauser, M. 1993. Introduction. In Steiner, D. and Nauser, M. (eds). *Human ecology: fragments of anti-fragmentary views of the world*. London: Routledge, pp. 1–12.

Stoddard, R., Blouet, B. and Wishart, D. 1986. *Human geography: people, places and cultures*. New Jersey: Prentice Hall.

Taylor, G. 1953. *Geography in the twentieth century*. London: Methuen.

Toye, J. 1987. Development studies and change in contemporary Britain. *World Development*. 15: 503–15.

Toynbee, A. 1966. *Change and habit: the challenge of our time*. London: Oxford University Press.

Turner, B. 2002. Contested identities: human-environment geography and disciplinary implications in a restructuring academy. *Annals of the Association of American Geographers*. 92: 52–74.

UNCED (United Nations Conference on Environment and Development). 1992.

Report of the United Nations Conference on Environment and Development, Rio de Janeiro, 3–14 June 1992. New York: United Nations.

van Benthem van den Bergh, G. 1986. The improvement of human means of orientation: towards synthesis in the social sciences. In: Apthorne, R. and Krahl, A. (eds). *Development studies: critique and renewal*. Leiden: E.J. Brill, pp. 109–35.

Wackernagel, M. and Rees, W. 1996. *Our ecological footprint*. Philadelphia: New Society Publishers.

(WCED) World Commission on Environment and Development. 1987. *Our common future*. Oxford: Oxford University Press.

White, C. and Renner, G. 1936. *Geography: an introduction to human ecology*. New York: D. Appleton-Century.

Wilbanks, T. 1994. Sustainable development in geographic perspective. *Annals of the Association of American Geographers*. 84: 541–56.

Young, G. (eds). 1983. *Origins of human ecology*. Stroudsberg: Hutchinson Ross.

Zimmerman, M. 1993. General introduction. In: Zimmerman, M. (ed). *Environmental philosophy: from animal rights to radical ecology*. New Jersey: Prentice Hall, pp. v–x.

6. Environmental, ecological and behavioural economics

Jack L. Knetsch

Much of the economic analysis of environmental issues remains wedded to conventional assumptions of standard economic theory. The presumed contribution of ecological economics is to point to the underachievements of traditional analysis and to call more explicit attention to a wider view of environmental values and conflicts.

However, with respect to the many results from behavioural economics research, ecological economics remains as immune to the potential offered by new findings and insights as the most narrow of conventional environmental economics. Even a cursory review of papers in *Ecological Economics*, new books and the Ecological Economics Society conference programmes reveals that findings such as people valuing losses much more than gains, discounting future gains at lower rates than future losses, and values being relatively insensitive to quantity and other attributes of environmental changes, are as fully unemployed in ecological economics as in the more traditional approaches.

The implications of the behavioural findings extend far beyond formal analyses of benefits and costs. They also include the way that people think about and discuss environmental problems and possible resolutions.

ENVIRONMENTAL VALUATIONS

Many environmental policy debates and choices turn on how to pursue environmental goals amid competing claims. Economists have focused much of their interest on trying to sort this out by turning to monetary valuations, mostly in terms of how much people seem willing to sacrifice to obtain environmental benefits or to prevent present or future degradation. This has led to a fairly vast literature on valuation methods and estimates – and too much employment of research assistants, and a cottage industry of individuals ready to facilitate furthering of environmental damage claims and to supply numbers for benefit–cost analyses and feasibility studies for all manner of proposals. Much good has come out of this, not the least of which is a far wider understanding that economic values include non-market, or non-pecuniary, as well as market returns.

A main staple of current environmental economic analysis is an adherence to conventional assumptions of traditional economic theory – 'A core set of economic assumptions should be used in calculating benefits and costs' (Arrow et al. 1996: 222). Such admonishments invoking the dictates of conventional economic theory continue to be the reigning standard by which methods and proposals are tested and critiques of them are judged. Consequently, economists and other policy analysts – or at least those enjoying the benefits of continued employment and those asked for their advice on environmental matters – have continued to rely on standard models of economic behaviour and preferences. As Tetlock and Mellers observe, 'Many psychologists [and others] will find it difficult to appreciate the tenacious grip that rational-choice theory holds over economics' (2002: 94).

However, the large and growing body of empirical evidence provided by psychologists, decision analysts and an increasing number of economists indicates that some important behavioural assumptions, which form the basis of the standard theory and much environmental and other economic analysis, often provide neither a very good description of people's preferences nor very useful predictions of their reactions to real choices. And, not incidentally, the biases, omissions and other shortcomings of many economic analyses being revealed by recent behavioural findings may help to explain at least part of the popular discontent with economic assessments of such matters and people's frustrations over lack of adequate response to environmental problems and opportunities.

A well-documented, and particularly important, example for issues related to the environment has to do with the assumptions that the value of any entitlement is independent of the reference of having or not having it and is invariant to particulars of how choices are presented. The evidence, of course, indicates that rather than such procedural or context invariance, goods and services (including non-pecuniary ones such as environmental services) may have one value to an individual in one context and quite another value in a different context.

CONTEXT DEPENDENCE AND DIFFERING VALUATIONS OF GAINS AND LOSSES

Perhaps the most prominent example of the context dependence of economic values is the asymmetric valuation of gains and losses (Kahneman and Tversky 1979).[1]

It is generally agreed that the economic value of gains, environmental or any other, is correctly assessed by the maximum sums people are willing to pay (WTP) to obtain them. It is similarly agreed that the economic value of losses is appropriately measured by the minimum amount of compensation people are willing to accept (WTA) to endure them.

In practice, however, it is commonly assumed that the maximum sum people would pay (WTP) to gain an entitlement is, except for a normally inconsequential difference due to a wealth or income effect, equal to the minimum sum they would accept (WTA) to give it up: '. . . there is no basis consistent with economic assumptions and empirical income effects for WTP and WTA to exhibit sizable differences' (Diamond et al. 1993: 66). Consequently, '. . . we shall normally expect the results to be so close together that it would not matter which we choose' (Henderson 1941: 121). This remains the empirical assertion of choice, and continues to provide the rationale for current analyses and assessments of environmental values.

The evidence is, of course, sharply at variance with the conventional assertion of equivalence between the two measures of economic value. The findings – which have been reported in *all* of the world's leading economics journals, and those of related fields, for over two decades – suggest instead that people commonly value losses from two to four or more times more than commensurate gains.

The results of two within-person real exchange experiments are indicative of the findings. In one, a group of individuals were willing to pay an average of US$5.60 for a 50 per cent chance to win US$20, but the *same* individuals demanded an average of US$10.87 to give up the identical chance to win the same prize of US$20 (Kachelmeier and Shehata 1992). In another example, participants were willing to pay US$0.96 to acquire a widely available lottery ticket selling for US$1.00, but these same individuals demanded an average of US$2.42 to give up exactly the same entitlement (Borges and Knetsch 1998).

Consistent evidence of a reference effect has come from a wide array of survey studies, real exchange experiments and recordings of the choices made by individuals in non-experimental decisions (Kahneman et al. 1991). For example, a greater sensitivity of investors to losses is apparent in their hesitation to realize a loss by selling, which leads to the observed smaller volume of sales of securities that have declined in price relative to those for which prices have increased (Odean 1998; Shefrin and Statman 1985).

Many other studies have demonstrated that the valuation disparity is pervasive, usually large (though variable depending on the entitlements at issue and the further particulars of the context of the valuation), and not the result of income effects, wealth constraints or transaction costs (Kahneman et al. 1990; Knetsch et al. 2001): 'The evidence is irrefutable that bids based on willingness to accept (WTA) compensation will systematically exceed – often by a large ratio – bids based on willingness to pay' (Vatn and Bromley 1994: 140).[2]

The findings from the many empirical tests of the reference effect strongly support three related conclusions of particular importance to values associated with the environment. The first is that, contrary to conventional assumptions, a good does not have a single 'true' value that can be elicited with sufficiently clever measurement methods – it has differing values depending on the context of the valuation. The second is that a future outcome will have one value in the context of the sacrifice an individual would make to obtain it and another, larger, value in the context of the sacrifice the same person would make to avoid its loss. The third is that the choice of which measure of value to use in particular instances will usually be a matter of substantial practical importance.

CHOOSING THE WRONG MEASURE

A major practical implication of the very large differences between assessments using WTP and WTA measures is that the current near universal practice of using the WTP measure to assess, and to think about, the value of losses and reductions in losses, is almost certain to greatly understate the actual value of such changes. Losses are appropriately assessed by the WTA measure, not WTP, and the distinction is important.

A pervasive instance of the inappropriate choice of measure occurs in nearly all contingent valuation studies of environmental damages. The reason for using the WTP measure in such assessments is not any widespread belief that this is the correct choice. The opposite remains true, 'The conceptually correct measure of lost passive-use value for environmental damage that has already occurred is the minimum amount of compensation that each affected individual would be willing to accept' (Arrow et al. 1993: 4603). The inappropriate choice of the WTP measure to assess losses is instead due to: (1) a persistence in ignoring the evidence of a large difference between the measures, '. . . willingness to accept compensation should exceed willingness to pay, *if only trivially*' (Arrow et al. 1993: 4603, emphasis added); (2) the near absence of sanction, or even criticism of this practice – indeed, the opposite of praise and monetary reward for doing so remain the rule; and (3) the inability to elicit meaningful WTA values from respondents in contingent valuation surveys:

> Respondents will be far less familiar with the notion of receiving compensation for losing something . . . This is likely to cause far greater uncertainty and variability in answers to WTA questions than occurs with WTP questions. Therefore, the former are to be avoided in favour of the latter (Turner et al. 1993: 123).

Continuation of this mischievous practice of using the WTP measure to assess losses is also encouraged by a compatible alignment of the self-interests of parties directly involved in damage actions:

- Courts and other tribunal-like public agencies are pressed to base positions and decisions on numbers that appear objective.
- Plaintiffs recognize that the usual contingent valuation study will provide unreliable WTA responses and so desire to establish at least the smaller WTP quantum of damages, which tribunals will accept.
- Contractors hired to provide damage estimates can only conveniently produce WTP numbers and therefore claim their legitimacy
- Defendants are only too pleased to endorse a measure that will yield lower estimates over one that would give rise to liability for far larger assessments.[3]

The current practice of using the WTP measure rather than the more appropriate, and usually much larger WTA measure for losses, and reductions of losses, in not just contingent valuation but in other assessments as well, will in most cases give rise to systematic understatements of their value. This will lead to undue encouragement of activities with negative impacts, such as pollution and risks to health, as these losses will be underweighted. Similarly, too few resources will be devoted to avoiding environmental deterioration as the efficiency of alternative allocations will be biased against avoiding losses (Knetsch 1990).

Yet, in spite of the fairly obvious consequences of the use of WTP measure of losses, this has been, and remains, the nearly universal practice. In doing so, it is quite common to follow the quite dubious advice to simply rephrase a description of a loss to make it seem a benefit: '. . . there is a class of problems for which the WAC [willingness to accept compensation] format seems appropriate but which can be framed in WTP terms in a plausible way' (Freeman 1993: 179–180). For example, in an attempt to assess the monetary damages of an oil spill affecting coastal areas in western USA and Canada, people were asked, 'What is the most your household would be willing to pay in total over the next five years in higher prices for programmes that prevent oil spills, like those described above, along the West Coast over the next five years?'. The responses were then taken to provide a 'measure of the damage of the Nestucca oil spill' (RCG/Hagler, Bailly Inc. 1991: 6.3), which was used as the basis for a damage claim.

Many context-dependent valuations, and the basis of many choices and decisions, are functions of reference states. Whether a positive change in the provision of environmental services is a gain or reduction of a loss is, for example, dependent on what is taken as the reference. The distinction is important because reducing a loss will likely be much more valuable than providing a gain, and this can have a large bearing on the appropriate policy response.

The reference levels used to discriminate between gains and reductions of losses, and between losses and foregone gains, appear to be mostly a matter of what people regard as the expected or normal state (Kahneman and Miller 1986). This may be akin to the good neighbour test of what is regarded as acceptable and unacceptable behaviour within communities (Ellickson 1973). Contrary to many assertions, reference states and determinations of the most appropriate measure appear largely not to be a matter of extant legal entitlements (Knetsch 1997). Legal rights determine what claims receive recognition by the state and support a cause of action (usually injunctive relief or damage payments) of an injured party against a neighbour. The choice of economic measure is about another issue, one of choosing a metric that best reflects actual changes in welfare resulting from particular changes.[4]

Current practice is overwhelmingly to assert, without bothering with much explicit justification, an implicit reference position – to, for example, treat all positive changes as gains regardless of any evidence of the timing or nature of the taking of a prior claim. A better sorting out seems much in order.

DIFFERENT DISCOUNT RATES FOR FUTURE GAINS AND FUTURE LOSSES

There is general agreement that future outcomes are valued less than present outcomes, and, consequently, 'Both economic efficiency and intergenerational equity require that benefits and costs experienced in future years be given less weight in decision-making than those experienced today' (Arrow et al. 1996: 222). Further, there is also agreement that, apart from some intergenerational equity issues, outcomes expected to occur at different times in the future should be made comparable by discounting to a common time, with the discount rate 'based on how individuals trade off current for future consumption' (Arrow et al. 1996: 222).

Here again, in the case of discounting the value of future gains and future losses, analysts continue to rely on conventional time preference models of standard theory, which suggest that all future outcomes should be discounted at the same rate: '. . . social discount rates are not project specific, the same set of discount rates should be used in the evaluation of all projects' (Dasgupta et al. 1999: 53). There has been disagreement over what that single rate should be, but, in accord with economic orthodoxy, whatever rate is chosen is taken to be invariant to particulars or contexts of specific temporal tradeoffs.

However, the empirical evidence indicates that the traditional discounting models, which assume that people adjust their present and future consumption to a single interest rate, do not reflect people's real time preferences. While there are problems with many of the specific findings, having to do with reliance on responses to hypothetical questions and confounding with other variables, it appears clear that the conventional model falls far short. Rather than a single rate of time preference, the available evidence indicates, for instance, that people value future losses more than future gains (for example, Loewenstein and Prelec 1992; Thaler 1981), and use higher rates to discount over a time period in the near term than over a like delay in the far term (for example, Benzion et al. 1989).

Explanations for the many observed disparities between predicted and observed intertemporal choices have centred on capital market imperfections, transaction costs, less than full information, risk perceptions and aversions, and common problems of inadequate data to calibrate models. While no doubt important, behavioural findings suggest that context variables provide a more general determinate of how people trade off present and future gains and losses. The observed higher valuations of future losses than future gains, for example, is a predictable consequence of the pervasive asymmetric valuations of gains and losses (Knetsch and Gregory 2002).

The measure of sacrifice that yields the correct economic value of a gain is, as widely acknowledged, the maximum sum an individual would pay (WTP) to obtain it. It does not matter whether the gain is to be received now or in the future. The present value of a future gain,[5] like the value of an immediate gain, is measured by the maximum sum that an individual would pay now (a present loss) to receive an entitlement to the future benefit. This WTP is in the domain of gains for the future entitlement and losses of present wealth. As gains are expected to be worth less than losses for both the future good and the present sacrifice, people can be expected to be willing to pay relatively less for a future gain, meaning that the future benefit would be equivalent to a relatively smaller present sum. This lower WTP implies a high rate of discount for future gains.

In the same way, just as the value of a current loss is correctly measured by the minimum compensation demanded to accept it, the present value of a future loss is the compensation received now that would leave the individual as well off as without the future change. This is the WTA measure. As losses are weighed relatively more, this implies that the present compensation would need to be larger to accept a future loss, making the future outcome equivalent to a larger present value and thereby implying a relatively lower discount rate for future losses.

Differences in rates of time preferences are then to be expected, as they follow directly from the valuation disparity and the difference in the appropriate gain and loss frames for assessing the present value of future gains and future losses. And this is what the empirical evidence confirms, as indicated, for example, in the finding that a group of high school students required compensation of US$1.09, on average, to delay use of a US$7 gift certificate by seven weeks, but were willing to pay an average of only US$0.52 to speed up its use by the same length of time (Loewenstein 1988).

Given that many environmental worries involve outcomes extending over time, and frequently long periods of time, the current use of invariant rates to determine present values may well provide seriously distorted views of people's preferences. To the extent that people discount the value of a future loss at a lower rate than a future gain, as the evidence suggests, this can have a major impact on designing and justifying environmental policies and actions, especially those intended to deal with such issues as global climate change, long-term storage of hazardous materials and unsustainable resource use.

CONTINUING NON-USE

Traditional behavioural assumptions of standard theory continue to guide both environmental economics and ecological economics: 'A failure to satisfy the requirements of economic theory would suggest that the appropriate preferences were not being measured' (Diamond 1996: 346). However, the results from what is now a vast array of tests have provided consistent findings that some of these common behavioural assumptions are very often quite wrong. Further, there is increasing evidence that policy design, damage assessments and environmental management could be materially improved with what now seem to be better readings of people's real preferences.

Thaler and Benartzi (forthcoming) provide a striking example of the benefits of taking advantage of behavioural findings. Instead of asking employees how much they would like to contribute to their pension fund out of their current salary, which frames this payment as a loss, they asked for contributions as a proportion of future salary increases, framing this as a far less aversive foregone gain. The result of this change, which involved real employees making actual pension fund decisions, was an over threefold increase in savings rates.

In spite of the large and fairly obvious implications of behavioural findings for environmental issues, there is little movement of environmental or ecological economists to take any similar serious note of them. There remains an almost total absence of any accounting, or even acknowledgement, of these findings in debates over environmental values, in valuation exercises, in the design of environmental policies, or even in environmental economics texts and workshops conducted throughout the world with the announced purpose of introducing people to the latest findings and techniques of environmental assessments.

It is not just the parties directly involved who are affected by damage assessments based on inappropriate measures; all live with the consequences of poor policies based on poor information. And these are just parts of the continuing levy of procrastination.

There are a number of reasons for the lack of much attention to behavioural findings in dealing with environmental matters (Knetsch 2000), but most appear to centre on the incentives provided to people and what they then perceive as their self-interest. One example is the self-censorship, conformity, and going along with the tried if not the true, resulting from restraints imposed by what has become known as group-think. This appears to be exacerbated by the growing awareness of the positive impacts on career success of being perceived as a 'good team member'. Another example is exemplified by two quotes: 'If I put this in no one would adopt my books', by a very successful economics text writer; and, 'Some ideas may be too novel or different to be accepted readily', by a knowledgeable senior economist in a public environmental control agency. Both seem correct, and both characterize the incentives leading to the present state of non-use of newer behavioural findings.

Given the incentives that presently discourage use of behavioural insights, a marked change in the potential costs and benefits facing individuals might well prod some socially beneficial changes. While there are no doubt many things that might be done to further this aim, two seem to be both practical and offer some promise or hope. One is more replications of important findings under differing circumstances and conditions so that the weight of evidence becomes increasingly overwhelming and more difficult to dismiss.

The other is to increase the costs of persisting with the status quo and decrease the cost of change by challenging more assertions and justifications for decisions that are inconsistent with the behavioural evidence. The history of benefit–cost analysis is mildly encouraging on this score. Abuse of the principles that make such exercises worth while are common, and few who follow the practical application of such analyses do not marvel at the ingenuity of project proponents to rationalize procedures to gain outcomes they favour. Yet, at least in some countries and in some institutions, there has been a tradition of informed critique, which has had marked beneficial impacts on analysts' motives – most do not want to be seen to be knowingly doing things poorly or wrong.

NOTES

1. This early and well-known 'Prospect theory' paper by Kahneman and Tversky calling attention to the disparity between valuations of gains and losses is reputed to be the most often cited paper ever published in *Econometrica* (Laibson and Zeckhauser 1998), a testament to its importance and range of applicability.
2. Hanemann (1991) has correctly pointed out that standard theory can, under particular conditions, allow for a large difference in gain and loss values for an identical entitlement. These include a positive income effect and a lack of substitutes for the good at issue. However, large

differences have been observed under conditions that violate those required for this standard theory explanation. The reference effect is, as Hanemann notes, 'a different phenomenon' (1991: 645), but it seems to be a far more general explanation for the pervasive differences observed in the numerous tests and in common experience than the narrow possibilities offered by standard theory.
3. Where, it might be asked, are the objections of academics, environmental interest groups, research institutes and others claiming to have an interest in improving the collective weal?
4. Individual cases of which party prevails over the other are, of course, settled in accord with existing legal entitlements. However, the assignment of entitlement used to settle disputes and to provide guidance to resource users would contribute most to social welfare if they correspond to people's reference for judging gains and losses. A lack of correspondence can compromise socially useful incentives – a problem made worse by the valuation disparity, as entitlements are unlikely to be changed through voluntary exchanges.
5. A future gain may take various forms, including a gain, an increase in a gain or delay of a loss. While all may be a future gain, there seems to be little reason to expect people to have the same specific rate of time preference for all of them.

BIBLIOGRAPHY

Arrow, K., Solow, R., Leamer, E., Portney, P., Randner, R. and Schuman, H. 1993. Report of the NOAA Panel on Contingent Valuation. *US Federal Register.* 58 (10): 4602–14, 15 January.

Arrow, K., Cropper, M.L., Eads, G.C., Hahn, R.W., Lave, L.B., Noll, R.G., Portney, P.R., Russell, M., Schmalensee, R., Smith, V.K. and Stavins, R.N. 1996. Is there a role for benefit–cost analysis in environmental, health, and safety regulation? *Science.* 272: 221–2, 12 April.

Benzion, U., Rapoport, A. and Yagil, J. 1989. Discount rates inferred from decisions: an experimental study. *Management Science.* 35: 270–84.

Borges, B.F.J. and Knetsch, J.L. 1998. Tests of market outcomes with asymmetric valuations of gains and losses: smaller gains, fewer trades, and less value. *Journal of Economic Behavior and Organisation.* 33: 185–93.

Dasgupta, P., Maler, K-G. and Barrett, S. 1999. Intergenerational equity, social discount rates, and global warming. In: Portney, P.R. and Weyant, J.P. (eds). *Discounting and intergenerational equity.* Washington, DC: Resources for the Future, pp. 51–77.

Diamond, P. 1996. Testing the internal consistency of contingent valuation surveys. *Journal of Environmental Economics and Management.* 30: 337–47.

Diamond, P.A., Hausman, J.A., Leonard, G.K. and Denning, M.A. 1993. 'Does contingent valuation measure preferences? Experimental evidence. In: Hausman, J. (ed). *Contingent valuation: a critical assessment.* Amsterdam: Elsevier Science Publishers, pp. 41–89.

Ellickson, R.C. 1973. Alternatives to zoning: covenants, nuisance rules, and fines as land use controls. *University of Chicago Law Review.* 40: 581–781.

Freeman, A.M. 1993. *The measurement of environmental and resource values – theory and methods.* Washington, DC: Resources for the Future.

Hanemann, W.M. 1991. Willingness to pay and willingness to accept: how much can they differ? *The American Economic Review.* 81: 635–47.

Henderson, A.M. 1941. Consumer's surplus and the compensation variation. *Review of Economic Studies.* 8: 117.

Kachelmeier, S.J. and Shehata, M. 1992. Examining risk preferences under high monetary incentives: experimental evidence from the People's Republic of China. *The American Economic Review.* 82: 1120–40.

Kahneman, D., Knetsch, J.L. and Thaler, R.H. 1990. Experimental tests of the endowment effect and the Coase Theorem. *Journal of Political Economy.* 98: 1325–48.

Kahneman, D., Knetsch, J.L. and Thaler, R.H. 1991. The endowment effect, loss aversion, and status quo bias. *Journal of Economic Perspectives.* 5: 193–206.

Kahneman, D. and Miller, D.T. 1986. Norm theory: comparing reality to its alternatives. *Psychological Review.* 93: 136–53.

Kahneman, D. and Tversky, A. 1979. Prospect theory: an analysis of decisions under risk. *Econometrica.* 47: 263–91.

Knetsch, J.L. 1990. Environmental policy implications of disparities between willingness to pay and compensation demanded measures of value. *Journal of Environmental Economics and Management.* 18: 227–37.

Knetsch, J.L. 1997. Reference states, fairness, and choice of measure to value environmental changes. In: Bazerman, M., Messick, D., Tenbrunsel, A. and Wade-Bensoni, K. (eds). *Environment, ethics, and behavior.* San Francisco: Lexington Press, pp. 13–32.

Knetsch, J.L. 2000. Environmental valuations and standard theory: behavioural findings, context dependence, and implications. In: Tietenberg, T. and Folmer, H. (eds). *The international yearbook of environmental and resource economics 2000/2001.* Cheltenham: Edward Elgar, pp. 267–99.

Knetsch, J.L., Tang, F-F. and Thaler, R.H. 2001. The endowment effect and repeated market trials: is the Vickrey Auction Demand revealing? *Experimental Economics.* 4: 257–69.

Knetsch, J.L. and Gregory, R.S. 2002. Discounting future gains and future losses: further evidence of the context dependence of time preferences. Working Paper. Simon Fraser University.

Laibson, D. and Zeckhauser, R. 1998. Amos Tversky and the ascent of behavioral economics. *Journal of Risk and Uncertainty.* 16: 7–47.

Loewenstein, G.F. 1988. Frames of mind in intertemporal choice. *Management Science.* 34: 200–214.

Loewenstein, G.F. and Prelec, D. 1992. Anomalies in intertemporal choice: evidence and an interpretation. *The Quarterly Journal of Economics.* 107: 573–97.

Odean, T. 1998. Are investors reluctant to realize their losses? *The Journal of Finance.* 53: 1775–98.

RCG/Hagler, Bailly, Inc. 1991. Contingent valuation of natural resource damage due to the Nestucca oil spill: final report. Boulder, Colorado, USA.

Shefrin, H.M. and Statman, M. 1985. The disposition to sell winners too early and ride losers too long: theory and evidence. *The Journal of Finance.* 40: 777–90.

Tetlock, P.E. and Mellers, B.A. 2002. The great rationality debate. *Psychological Science.* 13: 94–8.

Thaler, R.H. 1981. Some empirical evidence on dynamic inconsistency. *Economic Letters.* 8: 199–207.

Thaler, R.H. and Benartzi, S. Forthcoming. Save more tomorrow: using behavioral economics to increase employee saving. *Journal of Political Economy.*

Turner, R.K., Pearce, D. and Bateman, I. 1993. *Environmental economics.* Baltimore, Maryland: The Johns Hopkins University Press.

Vatn, A. and Bromley, D.W. 1994. Choices without prices without apologies. *Journal of Environmental Economics and Management.* 26: 129–48.

7. Economic psychology and ecological economics[1]

Stephen E.G. Lea

This chapter reflects on two unconventional approaches to the study of economics and to consider how they might be brought into closer relation. The underlying belief driving the chapter is that, if the world is to have a future at all, we have to revolutionize our understanding of economics. Obviously, given that apocalyptic context, I do not mean only, or even mainly, our academic understanding, but the way in which individuals and businesses construe and carry out their everyday economic tasks. But those everyday processes are reflected in, and in part reflect, the academic discipline of economics.

This chapter brings together two interdisciplinary critiques of that academic discipline, from, as it were, above and below. From above, we need to recognize that the whole system of human activities that collectively constitute 'the economy' forms just one part of a much larger system, the planetary ecology. Economic activity depends on the natural environment at every stage, from the procurement of its raw materials to the disposal of its waste materials. But its dependence is truly systematic, in the sense that causality runs in both directions. At least for the last few thousand years, and to a rapidly accelerating extent, human economic activity has been not just constrained by the ecosystem, but has been increasingly modifying it.

From below, we equally need to recognize that the economic system depends, again at every stage, on individual human beings. At every stage of the economic process, individual people are producing and consuming the goods and services that are involved; if they were not, there could be no economy. And once again, the dependence is systematic: individuals' economic behaviours construct the economy, but the economy acts as a powerful determining variable on the behaviour and mental life of each individual who lives within it.

Both conventional academic economics and the everyday practice of those who run businesses and manage national and international economies largely ignore the ways in which economics is embedded in ecology and embeds psychology. But the wider academic community has not altogether ignored them. A number of interdisciplinary areas of study and research have sprung up to look at these difficult interfaces between economics and ecology, on the one hand, and psychology, on the other. This chapter looks at two of them, which go by the names (which are titles self-consciously adopted by their practitioners as well as straightforward descriptions) of ecological economics and economic psychology.

Although these two approaches come at economics from opposite directions, they have some important points in common, which not only link them together, but also link them to the themes of this book. First, and most obviously, both are sometimes critical of conventional economics. Second, both have an orientation towards a greater consideration of values and ethics. Ecology is perhaps the ethical *cause celèbre* of our time, largely ignored by all moralists until halfway through the twentieth century but now possibly the hottest moral issue for many people, especially young people, in the 'advanced' countries. Economic psychology is not so inherently a values-driven activity. But of course moral values have to reside within individuals if they are to be translated into economic behaviour, and since conventional economics largely ignores such values, the fact that real people actually possess them is commonly a feature of psychologists' critiques of economic theory.

This chapter therefore sets these two interdisciplinary activities, each of which operates somewhere on the critical fringe of modern economics, alongside each other. But the aim is not just to compare them, but rather to look at the ways in which they interact, since together they may constitute a more powerful critique of the conventional economic approach than either can separately. So, as well as looking at the ways in which economic psychology currently interacts with ecological economics, the chapter moves on to look at ways in which that interaction could be extended and made more fruitful. It starts by giving a very brief overview of the two fields, and looks at some similarities, differences and complementarities between them. It then looks at some fields of economic psychology research that are, or ought to be, important to ecological economics, before identifying possible future interactions.

WHAT IS ECOLOGICAL ECONOMICS?

The following is very much a sympathetic outsider's view of ecological economics. There are of course several textbooks that will give a fuller picture (for example Söderbaum 2000), and what I am doing here is focusing on those areas that are most relevant to an interaction with economic psychology. I hope that ecological economists will at least recognize their discipline in the following discussion.

Ecological economics is much more than the economics of the natural environment. In intent, it is a truly interdisciplinary pursuit, and it is also a self-consciously values-driven one. It aims to recognize that human economic affairs are necessarily embedded into a wider ecological context, which constitutes the essential foundation of our economic life, contributes to economic production, constrains what is economically possible and is affected by economic activities. It overlaps with, but is distinct from, environmental economics. Environmental economists might try to assess the economic benefits of particular features of the environment, or to conduct an environmental cost–benefit analysis of a proposed economic development. Ecological economists, by contrast, would want to judge an economic development on the basis of its ecological sustainability, taking the view that only sustainable developments are economically possible in the long run.

Ecological economics is thus a non-standard economics. Although the largest group of its practitioners are trained as economists, ecological economists would in general not feel themselves bound by the mindset of neoclassical economics, and indeed they are frequently critical of it (as several chapters in this book evidence). In particular, they see the limits on economic activity that are set by the ecology of the planet as a first, rather than an outermost, consideration in any economic analysis. In consequence, they bring to centre stage what conventional economics refers to as the 'externalities' of an economic process – the costs it imposes on (or, more rarely, the benefits it yields for) those not primarily involved in it as buyers or sellers. Furthermore, ecological economics is not committed to materialism in the same way as conventional economics. One of the foundations of microeconomic theory is the 'axiom of greed', the assertion that, other things being equal, the economic welfare of an individual is increased if his or her consumption increases. There are of course ways within neoclassical economics of finessing this assumption, in order to accommodate the 'tastes' of those who voluntarily forego consumption, either out of philosophical asceticism or in order to reduce their impact on the environment. But ecological economics puts the uncertainty of the link between consumption and welfare into the centre of its thinking, instead of marginalizing it.

All this means that ecological economics is automatically committed to the idea of multiple motives. Of course, all economics has to deal with the trade-off between incompatible desires. But conventional economic analysis does so by reducing all desires to a single dimension of utility. A values-driven economics cannot do this; it has to recognize that some desires are not just incompatible but incommensurable. Economic agents – both people and firms and other institutions – operate under multiple motives that cannot be traded off against each other.

Another respect in which ecological economics is unconventional is that, because of its focus on real ecosystem problems, it necessarily operates in a real rather than an abstracted world. That is to say, it recognizes the essential value of data. This is partly because much practical ecological economics has grown out of agricultural economics, which has always been the most data-driven part of economic science. But it is mainly because it is much too easy to show that there is some theoretical ecological constraint on economic development. The argument only becomes interesting if we can show that the constraint applies in the here (or near) and now (or soon), in the quantitative circumstances of the current local economy. That in turn can only be demonstrated with the aid of the quantitative current local facts.

All this means that ecological economics, if undertaken seriously, is undoubtedly more difficult than conventional economics. It is easier to assume that there are no boundaries on economic development; it is easier to assume that all values can be subsumed into one; it is easier to construct theories in the abstract than to find ways of collecting data to test them. Nonetheless, ecological economics has enjoyed considerable success in recent decades, certainly in terms of institutional development, with textbooks and courses appearing worldwide and regular, well-attended international conferences, but also in terms of practical application. Governments and other authorities who face serious decisions with grave environmental consequences are willing to consult those who are able to place an economic analysis within a formal and responsible ecological framework.

AND WHAT IS ECONOMIC PSYCHOLOGY?

This too is a very cursory introduction to a field that has whole texts (for example Lea et al. 1987; Lewis et al. 1995; Webley et al. 2001) devoted to it. Unlike my glance at ecological economics, however, this is an insider's rather than an outsider's view. It is always necessary to remember, however, that economic psychology is one of those activities that many people do without recognizing that they are doing it. So, quite a few of the authors I cite as contributing to economic psychology might not think of themselves as economic psychologists – primarily, or even at all.

The first thing to say about economic psychology is that it too is a highly interdisciplinary study. It is not just a branch of psychology, and nor is it a branch of economics; economic psychologists are concerned to apply the concepts and methods of both disciplines to problems where they both have something to say. It is concerned with the areas where economics and psychology meet, or at least where they should meet. So economic psychologists are involved with all aspects both of individuals' economic behaviour and of the economy's impact on the individual.

This meeting is clearly a two-way process, and van Raaij (1981) and Lea et al. (1987, chapter 20) both presented formal paradigms that recognize that; Lea et al. refer to a process of 'dual causation'. The individual and the economy form part of a system, each influencing the other, and disentangling the lines of causality is always difficult and can be impossible. It certainly cannot be done in the abstract. So, even more than ecological economics, economic psychology is strongly empirical. Some parts of it are almost 'economics as if the data mattered': economic topics pursued with the kind of empirical approach characteristic of psychology. But although economic psychology aims to be interdisciplinary, most of its practitioners have their initial training in one or other of its two parent disciplines. So, it is meaningful to ask what kinds of psychology and economics are involved in economic psychology. Let us look first at economic psychology as psychology.

Since work and buying are the two largest kinds of economic behaviour, logically, economic psychology should certainly include both consumer psychology and occupational psychology (Lea 1992), both of which are large and successful subdisciplines within psychology. In practice, however, those who call themselves economic psychologists are more often concerned with economic behaviours other than work and buying; or if they are concerned with work or buying, they are wanting to see them within the context of an individual's general economic behaviour, or the general impacts of the economy on the individual.

Methodologically, economic psychology has its roots in social psychology. From the more sociological side of social psychology, it derives research implements such as questionnaire surveys, individual interviews and focus groups. However, social psychology also has a strong experimental tradition, and economic psychology in particular has significant theoretical roots in decision theory, and these influences bring with them a more experimental methodological tradition.

Historically, many psychologists who have examined economic theory have been fairly horrified by what they have seen. The rationality assumptions that lie at the bottom of microeconomic theory seem to be theoretically implausible and empirically false. Nonetheless, it may be wiser for economic psychologists not to be overly critical of such assumptions, but to recognize the very different processes of theory formation that have historically gone on within economics (see Lea 1994). Similarly, economic psychology should not try to present itself as an imperialist movement, of psychologists wanting to take over traditional economic fields of study.

Although there is much of the psychology of work and buying that is not thought of as belonging within economic psychology, obviously both topics do take important places in the subject area. Particularly in the study of buying, there is some evident tension between those who work on applied projects, which verge towards market research and other commercial concerns, and those working in a more academic, perhaps policy-oriented context (Lea 2000).

What about economic psychology considered as a variety of economics? In this context, it is more or less equivalent to 'behavioural economics' (see Knetsch, Chapter 6, this volume), although this phrase is more often used in North America, while 'economic psychology' is more familiar in Europe. Economists interested in psychological analyses are often even more critical of conventional economics, and in particular the use of rationality assumptions, than psychologists are. They tend to be involved with concepts like bounded rationality, multiple utilities and interpersonal utility, all of which strike at the heart of the way neoclassical economics uses the rationality assumption. Linked to this point is the fact that some influential experimental economists are involved in interdisciplinary work with psychologists. Experimentation on individuals leads inevitably to questioning the rationality assumption, which at best only works as an approximation applicable over large populations. Curiously, experimental economists have not been much influenced by experimental social psychologists in their methodology. Indeed, they have somewhat reacted against common psychological practices like misleading subjects about the purpose of the experiment, or using hypothetical scenarios. Their strong views on these topics, as well as some of the situations they have introduced (the ultimatum game, for example see Güth and Tietz 1990; Thaler 1988) have had a substantial influence on economic psychologists with a more psychological training, and even on mainstream psychology.

A further stream of economic thinking that has entered economic psychology is what is often called 'socio-economics'. This owes its foundation to the US economic sociologist Amitai Etzioni, and particularly to his book *The moral dimension* (Etzioni 1988). In many ways the book is more of a hybrid of sociology and economics than of psychology and economics, but it has had a strong influence on psychologists. It is interesting in the context of the present chapter because, like ecological economists, those who call themselves socio-economists are strongly interested in multiple motives and are also strongly values-driven. The driving idea in *The moral dimension* is that there are moral motivations to economic actions that are incommensurable with utilitarian considerations.

Although the title 'economic psychology' is at least a century old, going back to the work of the French social psychologist Gabriel Tarde (1902), it did not come to much prominence until after World War II. It was brought into currency by George Katona, a Hungarian-American gestalt psychologist who became involved in US economic policy formation during the war. Katona (1975) summarizes much of his data. His approach could almost be described as 'econometrics with added psychometrics'; he was interested in using psychological assessments of consumers' and business people's mood to improve forecasting of the macroeconomic trends in the economy. This has become part of the standard apparatus of economic prediction (see, for example, Biart and Praet 1987; Carrol et al. 1994), although debate continues as to whether psychological measures contribute anything that could not, in principle at least, be captured by economic statistics (for example Vanden Abeele 1983; Acemoglu and Scott 1994); for further discussion, see Webley et al. (2001, chapter 5).

COMMON GROUND AND COMPLEMENTARITIES

So what common ground do ecological economics and economic psychology have, and how do they fit together in ways that might benefit both? Among the themes that are common in both, we could include rejection of the axiom of greed; recognition of the importance of multiple motives or multiple, incommensurable utilities; recognition of the importance of interpersonal (including transgenerational) utilities; an interest in time and inter-temporal choice; a tendency towards 'real-world' empirical work and action research; and the use of experimental games. Some of these have already been discussed, but one or two need a little more explanation.

'Interpersonal utilities' is a long way of saying that each individual's welfare is influenced by the welfare of other people. We cannot fully explain any kind of giving without invoking some such concept. Giving falls into two kinds: personal giving, to family and friends, and charitable giving, where the beneficiary may be completely unknown. Economic psychologists have been particularly interested in giving, partly because it has long been a topic of concern in social science (for example Mauss [1925] 1954), partly because it does seem to violate the axiom of greed, and partly just because its study has turned up some reliable, interesting and slightly odd phenomena. Environmental charities and pressure groups have become major players in the 'market' for charitable giving, so this is already a point of contact with ecological economics. However, the most interesting relationship between the economic psychology of giving and ecological concerns is the issue of inter-generational transfers. A great deal of giving (both personal and charitable) occurs between generations, typically though not always from the older to the younger. One particular form of giving, bequeathing, is necessarily intergenerational, and furthermore shows a concern for what happens after an individual's own welfare has ceased to be relevant. Concern for the planetary ecology necessarily requires the same sort of involvement in a future that the individual will never live to experience. Although an individual may enjoy, and set a monetary value on, a pollution-free environment now, it requires a different kind of motivation to be concerned that the environment should be pollution-free in a century's time.

This brings in the question of inter-temporal choice; that is, choice between benefits that are delivered at different times. The entire theory of saving, debt and investment depends on an analysis of inter-temporal choice, and this has proved to be an area where economic theory on its own fails, and an interdisciplinary approach has proved much more successful (see Wärneryd 1999). In the light of the concerns of ecological economics, it is interesting to note that people are typically much less future-oriented than simple economic theory would suggest that they should be – although, on the other hand, the data on saving over the life span cannot be fully explained without taking the bequest motive into account.

What about complementarities? What can economic psychology offer to colleagues interested in ecological economics? First, and most obviously, there are well-established research techniques that should be of value. Although ecological economics remains firmly rooted in economics, its interest in data means that it does quite often need measurement at the individual, not just the societal, level. Economic psychologists have established ways of measuring attitudes towards various economic phenomena, the kinds of multiple values that are relevant to economic decisions, and constructs like time horizons that influence inter-temporal choices.

Second, in some fields there is a major resource of empirical knowledge. Consumer behaviour, at both the individual and the macro level, has been studied in detail, and we have both a large body of data and elaborate theories of why people choose to buy one product rather than another. In the next section we show that this has immediate implications for ecological concerns.

Conversely, economic psychology can also gain from ecological economics. For a complete economic psychology, we need a much better understanding of the actual economic and ecological impacts of individuals' behaviour, and the techniques for assessing these are developing rapidly in ecological economics. Furthermore, many economic psychologists work in fields (such as tax, social security, gambling, debt and poverty) that are highly relevant to social policy, and they could exchange lessons with ecological economists on the difficult art of translating behavioural knowledge into policy recommendations and getting those recommendations heard.

ECOLOGICAL ISSUES IN CURRENT ECONOMIC PSYCHOLOGY

So, what kinds of current research in economic psychology should be of particular interest to ecological economists? A quick survey of the papers presented at the annual conferences of the International Association for Research in Economic Psychology suggests that about 5 per cent of papers have clearly ecological themes. They tend to focus on psychological variables that relate to environmental concerns and either influence or are influenced by the economy. Examples of such variables include perceptions, social representations, attitudes, habits, motivations, information, commitment, time preferences, ethics, attention, gender and quality of life. A second major theme concerns economic and policy mechanisms that impact on the environment, including taxes, externality charges, marketing, durability and contingent valuation.

Looking in more detail at current research, I want to gather together some studies under a general title: 'green motivation'. As we have already seen, both ecological economics and economic psychology differ from standard, neoclassical economics in recognizing multiple, incommensurable, economic motivations. In the ecological context, the obvious possibility is that there is a motivation to conserve and favour the environment irrespective of, or perhaps at the cost of, its pecuniary worth. To what extent has research in economic psychology identified the characteristics and impacts of such 'green motivation'? This question is explored in more depth in Webley (2000); here I am taking a broader brush approach, to fit it into the framework of my discussion of the relation between economic psychology and ecological economics.

It is obvious that 'green' issues have become increasingly salient throughout the latter half of the twentieth century. Many people express 'green' attitudes; some vote for explicitly Green parties. If people are serious about those attitudes, we would expect them to express them in their economic life. Among the ways through which they could do so are job choice (which brings in occupational psychology), commodity choice (which brings in consumer psychology) and investment choice (which brings in economic psychology in the narrower sense).

Surprisingly, little is known about the green employee. Bauer and Aiman-Smith (1996) showed that a pro-environmental stance decreased an individual's intention to seek employment at all, perhaps because 'green consumers' tend to have anti-business attitudes (Zinkhan and Carlson 1995). However, Bauer and Aiman-Smith also found a corporate pro-environmental stance increases a firm's attractiveness to all potential employees, not just those with identifiable green attitudes. Much more is known about the green consumer (Beckmann 1999). Recent psychological (and other) work has concentrated on the translation of green attitudes into actual green consumption (this is of course one of the traditional concerns of social psychologists), the credibility of green marketing, and some specific green consumption behaviours such as recycling (Sterner and Bartelings 1999).

In keeping with many other results in applied social psychology, it has been found that general green attitudes have small (though significant) influence on consumer behaviour, while more specific attitudes and beliefs are more predictive. In terms of general attitudes, for example, in a US sample, Ozanne et al. (1999) found that women are more environmentally aware than men and are more likely to be green consumers. At the more specific level, the belief that green consumer choices will be effective is a strong predictor of whether or not a consumer will make such choices (for example Mainieri et al. 1997; Roberts 1996).

Green buying can be encouraged by social marketing (Shrum et al. 1995a). But the typical price premium that consumers will pay for a certificated green product is only about 10 per cent, although this is affected by price and income (Blake et al. 1997; Spinazze and Kant 1999). Certification is obviously an important factor in the credibility of green marketing claims. At least in the earlier period of green marketing, many claims were in fact untrustworthy (Davis 1992; Welsh 1993). Government and self-regulatory bodies have addressed this (Scammon and Mayer 1995), but consumers differ in degrees of scepticism towards such claims (Mohr et al. 1998) and green consumers tend to be sceptical of all advertising (Shrum et al. 1995b). Consumers are commonly more enthusiastic about certification schemes than producers (Spinazze and Kant 1999).

A particularly interesting case of green buying is consuming green electricity. The 'common carrier' provisions that have accompanied the privatization and enhanced competition that governments have enforced on the energy supply market have made it practicable for both specialist and general energy firms to offer 'green' electricity in (at least) the USA, the UK and Australia. Consumers who choose green electricity are assured that power quantitatively equivalent to their usage will be bought by the supply company from generators using sustainable technologies, such as wind, water, solar or landfill gas. While there is already evidence for the potential of this market (Elliott 1999; Stanord 1998), and some evidence that demand is increasing 'green' generation (Lamarre 1997), there is as yet no published evidence of the extent or durability of take-up or price elasticity.

The biggest consumption choice of all, of course, is house purchase. Economic psychology has been slow to investigate the housing market at all, and there is little evidence on the importance of green motivation in house purchase. While 'sustainable' houses have been built as research or demonstration projects, they are not yet available as a general consumer choice. However, housing choice has major ecological impacts. The biggest issue is probably location: a family's impact on the environment will be very different depending on whether they choose to live in an urban, suburban or rural area. The choice of a rural location can be driven by ecological, 'self-sufficiency' concerns (for example Librova 1996). But if combined with urban employment, it inevitably leads to increased commuting; the evidence is that though people recognize this as a cost (personally as well as environmentally), it is one they will pay for the sake of a lifestyle appropriate to some stages of their lives (for example Kendig 1984).

It is one of the constant themes of economic psychologists that work and buying do not exhaust the psychologically interesting kinds of economic behaviour. Investment is one of the relatively ignored areas that has been the subject of much interesting research recently, and within it the idea of the 'green investor' has been given some attention. As Webley (2000) explains, investment that pays attention to environmental concerns is an important subset of ethical investment, which in turn has been growing both in terms of market share and as a subject for academic interest. For example, one major research project looked in detail at ethical (including green) investment using surveys and experimental simulations, and taking as participants actual investors including some who have made the choice to invest in 'ethical' funds (see Lewis et al. 1998). Most ethical investment takes the form of putting money in unit trusts (mutual funds) that guarantee to avoid companies that engage in particular kinds of business, and in many cases business activities thought of as environmentally damaging are included in the excluded categories. As is now well known, such ethical funds typically do as well as or better than general funds. It turns out that most ethical investors are ethical only to an extent: they have only marginal resources in ethical funds or say they would only take a small loss to remain in such funds. Nonetheless, those who actually hold ethical investments believe 'it makes a difference' to do so; presumably those who do not hold that belief do not take the risk of investing in ethical funds – recall the parallel result in ethical buying (for example Roberts 1996).

CONCLUSIONS AND QUESTIONS

What can we conclude from this brief survey of green motivation in individual economic behaviour? It seems that there is quite a widespread willingness to engage in such behaviour, but if this generally favourable attitude is to be translated into behaviour, it is necessary that people should believe that their behaviour will actually have an effect. There is scepticism about commercial claims to be green, and 'false prospectuses' are likely to be exposed. But even enthusiasts, who believe that their behaviour will make a difference, only act green 'at the margin'. Figures around 10 per cent keep recurring, as the premium that people will pay for a green product, the loss they will carry to make a green investment or the proportion of their transactions that they will make on a green basis.

These conclusions lead directly to some questions, which economic psychologists are ill-equipped to answer, but ecological economists might well be able to respond to. Will such marginally green economic behaviour have any economic impact? It is easy to guess that it may well be too marginal. So how big a margin would be needed? What institutional changes would give the ecologically, aware individual more leverage? Such questions are the stuff of interdisciplinary research. Both ecological economics and economic psychology are already areas of interdisciplinary study. How can we work together to answer these and other questions of critical environmental concern?

Finally, how do these conclusions and questions bear on larger questions of integration between disciplines? I argued at the beginning that the economy interacts, as a system, with two other systems, from above and below – with the planetary ecosystem and the psychological system of the individual. What we see is that this is not a simple hierarchy of systems of ever larger, or ever smaller, scale. Rather, it is a matter of a triangular interaction. The larger concerns of the ecosystem will only be incorporated into the theory and practice of economics in so far as they are also the concerns of individual people. Ecology, psychology and economics need to go hand in hand.

NOTES

1. An earlier version of this chapter was presented to the International Society for Ecological Economics conference, Canberra, July 2000. I am grateful to Mike Young of CSIRO in Australia for that opportunity, and to Roberto Burlando and Paul Webley for their comments and discussion. The chapter is an edited version of an article that appeared in *World Futures*, Volume 56: 15–29 (used with permission). — *no date*

REFERENCES

Acemoglu, D. and Scott, A. 1994. Consumer confidence and rational expectations: are agent's beliefs consistent with the theory? *Economic Journal*. 104: 1–19.

Bauer, T.N. and Aiman-Smith, L. 1996. Green career choices: the influence of ecological stance on recruiting. *Journal of Business and Psychology*. 10, 445–58.

Beckmann, S.C. 1999. Ecology and consumption. In: Earl, P.E. and Kemp, S. (eds). *The Elgar companion to consumer research and economic psychology*. Cheltenham: Edward Elgar. pp. 170–75.

Biart, M. and Praet, P. 1987. The contribution of opinion surveys in forecasting aggregate demand in the four main EC countries. *Journal of Economic Psychology*. 8: 409–28.

Blake, D.E., Guppy, N. and Urmetzer, P. 1997. Canadian public opinion and environmental action: evidence from British Columbia. *Canadian Journal of Political Science*. 30: 451–72.

Carroll, C.D., Fuhrer, J.C. and Wilcox, D.W. 1994. Does consumer sentiment forecast household spending? If so, why? *American Economic Review*. 84: 1397–1408.

Davis, J.J. 1992. Ethics and environmental marketing. *Journal of Business Ethics*. 11: 81–7.

Elliott, D. 1999. Prospects for renewable energy and green energy markets in the UK. *Renewable Energy*. 16: 1268–71.

Etzioni, A. 1988. *The moral dimension*. New York: Free Press.

Güth, W. and Tietz, R. 1990. Ultimatum bargaining behavior: a survey and comparison of experimental results. *Journal of Economic Psychology*. 11: 417–49.

Katona, G. 1975. *Psychological economics*. New York: Elsevier.

Kendig, H.L. 1984. Housing careers, life cycle and residential mobility: implications for the housing market. *Urban Studies*. 21: 271–83.

Lamarre, L. 1997. Utility customers go for the green. *EPRI Journal*. 22: 6–15.

Lea, S.E.G. 1992. Editorial: on parent and daughter disciplines: economic psychology, industrial psychology and consumer science. *Journal of Economic Psychology*. 13: 1–3.

Lea, S.E.G. 1994. Rationality: the formalist view. In: Güth, W. and Brandstätter, H. (eds). *Essays in economic psychology*. Berlin: Springer-Verlag. pp. 71–89.

Lea, S.E.G. 2000. Making money out of psychology: Can we predict economic behaviour? *The Psychologist*. 13: 408–12.

Lea, S.E.G., Tarpy, R.M. and Webley, P. 1987. *The individual in the economy*. Cambridge: Cambridge University Press.

Lewis, A., Webley, P. and Furnham, A.F. 1995. *The new economic mind*. Brighton: Harvester Wheatsheaf.

Lewis, A., Webley, P., Winnett, A. and Mackenzie, C. 1998. Morals and markets: some theoretical and policy implications of ethical investing. In: Taylor-Gooby, P. (eds). *Choice and public policy: the limits to welfare markets*. London: Macmillan. pp. 164–82.

Librova, H. 1996. The decentralisation of settlements – vision and reality: 1. visions, attitudes to the countryside and potential migration in the Czech Republic. *Sociologicky Casopis*. 32: 285–96.

Mainieri, T., Barnett, E.G., Valdero, T.R., Unipan, J.B. and Oskamp, S. 1997. Green buying: the influence of environmental concern on consumer behavior. *Journal of Social Psychology*. 137: 189–204.

Mauss, M. 1954. *The gift: forms and functions of exchange in archaic societies*. London: Routledge & Kegan Paul.

Mohr, L.A., Eroglu, D. and Ellen, P.S. 1998. The development and testing of a measure of skepticism toward environmental claims in marketers' communications. *Journal of Consumer Affairs*. 32: 30–55.

Ozanne, L.K., Humphrey, C.R. and Smith, P.M. (1999). Gender, environmentalism, and interest in forest certification: Mohai's paradox revisited. *Society and Natural Resources*. 12: 613–22.

Roberts, J.A. 1996. Green consumers in the 1990s: profile and implications for advertising. *Journal of Business Research*. 36: 217–31.

Scammon, D.L. and Mayer, R.N. 1995. Agency review of environmental marketing claims – case-by-case decomposition of the issues. *Journal of Advertising*. 24: 33–43.

Shrum, L.J., Lowrey, T.M. and McCarty, J.A. 1995a. Applying social and traditional marketing principles to the reduction of household waste – turning research into action. *American Behavioral Scientist*. 38: 646–57.

Shrum, L.J., McCarty, J.A. and Lowrey, T.M. 1995b. Buyer characteristics of the green consumer and their implications for advertising strategy. *Journal of Advertising*. 24: 71–82.

Söderbaum, P. 2000. *Ecological economics*. London: Earthscan.

Spinazze, M.C. and Kant, S. 1999. Market potential for certified forest (wood) products in Ontario, Canada. *Forestry Chronicle*. 75: 39–47.

Stanord, A. 1998. Liberalisation of the UK energy market: an opportunity for green energy. *Renewable Energy*. 15: 215–17.

Sterner, T. and Bartelings, H. 1999. Household waste management in a Swedish municipality: determinants of waste disposal, recycling and composting. *Environmental and Resource Economics*. 13: 473–91.

Tarde, G. 1902. *La psychologie économique*. Paris: Alcan.

Thaler, R.H. 1988. Anomalies: the ultimatum game. *Journal of Economic Perspectives*. 2 (4): 195–206.

vanden Abeele, P. 1983. The index of consumer sentiment: predictability and predictive power in the EEC. *Journal of Economic Psychology*. 3: 1–17.

van Raaij, W.F. 1981. Economic psychology. *Journal of Economic Psychology*. 1: 1–24.

Wärneryd, K.-E. 1999. *The psychology of saving : a study on economic psychology*. Cheltenham: Edward Elgar.

Webley, P. 2000. Motivations for ethical choices in economic contexts. *World Futures*. 56: 263–78.

Webley, P., Burgoyne, C.B., Lea, S.E.G. and Young, B.M. 2001. *The economic psychology of everyday life*. Hove: Psychology Press.

Welsh, D.F. 1993. Environmental marketing and federal preemption of state-law – eliminating the gray behind the green. *California Law Review*. 81: 991–1027.

Zinkhan, G.M. and Carlson, L. 1995. Green advertising and the reluctant consumer. *Journal of Advertising*. 24: 1–6.

Q57

Q58

8. A policy orientation as integrative strategy

Stephen Dovers

Increasingly, sustainability and interdisciplinarity are words used in close proximity. But how to pursue interdisciplinary, or integrative, research and policy formulation is poorly understood and only quite recently taken up as a significant challenge. This chapter discusses the prospects and practicalities of using a 'policy orientation' to advance integrative scholarship and practice in the sustainability field, not as an answer to the challenge but as one strategy among many to be developed. After a brief discussion of drivers and variants of integration and interdisciplinarity,[1] the meaning of a policy orientation is discussed and the nature of policy problems in sustainability explored. Then, three variants of such an orientation are explored a little further: policy processes and cycles; policy instrument choice and policy monitoring and learning. The chapter concludes with a note on the potential for a policy orientation as a process for interdisciplinary understanding.

The chapter has a twofold aim. First, to propose a policy orientation as a focus for enhancing interdisciplinary activity concerning sustainability. To do this, the construction of 'policy' spreads the focus from predefined policy problem agendas, applicable to linear, applied research, towards deeper exploration of policy problems and processes inviting contributions from a wider range of disciplines. Second, and subsidiary to this, to present a policy perspective on sustainability that may sharpen the interest of other disciplines so that policy understanding and effectiveness, at present not optimal with respect to sustainability, can be improved by their attention. The chapter does not seek to propose a definitive integrative strategy, but rather to explain the rationale for a general direction and some possible pathways within that.

WHY INTEGRATION AND INTERDISCIPLINARITY?

It has become almost axiomatic that sustainability, either as an intellectual or policy challenge, demands integrative or interdisciplinary approaches. Significant sustainability issues, for example greenhouse, biodiversity, integrated land and water management, or population-environment linkages, continue to test intellectual and policy capacities, and prove difficult to comprehend let alone solve with existing tools and approaches. Sustainability issues, and explicitly our policy construction of how to respond to them, demand connection of social, economic and ecological understanding and policy over the long term, being concerned with interdependent natural and human systems (that is shorthand of course for many human and many natural systems, each complex and interlinked). More broadly, the ever-increasing specialization between and even within disciplines has led to desires for reintegration of knowledge and efforts, not just in the sustainability field. The drivers of interdisciplinarity, therefore, include a practical problem focus (sustainability as modern issue) as well as intellectual curiosity. Moreover, the drive does not come from only within the academic domain, but from policy agencies, governments and the general community who are increasingly involved in resource and environmental management.

Both in response to and as part of the drive for integration, a number of interdisciplinary ventures have begun in recent years, explicitly targeting the relationships between people and nature, or sustainability: ecological economics, environmental history, green social theory, environmental philosophy, environmental politics and so on (for a selective survey, see Becker and Jahn 1999). Sustainability in itself may eventually become a recognizable interdisciplinary domain. These endeavours vary significantly. Some are explicitly interdisciplinary, policy-focused and target sustainability, such as ecological economics in its broader manifestations, whereas others focus more on narrower constructions of 'environment', are largely carried out by members of a discipline seeking to better comprehend environment and do not focus on policy. An example of such is environmental history, although there is a growing strand within that enterprise seeking to both comprehend the modern sustainability agenda and connect better with contemporary policy concerns (see Dovers 2000). The interdisciplines also vary greatly in their assumptions about human-natural system interactions, theoretical and methodological approaches, data used, modes of communication, spatial and temporal scales and more besides. Indeed, the interdisciplines attending sustainability probably vary as much as the original disciplines from which they were spawned. As yet, these 'interdisciplines' remain largely unconnected, a situation that should be reversed to expand the opportunities for mutual learning about both sustainability and the art and craft of integrative research and problem-framing. For such connections to be built and for constructive discourse to occur, bases for communication are required and the policy orientation proposed here is one candidate.

However, it must be noted that integrative approaches are not *always* necessary for advancing sustainability, despite having become a requisite password at workshops. When existing, single-discipline theory or methods fail demonstrably to gain purchase on a sustainability problem, something else is required. That something else may come from another, single discipline, or it may be new and integrative. Single or multidisciplinary approaches – the latter being additive, not integrative – are useful and sufficient for many problems. But it would be a mistake to always assume that failure to advance a problem does not mean that single-discipline approaches are inadequate, as opposed to having not been well or sufficiently applied, or ignored. Careful justification of the need for an integrative approach in any given context should be accepted, and expected, as part of the problem-framing process as well as the later investigative process.

When is interdisciplinarity truly interdisciplinary? For example, some ecological economics operates as corrective at the margins of neoclassical economics, taking sometimes quite simple perspectives from, say, ecology, and bending economic orthodoxy to comprehend this, but not bending it too far. Other efforts seek to integrate ecology and economics (often, but not mostly, these are shorthand for a larger range of disciplines), in the process transforming both and maybe creating something newer and larger again. That provides a key test for genuine interdisciplinarity – *tranformative potential*. If the operating assumptions and epistemological commitments of a discipline are not open to question, then interdisciplinarity is not being attempted (see, for example, Schoenberger 2001). Becker et al. (1999: 12) propose a three-way typology of interdisciplinarity that exposes this further and moreover invites explanation of a 'policy orientation' as integrative strategy:

- goal-oriented multidisciplinarity;
- problem-oriented interdisciplinarity;
- self-reflexive transdisciplinarity.

The progression from less to more integration is clear and useful. The first might be crudely typified by an environmental impact statement or similar project undertaken by a team of different disciplinarians, being additive but not integrative. The second and third may be difficult to separate in practice. Reflexivity can be held to be roughly equivalent in intent as (potentially) 'transformative' above. Once that key point is accepted, the 'trans' versus 'inter' debate might be dispensed with as semantic. However, I propose it is a mistake to assume that being 'problem-oriented' means a less profound interdisciplinary engagement, or that it is mutually exclusive of reflexivity or transformative potential. It depends on what constitutes a 'problem', which I would take to include a substantive sustainability issue, a theoretical or methodological challenge or identified difference in disciplinary constructions, as well as a problem-taken-as-given in the sense of 'applied' research. In this sense, not only is a problem orientation a possible means for reflexivity and disciplinary transformation (and thus of interdisciplinarity), but I suggest a precondition of useful activity. We need to engage in processes of joint problem-framing – and all the messiness and interaction that will require – to advance thinking, not problems already defined and delivered whether by policy-makers or other disciplines. Without well-discussed and significant points of interaction, we may only ever circle or bypass each other without genuine or sustained engagement.

The difficulties of interdisciplinary engagement, both practical and intellectual, are large, and more so when transformative engagement is entertained. Across the big three divides of social and natural sciences and the humanities, the divides in construction and approach are sometimes immense. Within those larger domains they can be just as daunting, as, for example, economists and lawyers might find when they collaborate. However, the divides occur at much deeper levels than that, in fact right through individual disciplines. An ecological *economist* may find it easier to communicate and work with an ecologist than with a strict neoclassicist who may well regard ecological economics as apostate. *Intra*disciplinary variation and divisions are apparent to us in our own disciplines, but we can too often assume that other disciplines are unitary – hence the commonly heard exclamation in a formative interdisciplinary team, that 'we need a [insert disciplinarian]'. But what sort? An empirical, community ecologist is a different colleague than an ecosystem theorist, as distant as black-letter law is from sociology of the law or applied law-in-context research. The choice of a colleague can be a crucial yet unwitting choice of subdiscipline, predetermining the questions asked, methods and data used and conclusions reached.

This pervasiveness of division and difference emphasizes the need for well-considered points of interaction (Pawson and Dovers, forthcoming). Sustainability's imperative (and core to ecological economics) of being integrative/interdisciplinary *and* policy-oriented demands a point of interaction that invites a problem orientation with transformative and collaborative potential, as opposed to just bringing the existing tool kit to bear on someone else's problem. The next section explores sustainability problems to this end.

SUSTAINABILITY AND POLICY PROBLEMS AND PROCESSES

Becker et al.'s version of 'problem orientation' as non-transformative holds true when problem-framing is not part of the integrative research process, but rather has been already done elsewhere (often by an agency or interest group). To frame the problem collaboratively, hopefully exposing new or at least differently construed dimensions, means that sustainability 'issues' cannot be taken as given, but rather their deeper attributes must be explored thoroughly, well before the 'research problem/s' are defined. Joint discussion and analysis of the *nature of sustainability problems* is an initial step, one which may well be a worthy research project in its own right. To discuss the nature of sustainability problems, we can focus on the underlying attributes of these problems. The following is one iteration (other versions are possible and desirable) (Dovers 1995a, 1997):

- broadened and variable spatial scales;
- deepened and variable temporal scales;
- the possibility of ecological limits to human activity;
- irreversible and/or cumulative impacts;
- complexity within and connectivity between problems;
- pervasive risk and uncertainty, often not amenable to probabilistic analysis;
- new moral dimensions (other species, future generations);
- 'systemic' causes, embedded in patterns of production, consumption, settlement and governance;
- important resources and environmental assets not traded in formal markets and not easily assigned a monetary value;
- difficulty in separating public and private costs and benefits of resource use and policy and management interventions;
- lack of uncontested research methods, policy instruments and management approaches;
- poorly defined policy and property rights and responsibilities;
- strong demands and justification for increased community participation in policy and management;
- sheer novelty as a suite of policy problems.

Not every sustainability problem displays all these, but many display at least several in combination. This is the basis of the claim that significant sustainability problems are different in kind and perhaps in degree than those public policy problems with which we are more familiar and against which we have shaped our analytical and prescriptive capacities. In the language of public policy, they are definitely 'wicked' as opposed to well-defined or familiar problems. There is thus a prima facie case that traditional policy-oriented disciplines – economics, law, public policy, political science and so on – and the approaches to policy they underpin will lack purchase on sustainability problems. Hence interdisciplinarity.

Such attributes invite different disciplines to expose and compare (if never fully reconcile) their different perspectives, and to recognize that greater purchase on a problem with multiple attributes (which will be the normal situation) demands multiple inputs. Two important and inviting realities emerge easily enough. First, to comprehend a problem with multiple troublesome attributes, multiple disciplinary perspectives are required. An economist may have less to say about novel moral dimensions than a philosopher, but more than a historian about non-valued resources. A lawyer might be more help on property rights than an anthropologist and so on. That is intuitively obvious, of course, but working around problem attributes may provide a more robust basis for subsequent engagement than simple recognition that, for example, biodiversity begs the attention of ecologists and economists (and more besides). Second, most attributes beg the contribution of more than one discipline. Systemic problem causes – the eighth attribute listed above and perhaps the most problematic of all – begs economic investigation, but legal, political science, historical and planning ones as well. Similarly, extended and variable spatial and temporal scales invite consideration of the scales understood (or not) by different disciplines and for different reasons. For example, economics focuses on individuals, firms and national economies over relatively short time frames, whereas lawyers or ecologists conceptualize and investigate the world over markedly different scales (than economists and each other).

Moreover, a focus on underlying problem attributes may allow a greater degree of cross-problem and cross-sectoral analysis within the sustainability field and connections with accrued understanding or contemporary challenges within other policy fields. Although there may be large apparent variations across substantive issues (biodiversity, energy management, catchment management and so on) or policy sectors (natural resources, emergency management, public health and so on), problem attributes will often be similar. Recognition of this may expand the scope for both interdisciplinary inquiry as well as exchange of practical policy experiences and ideas. For example, rights markets in natural resources are popular these days, if in theory and advocacy more than in implementation. Generally portrayed as 'economic' instruments, rights markets are, in fact, mixed legal and economic instruments (and, moreover, potentially deep institutional changes). Lawyers and economists (at the very least) can be expected to have rather different constructions of such markets that bear exposure and integration. And, in an area of few markets of any longevity and, due to that and to poor monitoring and evaluation of the functioning of these markets, sparse empirical data, linking attention across resource sectors (for example tradable water rights, individual transferable quota (ITQs) in fisheries, pollution credits) enlarges the data set and analytical scope.

Policy problems do not exist in simple isolation, but are dealt with in *policy processes* that either already exist or ones we are currently developing or proposing for the future. It is quite widely accepted even in the policy statements of many governments that our existing policy processes, and the institutional arrangements that support these, are inadequate with respect to sustainability. What they should look like is hotly debated, but the following broad transitions reflect much of the literature and policy debate:[2]

- from short-term management interventions in particular places, to sophisticated management regimes connecting these interventions across time and landscapes;
- from short-term and narrow policy instruments and programmes, to improving the capacity of underlying policy processes;
- from marginal organizational change, to deeper change of institutional settings;
- from reshuffling government departments and portfolios from the top down, to new forms of governance defined by partnerships between science, government, markets and community;
- from public participation via short-term programmes with little devolved power, to long-term status and resource commitments for participatory approaches to resource management.

This entails a more profound policy and institutional response to sustainability, where policy institutional responses will be characterized by greater persistence in policy experiments, more clearly stated purpose through widely accepted principles, emphasis on information generation, ownership and use, inclusiveness of a range of stakeholder interests and flexibility and experimentation over time (Dovers 2001). It reflects the potential for a 'deeper' framing of sustainability problems that the attributes defined earlier might allow. Similar comments can be as with the attributes: the above transitions invite an array of disciplinary inputs and might be used to give structure to interdisciplinary interaction. The introduction of policy processes as opposed to discrete problems handled therein also serves to introduce the first of three variants of a policy orientation which is discussed in the following section.

VARIANTS OF A POLICY ORIENTATION

Within this broad yet hopefully cogent construction of a policy orientation, particular endeavours would wish to focus more sharply, while nonetheless maintaining cognizance of the wider policy arena. Three such possible variants or foci are presented below as examples (very sketchily, and summarizing fields of some complexity). These are ones where it is apparent that, first, different disciplines might have usefully different understandings and, second, that in most cases we do not do very well in terms of advancing sustainability policy (for a summary Australian assessment of such policy adequacy, see Dovers 2002). At one level, these three possible policy foci would be discernible from a standard public policy text (for example Howlett and Ramesh 1995), but at another, while perhaps obvious in public policy, they are not always perceived as such by other disciplines, or conceptualized as potential interdisciplinary meeting places. As with the problem-framing perspective above, they also serve to invite attention from disciplines that do not traditionally have a policy orientation.

Policy Cycles and Systems

A policy orientation can too easily to be taken as only located within one small component of the policy system. Commonly, 'policy' is construed in terms of a policy debate, policy statement, choice of policy instrument or, to cite a common, simple definition of policy, what governments do and by inference what scientists and other researchers do not. Linear, problem solving constructions of policy ('rational-comprehensive') have waned over the years, replaced first by ('incremental') approaches, and more commonly by those existing between these two extremes that emphasize policy cycles, processes, systems and sub-systems. Countless diagrammatic, conceptual and textual representations exist in the literature, all emphasizing messiness, complex information flows, iteration, embeddedness in political systems, feedbacks and cyclic processes, and above all that a particular policy event (a statement, a newly applied instrument and so on) is but one component of a more complex system. Figure 8.1 sets out such a construction of a broader policy process, in this case specifically for sustainability. This is not a model of how things do or should happen, but a heuristic device or checklist for the components of a reasonably complete policy process in the sustainability domain. For the purpose here, reference to Figure 8.1 (as one of numerous possible representations of policy processes) serves to emphasize some key points both about policy problems in sustainability and the possible role of interdisciplinarity. Not only can better policy be made acting on this recognition, but the potential of a broader policy orientation as integrative strategy in an intellectual sense becomes clearer.

If conceptions of policy are indeed insufficient without comprehension of the total policy system, as the disciplines of public policy and political science would attest, then a by now thoroughly expectable (for this chapter) point can be made – understanding of that system demands multiple disciplinary perspectives. It definitely requires more than only those recognizable policy-oriented disciplines such as public policy, public administration, law and economics. Taking a few elements of the model in Figure 8.1, the following linking of disciplines with elements of the policy process indicates the obvious (noting

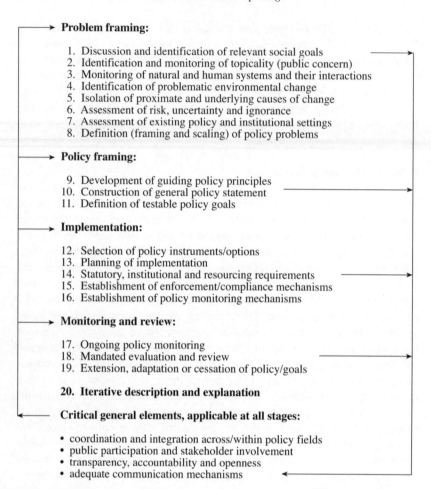

Problem framing:

1. Discussion and identification of relevant social goals
2. Identification and monitoring of topicality (public concern)
3. Monitoring of natural and human systems and their interactions
4. Identification of problematic environmental change
5. Isolation of proximate and underlying causes of change
6. Assessment of risk, uncertainty and ignorance
7. Assessment of existing policy and institutional settings
8. Definition (framing and scaling) of policy problems

Policy framing:

9. Development of guiding policy principles
10. Construction of general policy statement
11. Definition of testable policy goals

Implementation:

12. Selection of policy instruments/options
13. Planning of implementation
14. Statutory, institutional and resourcing requirements
15. Establishment of enforcement/compliance mechanisms
16. Establishment of policy monitoring mechanisms

Monitoring and review:

17. Ongoing policy monitoring
18. Mandated evaluation and review
19. Extension, adaptation or cessation of policy/goals

20. Iterative description and explanation

Critical general elements, applicable at all stages:

• coordination and integration across/within policy fields
• public participation and stakeholder involvement
• transparency, accountability and openness
• adequate communication mechanisms

Figure 8.1   A framework for policy analysis and prescription for
sustainability and resource and environmental management

that whole disciplines are suggested, when in fact subdisciplines would be the more appropriate taxonomic level, but the point is made nonetheless):

• 3–5. *Monitoring human and natural systems, problem identification –* information sciences, demography, ecology, meteorology, oceanography, geomorphology, environmental chemistry (and other natural sciences), public policy, law, economics, geography, public health, psychology.

- 6. *Uncertainty* – philosophy, information sciences, mathematics, statistics, ecology and other natural sciences, public policy, law, political science, psychology.
- 7. *Assessing existing policy* – political science, economics, public administration, public policy, law, history, planning, institutional and organizational theory.
- 13–14. *Implementation* – public administration, law, institutional theory, public policy, accounting, geography, sociology, psychology, history, institutional and organizational theory.
- 15. *Compliance/enforcement* – law, economics, planning, public policy and administration, psychology, education, communications, sociology.

Yet, although obvious, it is not clear that all disciplines recognize this, as a result of either not thinking very much about policy or of concentrating too fixedly on one, minor element or sub-element. At worst, an economist may only be concerned with one class of instrument (market mechanisms, perhaps?), or a lawyer blind to anything except the administration of recent regulations. They, or more likely perhaps a natural scientist, might dismiss the rest of the process as 'politics', in a derogatory sense.[3] A broader construction of what 'policy' means allows engagement on such issues, and the general point can be sharpened with reference to more specific elements within the policy process.

Policy Instrument Choice

For many practically minded economists, policy instrument choice is the sharp and interesting part of policy. It is also, in the context of environment and sustainability, where economists have entered or should enter into important discussions with other disciplines. However, those discussions, at least in the public arena, have often been simplistic, entailing comparative arguments for the relative merits of regulatory, educative and market-based policy interventions. As a mode of interaction between, for example, lawyers, psychologists and economists, such exchanges amount to an uninformed trading of blows rather than a revealing discourse. For policy instrument choice to be a focus for interdisciplinary engagement, a number of unremarkable yet too often strangely overlooked things need to be taken into account (Dovers 1995b):

- There are more than a few instrument classes, and certainly more than regulations, education and market mechanisms. Common law, monitoring, research and development (R&D), covenants on property, intergovernmental agreements, information flow, various assessment procedures, self-regulatory mechanisms, community-based resource management regimes, institutional or organizational change, adjustment of existing, distorting policy settings – these and other general classes of policy response are just as significant.

- Beyond this, there are menus-within-menus, where broad instrument classes contain a rich and varied set of options. 'Market mechanisms' is a meaningless term when it covers such different options as input and output taxes and charges, performance bonds, resource use charges, tradable resource rights and subsidies. Likewise, 'education' means nothing if not specified – broad public education, or that targeted at sub-populations, formal curriculum change, technical training and so on.
- Instrument choice should be, but rarely is in practice, undertaken on the basis of selection criteria suited to the policy field. For sustainability these include information requirements, dependability, cost and efficiency, distributional impacts, antidotal versus corrective potential, flexibility, enforcability, institutional and political feasibility, social acceptability and communicability. Of course, no single discipline can competently deal with more than one or two criteria.
- Even with specific instruments, a range of disciplinary expertise will be relevant if not crucial. For example, rights markets are, in part, economic instruments, but also legal and institutional and, therefore, the promotion and design of, say, ITQ or water trading systems demands more than just economic skills. The same holds for most other instruments.
- It is rarely the case that one specific instrument is used in isolation but, rather, policies utilize a variable mix of instruments (for example a tax, with legal and administrative basis, communicated through an education campaign, enforced through regulation).
- However, there are *universal* instrument classes that must be a part of any policy response, whether pre-existing or new. Where the rule of law is important, where people need to know what is happening, and where humans only achieve things via institutions, these are a legal basis, an educative component and an institutional setting.
- From this, it is crucial to understand that the law offers more than strict regulatory instruments (or 'command-and-control' as economists seeking to tilt the playing field towards their favourite instruments would have it). Statute, common and customary law serve to shape agency objectives, ensure due process in decisions, guarantee transparency and create opportunities for persistent public participation (Dovers 1999).

So, no one instrument class is 'better', nor indeed is any particular instrument, but may be more or less appropriate in a given context. It is perhaps helpful to view all policy instruments as *information* – pleas, threats, warnings, signposts, moral exhortations – designed to change the behaviour of individuals, households, firms or institutions. Instrument choice thus becomes identification of the most appropriate media 'mix' for delivering the message, and varied mixes across contexts accepted as an interdisciplinary task given the variety of instruments and criteria. Construed in this way, no single discipline can ever offer more than a very partial insight into instrument choice, either generally or in any one situation.

Policy Monitoring and Learning

The third sub-variant of a policy orientation to be noted here is at once obvious and startlingly under-attended in both the intellectual and policy domains. That we would wish to know if our policy interventions work or not and why is intuitively obvious. That careful monitoring and evaluation of policy is, in fact, quite rare is grossly unfortunate. Generally, May (1992: 350) stated that deliberate and sustained policy learning is 'advocated but not adequately conceptualised', while Lee (1993: 185) put it that, in the sustainability arena, 'deliberate learning is possible, though surely uncommon, in public policy'. This disjunction should be a vehicle for interdisciplinary engagement given that the reasons for poor policy monitoring, evaluation and learning span many areas of specialist knowledge and potential explanation. For example, are biophysical impacts (or lack thereof) cryptic in some way? Is the administrative and institutional machinery of public policy deficient? Are monitoring and evaluation and what they might reveal lacking in scientific or political kudos and thus not undertaken? Are the data required not routinely gathered as they should be? Or, what context-specific combination of such factors applies? Dealing as it must with biophysical systems, production and consumption systems, the role of science in policy, and basic public administration, among other things, useful analysis of such possible reasons and prescription of response strategies require a span of disciplinary skills.

A deeper and potentially more engaging question is the nature of policy learning (for example Bennett and Howlett 1992; May 1992). Core to exploring this is the question of *who learns what*. Agency staff may desire operational lessons from a specific programme within a defined domain of implementation – learning in an instrumental mode – as might, for example, economists viewing the application of an economic policy instrument. Other members of the extended policy network might seek reflection on the social construction of policy problems and processes, or political lessons regarding agenda-setting and policy change.[4] These different modes of and justifications for policy learning are related but nonetheless qualitatively different and beg quite different approaches. However, such a construction refers largely to members of the policy community, who may or may not have (or utilize) a particular disciplinary allegiance and all that comes with it. Scientists and other epistemic communities have their own, perhaps less practical, reasons for learning, and seek different information over different scales of interest. These may have to do more with theoretical and methodological questions than the tactical or practical lessons sought by, for example, agency staff or sectoral stakeholders and activists. Clarification of such agendas in a given 'learning' context should be expected, and may prove a profitable arena for communication across disciplines.

CONCLUSION: POLICY ORIENTATION AS PROCESS OR PRODUCT?

The arguments put here for a policy orientation as an integrative mechanism are meant to be strongly suggestive and flexible, not absolute. As constructed here, the idea is formative and requires testing and intensive discourse to be advanced. However, that intensive discourse around disciplinary approaches to policy is a worthy end in itself as well as leading perhaps to better theory, method or policy outcomes. A policy orientation – or, rather, a variety of possible orientations as outlined here – should be viewed as a process of deepening interdisciplinary understanding as much as a means to the product of improved purchase in a practical sense.

One example of a potential discourse, in itself an important factor in progressing cross-disciplinary understanding, might occur between disciplines that are already policy-oriented and those that are not. Leaving aside the larger array of disciplines noted as relevant earlier, even a casual observer of sustainability problems would recognize the indispensable contributions of a range of disciplines. Take climate change, in the sense of understanding the process, the impacts and possible responses. From the natural sciences, atmospheric chemistry, physics, oceanography and ecology are crucial, as are, from the social sciences, economics, law and political science (there are others, but the sample will suffice). Of these, the three social science disciplines have long and perhaps even proud histories of direct, sustained engagement with policy (or, rather, with certain aspects of policy as that domain has been characterized here). That is, in large part, their reason to be. The three natural science disciplines, however, do not, but, of course, have a purchase on aspects of natural systems that no social science does.[5] Putting these orientations together – people and nature, or natural and human systems – is the point of interdsiciplinarity for sustainability, and the justification of ecological economics.

But when an explicit policy orientation is pursued, does that place disciplines with little previous engagement and thus understanding of policy at a disadvantage? Yes and no. On the one hand, getting up to speed on policy processes, generally and in the sense that other disciplines understand policy, is certainly a challenge for most natural sciences (as well as for some other disciplines, for example history). On the other hand, 'traditional' policy-oriented disciplines may have the reverse challenge of unsettling their previously treasured (or even forgotten) assumptions and resisting the easy route of reapplying existing theory and method. If sustainability problems are indeed different in kind, and the *prima facie* case of suspected inadequacy of traditional policy-oriented disciplines accepted, then trusting to their construction and approach may be ill-advised. Therefore, a policy orientation requires the impressive, accrued – and markedly varied – understandings of the policy-oriented disciplines, but also the ability of the natural sciences to propose challenges to that understanding, as well as the more recognized role of understanding natural systems. Discussions of such different starting points would be worthy in themselves to advance interdisciplinary understanding, as well as holding out the prospect of better policy. The proposed foci in this chapter – processes, instruments, policy monitoring and learning – would assist such discussions. Importantly, policy problem-framing, policy design, instrument choice and policy-monitoring and learning all require consideration afresh in each specific situation. While perhaps frightening, this requirement for context-specificity demands an ongoing interaction among disciplines (and other knowledge systems, and theory and practice), a prospect that can be construed as not frightening, but realistic and inviting.

For purchase on sustainability problems, multiple integrative strategies and mixes of disciplines will always be required and no single, superior approach, no 'science of sustainability', will emerge. Decades on, ecological economics, environmental history and numerous others will still be making sustainability a vibrant field of interest. As suggested earlier, the greater the links between these arenas, the greater this vibrancy and the greater the potential intellectual and policy advances. This chapter has suggested that, among this array of interdisciplines and interdisciplinary enterprises, a carefully pursued orientation towards the underlying nature of policy problems and processes in sustainability will increase this purchase, and perhaps function in the manner of – so to speak – an integrative strategy among integrative strategies.

NOTES

1. Interdisciplinary refers to the knowledge systems represented by formal disciplines, whereas integrative refers to the inclusion of other knowledge systems (community, indigenous, lay) as well. However, the two terms will be used interchangeably here. The emphasis here is largely on disciplines, although the need for and challenges associated with a wider integrative pathway are acknowledged.
2. The following characterization draws on a normal public policy perspective, and by the idea of 'adaptive' institutions, policy processes and management regimes, an extension of the ecological proposal for adaptive management, incorporating societal learning and institutional

dimensions and applied across sectors, jurisdictions and time; see Dovers 1999, 2001; Dovers and Mobbs 1997.
3. On the derogatory use of 'political' when applied to decisions or decision making processes, the instruction of Davis et al. (1993: 257) is apposite – 'Politics is the essential ingredient for producing workable policies, which are more publicly accountable and politically justifiable ... While some are uncomfortable with the notion that politics can enhance rational decision making, preferring to see politics as expediency, it is integral to the process of securing defensible outcomes. We are unable to combine values, interests and resources in ways which are not political'.
4. Policy learning by individuals and organizations takes place within and is strongly fashioned by underlying institutional systems, and these systems are complex, historically determined, prone to uneven rates of change and poorly understood. Cognizance of this is important, but is not covered here.
5. These judgements apply to the disciplines generally, while recognizing particular individuals or minor groups within disciplines who, in fact, have engaged with and developed particular understandings of the 'other' realm.

REFERENCES

Becker, E. and Jahn, T. (eds). 1999. *Sustainability and the social sciences: a cross-disciplinary approach to integrating environmental considerations into theoretical reorientation*. London: Zed Books.

Becker, E., Jahn, T. and Stiess, I. (eds). 1999. Exploring uncommon ground: sustainability and the social sciences. In: Becker, E. and Jahn, T. (eds). *Sustainability and the social sciences: a cross-disciplinary approach to integrating environmental considerations into theoretical reorientation*. London: Zed Books, pp. 1–22.

Bennett, C.J. and Howlett, M. 1992. The lessons of learning: reconciling theories of policy learning and policy change. *Policy Sciences*. 25: 275–94.

Davis, G., Wanna, J., Warhurst, J. and Weller, P. 1993. *Public policy in Australia*. 3rd edn. Sydney: Allen & Unwin.

Dovers, S. 1995a. A framework for scaling and framing policy problems in sustainability. *Ecological Economics*. 12: 93–106.

Dovers, S. 1995b. Information, sustainability and policy. *Australian Journal of Environmental Management*. 2: 142–56.

Dovers, S. 1997. Sustainability: demands on policy. *Journal of Public Policy*. 16: 303–18.

Dovers, S. 1999. Adaptive policy, institutions and management: challenges for lawyers and others. *Griffith Law Review*. 8: 374–93.

Dovers, S. 2000. On the contribution of environmental history to current debate and policy. *Environment and History*. 6: 131–50.

Dovers, S. 2001. *Institutions for sustainability*. Tela paper 7. Melbourne: Australian Conservation Foundation. (Available at www.acfonline.org.au/docs/publications/tp007.pdf).

Dovers, S. 2002. Sustainability: reviewing Australia's progress, 1992–2002. *International Journal of Environmental Studies*. 59: 559–71.

Dovers, S. and Mobbs, C. 1997. An alluring prospect? Ecology, and the requirements of adaptive management. In: Klomp, N. and Lunt, I. (eds). *Frontiers in ecology: building the links*. London: Elsevier, pp. 39–52.

Howlett, M. and Ramesh, M. 1995. *Studying public policy: policy cycles and policy subsystems*. Oxford: Oxford University Press.

Lee, K.N. 1993. *Compass and gyroscope: integrating science and politics for the environment*. Washington, DC: Island Press.

May, P. 1992. Policy learning and policy failure. *Journal of Public Policy*. 12: 331–54.

Pawson, E. and Dovers, S. Forthcoming. Environmental history and the challenges of interdisciplinarity: an Antipodean perspective. *Environment and History*.

Schoenberger, E. 2001. Interdisciplinarity and social power. *Progress in Human Geography*. 25: 365–82.

THIRD DIMENSION

Frameworks and Applications

9. Towards an ecological-economic theory of nature policy[1]

C. Martijn van der Heide, Jeroen C.J.M van den Bergh and Ekko C. van Ierland

Nature policy can be defined as the total of policies aimed at maintenance, restoration and sustainable development of ecosystems and landscape. This covers the protection of species and biodiversity, the use of renewable resources, land use and physical planning, acquisition, development and maintenance of nature areas, and policies for sustainable agro-ecosystems. Nature policy is a new term that has a wider connotation than terms like conservation, preservation and protection of nature. In our terminology, it also covers, among others, ecological networks, extensive and organic farming, recreation, and education and moral suasion to increase people's awareness of the vital importance of nature. We avoid here the term conservation policy, because it is mainly used in the narrower sense of maintenance of some or all of the components of biological diversity.

While it is widely recognized that nature policy should satisfy both certain ecological and certain economic criteria, a coherent theory on nature policy is still lacking (for example Barbier et al. 1994; Costanza 1984; Nijkamp 1976; Odum 1989; Primack 1998). Environmental economics can offer insight into the problems of conservation and development of nature and landscape. However, despite the theories of public goods and externalities, the standard theory of environmental policy offers insufficient understanding of appropriate policy measures for the restoration and conservation of nature. In fact, this chapter claims that nature policy greatly differs from environmental policy. Moreover, nature policy interacts with environmental policy, which may range from complementarity to conflict. This chapter discusses what theoretical and methodological approaches can assist in the analysis and formulation of nature policy.

Most environmental problems are expressed in terms of 'externalities' (or 'external costs') and, as a result, the traditional economic theory considers environmental policy to be based on optimization and internalization of externalities. In addition, resource economics traditionally focuses the attention on optimal allocation and efficient use of scarce resources (Dasgupta and Heal 1979; Field 2001; Hartwick and Olewiler 1998). These approaches are in sharp contrast with problems of sustainable conservation of nature and land-scape, which are – due to linkages between natural and economic systems – characterized by ecological and economic spatial and temporal phenomena. Though conservation issues straddle the divide between environmental, resource and ecological economics, the abstract theories of environmental policy and resource use are too far removed from the spatially and temporally complex reality of nature policy (see also Turner et al. 1997). Nevertheless, like environmental policies, nature policies ideally need to be consistent with multiple goals – sustainability, equity and efficiency (Turner et al. 1999). A convincing theory of nature policy, therefore, requires a balanced input of insights from ecology and economics.

One of the main roles of ecologists can be to inform policy-oriented social scientists about how biological diversity affects ecological processes and how these, in turn, influence goods and services provided by ecosystems. Unfortunately, scientific knowledge of genes, species and ecosystem func-tioning is still incomplete. As a result, the precise impacts of changes in the environment, such as losses of biodiversity, are difficult to predict. Moreover, ecological-economic interactions very often follow a complex spatial struc-ture. Ecologists can provide important spatial information about ecological structure to integrated modelling and analysis, and thus support the upgrading of spatial approaches to the study of nature policy by economics. Economists can contribute to the design of nature policies by explicitly incorporating ecological and landscape values into decision-making frameworks (Daily 1997). Economic analysis, therefore, can demonstrate the potentially high benefits of nature and biodiversity, and reveal more clearly the economic and social pressures that threaten it. Moreover, as there is a limited budget for nature policy, it is also a task of economists to assist in setting priorities among alternative nature policy and management options.

Our aim in this chapter is to clarify why it is so difficult to analyse nature policies from an integrative, interdisciplinary perspective with an emphasis on economic considerations and arguments. Our treatment is guided by the following research questions:

- What is the role of the standard theory of environmental policy in the analysis of nature policy?
- What are the ecological limits of the conventional economic approach to selecting nature investment priorities and which extensions can be proposed in order to explicitly incorporate scientific uncertainty and irreversibility into decision making?
- How important are spatial aspects for the analysis of nature policy? In this context, the role of integrated spatial modelling is studied by focus-ing on policy questions such as:

- What is the best shape for and the optimal size of nature reserves?
- Is it better to have a single, large nature reserve or many smaller nature reserves?
- What are possible interactions between integrated modelling and monetary valuation of natural systems and their components?
- How are the local and global benefits of nature policy distributed; that is, who reaps the benefits and who bears the costs of nature policy?

The organization of the chapter is as follows. Section 2 discusses the differences between nature and environmental policies and their complementarity or conflict, and considers the useful elements of the standard theory of environmental policy. Section 3 presents the main integrated ecological-economic approaches to the analysis of nature policy. Section 4 addresses the local and global benefits of nature policy, the valuation of these and the link between integrated modelling and monetary valuation. Section 5 concludes.

NATURE POLICY VERSUS ENVIRONMENTAL POLICY

Nature and environment refer to different aspects of reality. Likewise, nature policy (and management) is different from environmental policy. Environmental policy can, of course, be defined in a very broad sense as covering nature policy. However, the use of environmental policy in environmental economics refers predominantly to environmental pollution, linked to the emission of harmful substances and the generation of waste, that is the non-living dimensions of the environment.[2] This is illustrated by examples given in textbook treatments of environmental policy theory (for example Hanley et al. 1997; Kahn 1998; Perman et al. 1996). Nature policy, on the other hand, relates to conservation and development of nature and landscape, and thus is directly concerned with the living world. In a narrow sense, it has received less systematic attention in theory than environmental policy.[3]

Environmental policy creates the conditions under which nature policy operates. Successful nature policy requires a robust environmental policy. However, environmental and nature policy goals sometimes conflict. For example, the growing concerns about climate change have resulted in an increasing demand for renewable energy. However, the presence of wind parks adversely affects the aesthetic values of landscape, while hydroelectricity will inevitably lead to the destruction of ecosystems and wildlife. Of course, this could be avoided by taking all externalities into account which, unfortunately, is extremely complicated and, therefore, rare in reality. Another policy conflict occurs when environmental policy encourages extensive and environmentally friendly agriculture, which can require the conversion of natural areas into agricultural land. Furthermore, a strict separation of rural and urban development stimulates the concentration of human activities in economic 'hot spots', whose interactions lead to physical infrastructure (roads). As a result, natural habitats are in danger of being fragmented. This could be traded off against the disadvantages of urban sprawl. Further conflicts may arise when environmental policy focuses on avoiding human health and morbidity as opposed to nature conservation issues. Interestingly, the recent attention for ecosystem health includes efforts to synthesize human and ecosystem health issues (Costanza et al. 1992).

The complementarity between environmental and nature policy justifies the question of what insights the standard theory of environmental policy offers for the analysis of nature policy. The economic theory of instrument choice in environmental policy is focused on notions like externalities, common property (or open access) resources and public goods, witness problems of clean air and water, solid waste, public lands and natural resources. These instruments aim at influencing private decision-making in order to achieve a highly abstract social optimum, which is usually quickly replaced by a more modest, second-best case characterized by preset environmental goals that are attained at minimum private costs. Negative externalities, notably those caused by pollution, are the core of the economic theory of environmental policy. The source of an externality is typically to be found in the lack of a well-defined property right (Baumol and Oates 1988). When property rights are imperfectly defined, or enforced or non-transferable, markets fail to coordinate people's use of the environment. While the actions of one agent affect the well-being of other agents in an unintended way, there is frequently no incentive for the generator of this effect to consider it in its decision-making. Although it is possible that externalities show the characteristics of private goods, most externalities associated with the use of environmental assets are public in nature (Kahn 1998; Perman et al. 1996).

Many natural assets, such as species and ecosystems, are also characterized by the absence of fully defined property rights. Many of these assets are considered to be public or collective goods, or possess some features associated with such goods. Pure public goods have the characteristics of joint consumption and non-exclusion. Due to the non-exclusion attribute, a pure collective good cannot be marketed. Because it is impossible or at least very costly to deny access to a natural asset, markets fail to allocate resources with public good characteristics efficiently. This may be understood by noting that prices do not then signal the true scarcity of the asset (Hanley et al. 1997).

The standard classification of environmental policy in the traditional economic theory is (Baumol and Oates 1988): (1) economic instruments, such as taxes or 'effluent fees' on polluting activities; (2) information provision and moral suasion by public authorities and voluntary agreements; and (3) 'command-and-control instruments' involving explicit limitations on allowable levels of emissions and the use of specified abatement techniques. In particular the application of economic instruments allows policy-makers to proceed towards an 'internalization' – or more correctly an 'optimization' – of externalities created by the polluting sources (OECD 1999). Economic instruments can also be deployed to encourage sustainable nature management. Just as the creator of pollution should pay a tax or penalty of some kind. From this perspective it is justified, for example, for those who use nature to pay a price, for those who structurally damage nature to pay a compensation and for those who protect nature to appropriate the benefits that are provided to other people. In the latter case a price can be extracted from the beneficiaries. In this way, the allocation of property rights rectifies market failures and ensures against excessive depletion of resources and natural assets.

In addition to the overlap in approach between nature and environmental policy, the conservation and sustainable use of nature poses also challenges to the policy-maker that have distinctive and unique features. There are at least two reasons for this difference, namely (see OECD 1999):

- The causes affecting changes in nature and landscape, and these changes themselves, are diffuse and extremely complex in time and space, and rarely known with any precision, as opposed to the case of point externalities, where both the causes and the detrimental impacts are generally fairly well known.
- Most problems related to the loss of nature are the concern of a large number of actors with different objectives. This is in contrast to the political process of environmental policy where very often only two groups of actors are distinguished, namely the government and its officials, on the one hand, and industry, agriculture and the service sector, on the other (see Verbruggen 1994).

The formulation of nature policy is complicated, because the causes of nature loss and landscape degradation are multiple, and can be divided into proximate and underlying causes. The proximate causes, such as over-exploitation of species and land-use changes, are partly within the domain of natural sciences and partly within that of the social sciences, whereas the underlying causes, such as pressure of human population growth and the structure of property rights, are largely within the domain of the social sciences (for example Folke et al. 1996; van Kooten and Bulte 2000; Perrings et al. 1992). The proximate causes are better understood than the underlying causes, which are not clearly identifiable and, therefore, subject to debate. Separating all these causes is an impossible task, partly due to the many interlinkages that exist (van Kooten and Bulte 2000). It certainly is not possible to identify a single cause for the loss of nature.

Moreover, ecological processes operate at different spatial scales. Scaling up from small to large is, however, a non-linear process, so that spatial attributes vary with scale rather than being uniform. Recognizing that many ecological phenomena are fundamentally spatial processes requires a nature policy that involves these spatial aspects (Deacon et al. 1998). That is, nature policy needs to generalize the concept of a natural asset from a few target species to a larger set of ecological systems. Consequently, the policy needs to be flexible, adaptive and experimental at scales compatible with those of critical ecosystems functions (Holling et al. 1995; see also Spash 1999). In this respect, the analysis of habitat fragmentation is important. Habitat fragmentation – one of the major threats to nature that result from human activity – can be defined as a process that reduces a large continuous nature area or habitat into two or more fragments. The topic of habitat fragmentation is hardly addressed by the standard theory of environmental policy, which, in this context, is too general and abstracts from space. Ecological insights are therefore necessary, as spatial dynamics of ecological systems have given rise to the development of an explicitly spatial approach to ecological structure and processes in landscape ecology.

The other characteristic that distinguishes the problems of nature loss from classical environmental problems is a large number of stakeholders that affect nature, as well as are affected by its goods, services and losses. The main reason why generally more stakeholders are involved in nature than environmental policy issues is a 'multiple use' of natural or wilderness areas: various types of recreation, resource use (forestry, fishery), scientific research and so on. To manage nature properly is thus the concern of conservationists, entrepreneurs, local populations, and policy-makers. Each group of stakeholders has its own particular objective, which complicates the assessment of the benefits of nature policy. Problems linked to the implementation of policy measures result from stakeholders' pursuit of their perceived self-interests as well as from their imperfect knowledge of ecological and economic outcomes (Wills 1997). As a result, the large numbers of actors and the wide range of different objectives make coalition-building difficult and hamper an efficient monitoring and enforcement of nature policy measures.

We have shown that environmental policies can both complement and thwart nature policies. In order to prevent that, nature is subordinate to the goals of environmental policy, resulting in a further loss of nature; it is imperative that the two policies are geared to one another. The synergy that arises from this creates favourable conditions for both sustainable nature and environmental management. For example, a protected zone of forest can play an important role as a carbon sink, and thus contributes to greenhouse gas reduction. The forest, however, also provides ecosystems goods and services such as timber, generation and renewal of soil fertility, pollution control, protection of water catchment and wildlife reserves. This works also the other way around, since climate policy prescriptions for reducing greenhouse gas emissions can have positive impacts on decisions about conservation of natural areas and the species that live there. In conclusion, the relationship and distinction between nature and environmental policies is multifaceted and may differ from case to case. More even than environmental policy analysis, nature policy analysis requires a synthesis of the best insights from the natural and social sciences.

INTEGRATED ANALYSIS OF NATURE POLICY

In this section, we discuss the most important examples of integrated ecological-economic approaches that facilitate the incorporation of ecological concerns into conventional economic theory. We examine approaches that address practical nature policy problems. These problems include the following:

- the evaluation of the costs and benefits of government intervention through investments that have significant ecological implications;
- the analysis of the irreversible effects of many economic development projects, and an incomplete scientific knowledge of the consequences of nature loss;
- the ranking of biodiversity conservation priorities under a limited budget constraint;
- the spatial aspects that are often involved in the management of landscape and natural assets.

In order to address the problems, we focus on the following four integrated approaches, each of which deals with one particular problem: (1) cost–benefit analysis and the Krutilla–Fisher algorithm; (2) the safe minimum standards approach; (3) Weitzman's ranking criterion for biodiversity conservation; and (4) integrated spatial modelling.

Cost–Benefit Analysis and the Krutilla–Fisher Algorithm

Cost–benefit analysis (CBA) is the conventional neoclassical economic approach to quantifying and evaluating projects (Moran et al. 1996, 1997). The technique incorporates clear principles for assessing the net difference between the monetary costs and benefits over the lifetime of an investment.

The main criterion for project appraisal is economic efficiency, which under certain conditions is assured by applying CBA. However, the objective of nature policy programmes is not simply, or even principally, efficiency (van Kooten and Bulte 2000; Strijker et al. 2000). Nevertheless, if applied properly, CBA can play an important role in legislative and regulatory policy debates on protecting nature and landscape. CBA provides a useful framework for consistently organizing disparate information – without double-counting – which greatly improves the process and outcome of policy analysis (Arrow et al. 1996). Traditionally, CBA has been defined in terms of what the gains and losses are to society, and therefore the method offers an aid to decision-makers in evaluating public sector projects or projects with non-market environmental consequences (see Hanley and Spash 1993). It should be realized, however, that CBA cannot replace political judgement.

Although cost–benefit analysis is a widely practised technique of project appraisal, there are a number of difficulties posed by applying it to ecological and nature issues (see Hanley and Spash 1993; Perman et al. 1996). First, as already mentioned, many of the natural assets possess the characteristics of public goods. As a result, there are inherent problems in measuring benefits and costs in monetary terms. Second, determination of society's discount rate appears to be extremely difficult, whereas the outcome is usually very sensitive to its precise value (see, for example, Porter 1982; Turner et al. 1994). Third, conducting a cost–benefit analysis of a policy having significant ecological implications requires detailed knowledge of ecosystem functioning and complexity as well as (ir)reversibility of ecological changes. Unfortunately, this knowledge is often incomplete and qualitative in nature (Turner et al. 2000: 14). Traditional CBA is not equipped to address issues of ecological irreversibility and foregone preservation benefits, and therefore adaptations of the technique are required in performing an evaluation of major decisions regarding ecological and environmental issues.

Krutilla and Fisher (1975) proposed a new approach to handle the irreversible effects that many economic development projects have. Traditionally, the evaluation of a proposed development project that affects nature and environment is based on the assumption that the conservation of nature entails neither a cost nor a benefit. The fundamental point of the Krutilla–Fisher algorithm, however, is its rejection of the view that the profitability of a project is an adequate criterion for the acceptability of the project when it destroys ecological values. The algorithm furthermore explicitly recognizes asymmetric growth rates in development and preservation benefits, based on which foregone conservation benefits are treated as part of the costs of the economic development (Hanley and Spash 1993; Porter 1982). More specifically, benefits of protection are likely to increase over time as the natural environment decreases in quantity so that its 'scarcity rent' increases. In addition, there are several reasons to expect the demand for nature to grow when economies become increasingly materially affluent, for example, due to an increase in income and expenditures, higher education levels, and improved knowledge and understanding of the importance of ecosystems and biological diversity. Whereas the benefits of protection may grow, the benefits of economic development may fall over time. Especially the force of continuous technological progress will reduce the costs of existing, or even introduce entirely new, competitive technologies, thus eroding the benefits of the current economic project. This is in the algorithm represented by introducing an annual rate of decline in development benefits (Pearce and Turner 1990; Perman et al. 1996).

The Krutilla–Fisher model is an interesting integrated approach to irreversible economic developments. Another line of economic thinking on irreversible changes has been followed by Arrow and Fisher (1974). They developed the concept of a 'quasi-option value', which is the expected benefit of awaiting improved information derived from delaying exploitation (see also Henry 1974). As such, it is based on the uncertain future benefits, rather than on discounted net benefits. The essence of quasi-option value is that is attaches a value to nature conservation, derived under risk neutrality, given the expectation of the growth of knowledge (Graham-Tomasi 1995).

There are a number of problems with the Krutilla–Fisher algorithm (see Hanley and Spash 1993). First, although it is common in empirical studies to proxy the growth rate of preservation benefits by the growth rate in real per capita income and the rate of depreciation of development benefits by the rate of technological progress, these two growth rates may be different and generally unpredictable. Second, the initial values for benefits of nature conservation and economic development can already be difficult to estimate. Third, there is uncertainty about the preferences of the individual in the future. That is, foregone conservation benefits are measured using the preferences of current individuals, which may not reflect the preferences of future generations. Finally, the Krutilla-Fisher algorithm leads to a more conservation-oriented rule, one which is – due to its CBA basis – arrived at entirely on the grounds of economic efficiency. Most nature policy programmes, however, also have to deal with other goals, such as equity and sustainability, and the tradeoffs between them.

To summarize, the Krutilla–Fisher algorithm is modest in its way of ecological-economic integration. Further adjustments can be undertaken by adding ecological constraints to the approach, reflecting ecological thresholds and current knowledge of the relationship between ecosystem stability and biodiversity. In modelling terms this would then give rise to a constrained dynamic optimization approach.

The Safe Minimum Standards Approach

If economic development projects jeopardize ecological systems, the criterion of economic efficiency may be regarded as inappropriate. The reason for this is that efficiency supposes a level of accuracy of analysis, policy-setting, policy implementation and enforcement that is unrealistic. In the context of nature policy this is particularly the case as the ecological effects of current economic activities are complex, incompletely understood and subject to variable external conditions outside the control of humans – think of climatic dynamics. This problem is magnified because the consequences of current losses of nature extend far into the future. Among others, this leads to information problems, which cover ignorance about the identity and personal preferences of those who suffer from nature loss in the future as well as about future technologies and resource costs (Wills 1997). If striving for efficiency is no longer realistic, CBA becomes irrelevant and other concepts and methods of analysis are opened up.

When scientific uncertainty is extreme, a precautionary principle is rational (Gollier et al. 2000). In the context of nature policy the safe minimum standard (SMS) of conservation has been proposed to prevent as best as possible major irreversibilities (Crowards 1998; Perrings et al. 1992; Randall and Farmer 1995). An SMS approach to nature conservation represents a decision-making principle that suggests there be a presumption in favour of not harming the natural environment unless the costs of that action are intolerably high (OECD 1999; Randall and Farmer 1995). Some argue that this concept, which was introduced by Ciriacy-Wantrup in the 1950s and adopted and revitalized by Bishop (1978) in the 1970s, bridges the gap between economists and ecologists (see Spash, 1999). The SMS defines the level of preservation that ensures survival and implies a conservative approach to risk-bearing (Randall 1988). In effect, deciding to conserve today can be shown to be the risk-minimizing way to proceed given the presence of uncertainty about the consequence of nature loss (Hanley et al. 1997; Tisdell 1991). Due to scientific uncertainty about the consequences of using natural assets, an SMS approach shifts the burden of proof from those who wish to conserve to those who wish to develop (Norton and Toman 1997; Randall and Farmer 1995). The SMS approach is related to the precautionary principle, but it permits more scope for economic development. The barriers to economically rational actions that threaten the natural environment are lower under an SMS approach than when the precautionary principle is adopted (van Kooten and Bulte 2000; Wills 1997; for a full discussion of the precautionary principle, see Gollier et al. 2000).

The virtue of the SMS approach in circumstances of great uncertainty is that it places natural assets beyond the reach of routine tradeoffs. Unfortunately, the approach also has some problems. Perhaps the most serious limitation of SMS is that the priorities for nature conservation depend solely on the costs of conservation. That is, it disregards the available scientific information about biological diversity and its functions, and treats one gene, species or ecosystems as equal to another (Wills 1997). Furthermore, in order to make the concept of SMS operational, two aspects require special attention: the determination of the principles that identify a safe minimum standard, and the specification of what cost level is considered unacceptably high. Decisions regarding these two aspects, however, are political. As a result, the outcomes of a SMS approach depend very much on the societal or interest-group preferences of the persons who make these decisions (Turner et al. 1999).

Determining Priorities for Biodiversity Protection: Weitzman's Ranking Criterion

Saving all biodiversity is impossible, if only for a lack of funding. Setting protection priorities is thus inevitable, leading to the question of how most species can be supported or how a given amount of biodiversity can be protected against least cost. If, for example, the aim of Dutch nature policy is to increase biological diversity, it turned out that the development of nature in conservation areas is more cost-effective than nature-friendly farming (Strijker et al. 2000).

In an effort to address such questions, Weitzman (1998) derives the following criterion for setting priorities among biodiversity-protecting projects under a limited budget constraint:

$$R_i = (D_i + U_i) \left. \Delta P_i \right/ C_i.$$

Here, R_i represents the performance index of species i, D_i is the (genetic) distinctiveness of species i (meaning roughly how unique or different a species is), U_i denotes the direct utility associated with preservation of species i, and C_i is the cost of the protection project that increases the probability of survival of species i by ΔP_i.

Weitzman's criterion is based on the assumption that the loss of biological diversity due to the extinction of a species is exactly equivalent to the distinctiveness of that species. This means that the uniqueness of each species depends on the genetic distance between species. Uncertainty of extinction is introduced by defining P_i as the probability of survival of species i, and $1 - P_i$ as the probability of extinction of species i. These probabilities are exogenous, that is they originate from outside Weitzman's framework. The approach implies, for instance, that in a situation with two species and identical costs of protecting each species, identical utility and identical changes in survival probabilities, it is optimal to protect the species with the highest probability of survival – because this species is most distinctive (has the highest D_i). This leads to the interpretation that it is optimal to give priority to the protection of a less-endangered species instead of a more endangered species. This can be referred to as 'Weitzman's paradox' (Witting et al. 2000).

For analytical simplicity, Weitzman makes the essential assumption that the loss of a species has no, or a negligible, effect on the existence of other species. From an ecological point of view, this is either an unrealistic or a very specific assumption (Begon et al. 1996). It implies that Weitzman's ranking criterion holds mainly, and perhaps only, for *ex situ* conservation, which severely limits application of the criterion. For their survival in the wild, species depend very much on other species, through food web and ecosystem relationships (Polis 1998). Applying Weitzman's criterion to *in situ* conservation – which, according to Primack (1998), is the best strategy for long-term protection of biodiversity – can therefore lead to a non-optimal ranking of nature policies. This is illustrated by van der Heide et al. (2002a), who show that Weitzman's *ex ante* optimal policy is inconsistent with the *ex post* optimal policy when a certain type of interdependence of species is taken into account: an *ex ante* most preferred species *ex post* may in fact become the least wanted. The solution to 'Weitzman's paradox' is thus the inclusion of ecological insights in the ranking criterion.

Integrated Spatial Modelling

The most important interaction between human beings and biological diversity is the competition for land. Habitats suitable for species often compete with alternative uses, such as agriculture and economic development. In Europe, only 15 per cent of the land area remains unmodified by human activities (Primack 1998). Thus ecological-economic interactions are very often spatially determined, which justifies that analysis of these interactions be carried out in a spatial context. However, whereas natural sciences are placing increasingly emphasis on the importance of spatial factors in understanding ecological systems (for example Hof and Bevers 1998), mainstream (environmental) economics often uses less clear spatial boundaries and specifications. This difference is related to the fact that the size of the problem in terms of spatial, temporal and conceptual dimensions is often more explicit in natural than social sciences. The advantage of more micro-oriented approaches is that they allow for a higher resolution, that is a higher level of precision in measurement and description. A more aggregated approach usually goes along with less resolution and a loss of basic units and processes.

Costanza et al. (1997: xxii) go so far as to state that the integration of economics and ecology is hampered by the lack of space in economic theories and models. Although it is true that mainstream economics has largely assumed away space and spatial externalities between economic agents, the statement neglects the large area of spatial economics. This covers regional, urban and transport economics as well as spatial informatics – mainly the application of geographical information systems (GIS; see Scholten and Stillwell 1990). GIS applications are nowadays often considered as an essential input to integrated spatial models, because they allow the interaction between economic and ecological phenomena to be represented at a detailed spatial scale. It is not clear, however, that using a high spatial resolution will always be fruitful. Whereas many ecological and hydrological processes are amenable for a grid-based description, most economic processes operate at higher scales.

Landscape ecology, originating from an interaction between ecology, geography and land-use planning, has developed into a field that can provide important spatial information to integrated modelling. Turner (1998) presents a short introduction to landscape ecology. It studies the two-sided link between ecological processes and spatial patterns in the environment, taking account of the spatial heterogeneity of land cover, that is vegetation and habitat types. The spatial patterns of nature and environment change over time through various mechanisms: (1) regular and short-term natural causes like ecosystem succession, sedimentation, erosion and less regular causes like fires, pests and storms; (2) long-term evolution caused by local systems developing in different directions as a result of being spatially isolated for long periods of time; and (3) alterations in land use by human activities. The latter have especially caused fragmentation of nature, due to land clearing, land use, settlements and infrastructure.

Landscape ecology takes a grand perspective at a local or sometimes regional scale level, using models and GIS. It thus allows for concrete interaction with economic land-use-oriented models, in particular for linking the different spatial scales at which models in ecology and economics are commonly defined. In general terms, two approaches of land-use models are distinguished. One deals with the allocation of land between alternative uses. The second describes endogenous land use and vegetation cover modelling, aiming at habitat patch dynamics. In order to be able to assess the effects of economic activities on ecological systems in landscapes, it is essential to understand the (ecological) processes determining the landscape. There is a need for an integrated approach that focuses on the development of the countryside – possibly combining economic growth, employment and protection of nature and landscape. Such a framework can incorporate economic and ecological dynamics based on regulations and human decision-making processes, in order to understand the consequences for ecosystem and land-use configurations (Bockstael et al. 1995). For instance, integration of models can provide a framework for regulatory analysis in the context of risk assessment of nature use.

The regional and GIS approaches include elements from spatial economics, economic geography, urban economics and social geography. The use of GIS can then support a grid-based linking of, for example, hydrological, ecological and economic processes. On such a basis, spatial patterns and their evolution can be identified. Applications are usually at the ecosystem or regional scale, rather than at a global scale, due to barriers relating to the level of detail and the dimensions of models. GIS can be combined with analytical models in various ways, ranging from analytical integration to loose coupling based on consistent economic and ecological scenarios. Relatively few integrated models are actually analytically integrated in a GIS format as they would become very complex and multidimensional. Extension towards dynamic formulations is for these reasons even more limited. Examples of integrated spatial modelling are presented by van den Bergh et al. (2001), who consider the analysis and evaluation of land-use scenarios for the Vecht area, a wetlands region in the Netherlands, and by van der Heide et al. (2002b), who address ecological and economic consequences of defragmentation in the Veluwe, a natural park in the Netherlands.

Concluding Remarks

This section has discussed four integrated approaches: (1) cost-benefit analysis and the Krutilla–Fisher algorithm; (2) the safe minimum standards approach; (3) Weitzman's ranking criterion; and (4) integrated spatial modelling. In order to deal with the costs and benefits of government intervention through direct investment, a cost–benefit analysis can be applied. The Krutilla–Fisher algorithm adds a few ecological considerations to this analysis as it explicitly recognizes asymmetric growth rates in economic development and nature protection benefits. The SMS approach represents another supplement to traditional cost–benefit analysis. It places greater emphasis on the protection of nature and landscape by minimizing maximum possible losses to society wherever thresholds of irreversible damage are threatened and uncertainty over the benefits of nature protection exists. The ultimate objective of Weitzman's ranking criterion is to set biodiversity conservation priorities. Unfortunately, the criterion is based on unwarranted assumptions about independent survival probabilities of species. For this reason, Weitzman's general criterion only holds under a very strict condition: namely, in the absence of ecological relationships among species – a very unrealistic case indeed. Since many problems attached to the protection and sustainable use of nature and landscape are spatially determined, the issues of spatial scale and level are important for integrated modelling. Especially in the case of fragmentation, which is generally seen as one of the most critical threats to nature worldwide, spatial modelling is clearly an area for an integrated approach. Formulation of *in situ* measures, such as the establishment of nature reserves, cannot be fully addressed by ecological analysis alone. In fact, the allocation of limited financial, human and institutional resources is one of the most difficult aspects of *in situ* nature management.

Success at meeting the objectives of nature management depends on an adequate understanding of the social, political, economic and ecological context within which nature policy goals are pursued. It is important to realize, however, that due to incomplete scientific knowledge, nature policymakers must learn to deal explicitly with scientific uncertainty. Meanwhile, a continuous scientific effort should provide further insights into genes, species and ecosystem functioning as well as in the relationship between biological diversity and ecosystem stability. In addition, natural scientists must be forthright about past, present and future trends in nature loss, and the causes of these trends. Before making decisions on how to protect and realize sustainable use of natural assets, policy-makers should make choices about what assets need protection or can be sacrificed, where to protect and how to finance the required protection measures (de Kruijf et al. 2002).

Monetary valuation helps decision-makers to make informed decisions about nature policy where there are alternative ways of allocating scarce financial and other resources. That is, in order to divert these resources into nature management at the expense of other competing programmes, the benefits that flow from nature policy should be assessed and clearly expressed in monetary terms. We elaborate on the issue of the benefits of nature policy in the next section.

ASSESSMENT OF BENEFITS OF NATURE POLICY

In this section, we briefly address the benefits of nature policy, both from a global and local point of view. That is, we examine the distribution of the benefits of nature policy from the perspective of individual users of natural resources, nations, regional and local groups, and the international community. In addition, we consider various approaches to measuring these non-market benefits. Finally, we turn to the potential relationships between integrated modelling and monetary valuation.

Local and Global Benefits of Nature Policy

Since natural assets and biological resources are the pillars on which humanity builds civilizations, nature protection is consistent with self-interest (CBD

2000). It is of paramount importance to realize that the continued extinction of local populations of species contributes to loss of their neighbours, which may ultimately lead to spreading patterns of global extinction (Levin 1999). Although human activities such as the conversion of wilderness areas to agriculture may be to the benefit of a particular human individual or society, they threaten the continued flow of global services from nature (Swanson 1992). As a result, proper management of nature requires policy measures at all levels ranging from local to global. In fact, 'think globally, act locally' is a true measure of how nature conservation must take place (Primack 1998; see also Levin 1999). While most of the world's terrestrial and coastal biological diversity is located in the very tropical countries, which are among the poorest in the world, the major demands for their protection come from the wealthier countries. Nature policy that relies on a restrictive management of wilderness areas in developing countries, for instance, by denying access or charging of fees, would impose a large opportunity cost on the poorest groups who live near or within these areas (Munasinghe 1992). Consequently, local people may feel alienated from protection projects and refrain from supporting them.

On local and national scales consumptive benefits from nature, such as fresh water, meat and fish, and revenues from tourism and recreation, are the most significant, since these benefits directly affect subsistence and incomes of local communities. In contrast, non-consumptive benefits, such as aesthetic, spiritual and cultural-historical benefits, and indirect, often 'hidden' benefits from ecological processes, are extremely important from a global perspective (Wells 1992). Sustainable uses of natural assets will thus benefit local people, but some of the benefits accrue to the world as a whole. The global benefits, however, do not necessarily generate a cash flow; that is, they have the characteristics of global public goods. One way to encourage less loss of nature, then, is to create property rights and markets so that countries possessing the natural assets are able to appropriate the benefits they are providing for the rest of the world (Turner et al. 1994). Developed countries of the world often place a greater emphasis on the protection of nature than the poorer. Therefore, it seems fair and reasonable when developed countries provide incentives for developing countries to invest in the protection of the resources. The nature of these incentives will be a country's financial compensation for the global benefits generated by its biological resources. In other words, international institutions should provide mechanisms to channel payments to host states that invest in the protection of the global services from nature (Swanson 1992, 1995). In fact, this is exactly what was discussed at the Rio Convention on Biological Diversity in 1992. There it was agreed that the Convention would provide the poor countries with significant incentives, including financial assistance and biotechnology transfers from rich countries, reflecting the international benefits of nature protection (Wills 1997).

Methods for Valuing Natural Assets

Assigning a monetary value to the benefits of, or avoided damages due to, protecting nature can be done by a number of measurement techniques, based on either observed market behaviour (revealed preferences or indirect method) or stated preferences (direct method). The first type of approach seeks to recover an explicit relationship between individuals' willingness to pay for environmental quality and the demand for a market good (Shechter 1999). Stated preference methods consider an improvement of the environment and, through appropriately constructed questionnaires, they seek to directly measure the value of these improvements (Pearce and Turner 1990; Perrings 1995). As such, these methods derive a value by simulating or constructing a hypothetical market (Baarsma 2000).

The travel cost method (TCM), a revealed preference method, is one of the oldest valuation methods employed by environmental economists (Clawson and Knetsch 1966). It is especially useful for assessing the value of outdoor recreation in natural parks, and to this end, it has been widely used in the USA and to a lesser extent the UK (Perrings 1995). The underlying assumption of the TCM is that the incurred costs of visiting a national park, nature reserve, open space or any other recreational site are directly related to the benefits individuals derive from the amenities within the area, such as hiking, camping, fishing and swimming. The method involves using the value of time spent in travelling, the cost of travel (for example petrol costs) and entrance and other site fees as a proxy for computing the demand price of the environmental resource.

The hedonic pricing method (HPM) derives the value of environmental amenities, such as pollution and noise level, from actual market prices of some private goods. Just like the travel cost method, the HPM is based on observed behaviour. By far the most common application of HPM is to the real estate market. House prices are affected by many factors, not only by house characteristics like the number of rooms and the size of the garden, but also by the environmental quality of the surroundings, including proximity to natural or recreation areas and the quality and uniqueness of such areas. If the non-environmental factors can be controlled for, then the remaining differences in real estate prices are expected to be the result of environmental differences (Turner et al. 1994). Both the HPM and TCM take only use values into account and thereby omit any non-use value elements of the natural assets under investigation. Use values arise from the actual use of the natural environment. Non-use values exist when an individual, who does not intend to make use of a natural asset, would nevertheless feel a 'loss' if it were to disappear (Moran and Pearce 1997; Perrings 1995). As a result, these two techniques may underestimate the total economic value of such assets (Bateman 1993).

In the absence of appropriate data or interdependent market goods, applying an indirect method to value the benefits of biodiversity protection is either not possible or will lead to spurious results. Direct methods bypass the need to refer to market prices by asking people directly what their willingness-to-pay for a change in environmental quality is. This requires the presentation of a change scenario, for example, forest conservation, clearing of a forest, construction of a dam or the loss of certain animal species. The contingent valuation method (CVM) is the most used direct approach. It invokes a framework of a contingent (or hypothetical) market, used to indicate what individuals are willing to pay for a beneficial change or what they are willing to accept by way of compensation to tolerate an undesirable change (Pearce and Turner 1990; Shechter 1999). The main advantages of CVM are that it is capable of capturing non-use values related to nature and species, and that it can value policies before they are implemented (Baarsma 2000; Carson et al. 2001; Hanley and Spash 1993; Nunes et al. 2000). The difference between CVM and the other stated preference methods, such as conjoint measurement, welfare evaluation method and well-being evaluation method, is that in a CVM setting it is much easier to divide the total value into a use component and a non-use component. On the other hand, a major problem of CVM is that it elicits strategic answers, which is due to the fact that in a CVM setting very few incentives exist for people to express their true value. Alternative stated preference methods outperform the CVM on this point (Baarsma 2000; for further critics of CVM, see Diamond and Hausman 1994).

Valuation studies of natural assets have especially been conducted for species preservation, recreation and water management. In particular CVM can, in principle, be used for measuring the economic value of biodiversity and nature, although it should be recognized that this method will fail for those value categories that the general public has no experience with (Nunes and van den Bergh 2001). The literature on valuation is quite extensive and the number of studies quantifying the value of natural assets is rapidly expanding. Thorough overviews of the most important valuation studies are offered by Loomis and White (1996), Nunes et al. (2000), Nunes and van den Bergh (2001) and Woodward and Wui (2001).

Despite the common yardstick in the benefit valuation methods presented, none of them are panaceas; rather, each has its advantages and disadvantages. However, since nature policies entail costs, decision-making by policy-makers and the public at large regarding nature can benefit from the provision of monetary information on the expected benefits (or costs), as it improves the rationale for spending on such policies.

Valuation and Integrated Modelling

So far, integrated ecological-economic modelling and valuation of ecological goods and services have been largely separate areas of research. In order to make full use of the insights of either area, an interaction or even integration of modelling and valuation is needed. This can take a number of routes.

Values estimated in a valuation study can be used as a parameter value in a model study. Benefit or value transfer can assist in translating value estimates to other contexts, conditions, locations or temporal settings that do not allow for direct valuation in 'primary studies' (due to technical or financial constraints) (Brouwer 2000).

Models can be used to generate values under certain scenarios; in particular dynamic models can be used to generate a flow of (net) benefits over time, which can subsequently be transformed in a (net) present value. This can serve as a value relating to a particular scenario of ecosystem change or management (an example is van den Bergh et al. 2001).

Models can be used to generate detailed scenarios that enter valuation experiments, for example, CVM studies. An input scenario can describe a general environmental change, regional development or ecosystem management. This can be fed into a model calculation which, in turn, provides an output scenario with more detailed spatial or temporal information. The latter can then serve, for example, as a hypothetical scenario for valuation, which is presented to respondents in a certain format (graphs, tables, story, diagrams, pictures) so as to inform them about potential consequences of the general policy or exogenous change. Computer software can even be used in such a process.

Spatially disaggregate models can aggregate monetary values defined at the level of a certain disaggregate spatial patch or unit. This can support, for instance, cost–benefit and multi-criteria evaluation exercises at the total system level (see also van den Bergh et al. 2001).

The output of model and valuation studies can be compared. For instance, when studying a scenario for wetland transformation an individual can model the consequences in multiple dimensions (physical, ecological and costs/benefits), and aggregate these via a multi-criteria evaluation procedure, with weights being set by a decision-maker or a representative panel of stakeholders. Alternatively, respondents can be asked to provide value estimates, such as a willingness-to-pay for not experiencing the change. If such information is available for multiple management scenarios, then rankings based on either approach can be compared.

CONCLUSIONS

The protection and sustainable use of nature requires an approach that shares characteristics with environmental policy, but is different from it in a number of dimensions. This is due to the fact that problems of nature loss and degradation, and the formulation of nature policies, are characterized by elements of irreversibility, complex phenomena in time and space, uncertainty about the chain from genes to ecosystems functions and a large number of stakeholders with different objectives. This was the motivation for the approach adopted in this chapter, namely to develop a framework for theorizing about nature policy as well as developing operational methods for its analysis.

At the same time, it was stressed that nature policy must be complemented by adequate environmental policy measures, because of the dependence of natural assets on environmental conditions. Addressing the issue of nature priority-setting has become an area for an integrated ecological-economic approach. Many problems of nature priorities can be cast in terms of maximizing species richness in a geographic location under a limited budget constraint (see, for instance, Moran et al. 1996, 1997). Moreover, nature protection priorities have given greater impetus to the design and formulation of cost-effective nature policy measures. This implies that nature policy is formulated in terms of available information on costs, while the effectiveness is defined in non-monetary terms.

The disciplines of ecology and economy both play an important role in identifying efficient, effective and equitable policy options for nature management. Integrated ecological-economic approaches to nature policy allow presenting ecological results in terms that are directly relevant to management. Ecological approaches are typically descriptive and may provide, for example, arguments to plead the case of a single, large nature reserve rather than several small reserves. With economic tools, however, a policy-maker with a budget constraint can be informed about the optimal level of investment in each strategy. Ecologists, economists and possibly researchers from other disciplines must take up the challenge to provide further insight into the fundamental economic and ecological dimensions of nature and biological diversity. Getting the right mix of models, new theories, innovative approaches and practical examples will be the key to a successful identification of and solution to nature loss and landscape degradation.

Since much of the benefits of nature protection are likely to accrue to the people in developed countries, these countries have an important role to play. Large-scale north–south transfers of capital are essential to enable the developing countries to preserve habitats and to improve natural resource management. The Global Environmental Facility (GEF) provides a vehicle for the international financial assistance to developing countries for global nature protection efforts. However, the lack of participation in the GEF by governments limits the possibilities for the GEF's control and monitoring activities. There is a pressing need to increase the amount of money directly available for nature management activities. Where existing budgets cannot cover financial requirements to meet nature policy goals, countries should be able to seek international financial cooperation.

In economic terms, people living in or near a protected ecosystem often capture little benefit from preservation or sustainable resource use. The benefits of nature protection increase with the scale from local to regional to national to global. In contrast, the economic costs incurred as a result of nature protection prescriptions follow an opposite trend. The heaviest burden tends to be borne by people situated in rural areas, in the vicinity of protected areas. This creates an incentive problem. Poorly defined property rights or public goods' externalities result in market failures, which are widely regarded as the fundamental causes of nature loss and landscape degradation. The property rights' issue results in a lack of incentive for sustainable management and use of natural assets. In response to market failures, the assignment of property rights as a form of nature policy has often been suggested. It is important to realize, however, that government intervention may not always be a magic cure-all in correcting the market failure. With many competing social and economic objectives to be satisfied, such as employment, agriculture and economic growth, there are nearly always intervention failures, inefficient or uncoordinated regulations, policies and institutions that exacerbate adverse impacts on nature. Decentralization and self-organization may then be reasonable strategies of public action.

NOTES

1. The authors are grateful to David Stern for valuable comments on an earlier draft of this chapter.
2. Even if some elements typical of nature policy, such as safe minimum standards, are available to environmental policy-making, nature policy measures are no standard element of the economic theory of environmental policy (Baumol and Oates 1988).
3. The large number of nature valuation studies should not be confused with a policy theory of nature. In fact, the policy implications of valuation studies are very general and non-specific.

REFERENCES

Arrow, K.J. and Fisher, A.C. 1974. Environmental preservation, uncertainty and irreversibility. *Quarterly Journal of Economics.* 88: 312–19.
Arrow, K.J., Cropper, M.L., Eads, G.C., Hahn, R.W., Lave, L.B., Noll, R.G., Portney, P.R., Russell, M., Schmalensee, R., Smith, V.K and Stavins, R.N. 1996. Is there a

role for benefit–cost analysis in environmental, health, and safety regulation? *Science*. 272: 221–2.

Baarsma, B. 2000. Monetary valuation of environmental goods: alternatives to contingent valuation. PhD thesis, University of Amsterdam.

Barbier, E.B., Burgess, J.C. and Folke, C. 1994. *Paradise lost? The ecological economics of biodiversity*. London: Earthscan Publications Ltd.

Bateman, I. 1993. Valuation of the environment, methods and techniques: revealed preference methods. In: Turner, R.K. (ed). Sustainable environmental economics and management; principles and practice. London and New York: Belhaven Press, pp. 192–265.

Baumol, W.J. and Oates, W.E. 1988. *The theory of environmental policy*. 2nd edn. Cambridge: Cambridge University Press.

Begon, M., Harper, J.L. and Townsend, C.R. 1996. *Ecology: individuals, populations and communities*. 3rd edn. Oxford: Blackwell Science.

Bishop, R.C. 1978. Endangered species and uncertainty: the economics of a safe minimum standard. *American Journal of Agricultural Economics*. 60: 10–18.

Bockstael, N., Costanza, R., Strand, I., Boynton, W., Bell, K. and Wainger, L. 1995. Ecological economic modeling and valuation of ecosystems. *Ecological Economics*. 14: 143–59.

Brouwer, R. 2000. Environmental value transfer: state of the art and future prospects. *Ecological Economics*. 32: 137–52.

Carson, R.T., Flores, N.E. and Meade, N.F. 2001. Contingent valuation: controversies and evidence. *Environmental and Resource Economics*. 19: 173–210.

CBD. 2000. *Sustaining life on earth; how the Convention on Biological Diversity promotes nature and human well-being*. Montreal: Secretariat of the CBD.

Clawson, M. and Knetsch, J.L. 1966. *Economics of outdoor recreation*. Baltimore: The Johns Hopkins University Press.

Costanza, R. 1984. Natural resource valuation and management: toward an ecological economics. In: Jansson, A.-M. (ed). *Integration of economy and ecology: an outlook for the eighties*. Stockholm: Proceedings from the Wallenberg Symposia, pp. 7–18.

Costanza, R., Norton, B. and Haskell, B. (eds). 1992. *Ecosystem health: new goals for environmental management*. Washington, DC: Island Press.

Costanza, R., Perrings, C. and Cleveland, C.J. 1997. *The development of ecological economics*. Cheltenham: Edward Elgar.

Crowards, T.M. 1998. Safe minimum standards: costs and opportunities. *Ecological Economics*. 25: 303–14.

Daily, G.C. 1997. Valuing and safeguarding earth's life-support systems. In: Daily, G.C. (ed). *Nature's services; societal dependence on natural ecosystems*. Washington, DC: Island Press, pp. 365–74.

Dasgupta, P.S. and Heal, G.M. 1979. *Economic theory and exhaustible resources*. Cambridge: Cambridge University Press.

de Kruijf, H.A.M., van Ierland, E.C., van der Heide, C.M. and Dekker, J.M. 2002. Attitudes and their influence on nature valuation and management in relation to sustainable development. In: Rapport, D.J., Lasley, W.L., Rolston, D.E., Nielsen, N.O., Qualsec, C.O. and Damania, A.B. (eds). *Managing for healthy ecosystems*, pp. 127–43. Boca Raton, USA: Lewis Publishers.

Deacon, R.T., Brookshire, D.S., Fisher, A.C., Kneese, A.V., Kolstad, C.D., Scrogin, D., Smith, V.K., Ward, M. and Wilen, J. 1998. Research trends and opportunities in environmental and natural resource economics. *Environmental and Resource Economics*. 11 (3–4): 383–97.

Diamond, P.A. and Hausman, J.A. 1994. Contingent valuation: is some number better than no number? *Journal of Economic Perspectives.* 8 (4): 45–64.

Field, B.C. 2001. *Natural resource economics; an introduction.* Boston: McGraw-Hill.

Folke, C., Holling, C.S. and Perrings, C. 1996. Biological diversity, ecosystems, and the human scale. *Ecological Applications.* 6 (4): 1018–24.

Gollier, C., Jullien, B. and Treich, N. 2000. Scientific progress and irreversibility: an economic interpretation of the 'Precautionary Principle'. *Journal of Public Economics.* 75: 229–53.

Graham-Tomasi, T. 1995. Quasi-option value. In: Bromley, D.W. (ed). *Handbook of environmental economics.* Oxford and Cambridge: Basil Blackwell Ltd, pp. 594–614.

Hanley, N., Shogren, J.F. and White, B. 1997. *Environmental economics in theory and practice.* Houndmill and London: Macmillan Press Ltd.

Hanley, N. and Spash, C.L. 1993. *Cost–benefit analysis and the environment.* Aldershot: Edward Elgar.

Hartwick, J.M. and Olewiler, N.D. 1998. *The economics of natural resource use.* 2nd edn. Reading, MA: Addison-Wesley.

Henry, C. 1974. Option values in the economics of irreplaceable assets. Review of Economic Studies: Symposium on the Economics of Exhaustible Resources, pp. 89–104.

Hof, J. and Bevers, M. 1998. *Spatial optimization for managed ecosystems.* New York: Columbia University Press.

Holling, C.S., Schindler, D.W., Walker, B.W. and Roughgarden, J. 1995. Biodiversity in the functioning of ecosystems: an ecological synthesis. In: Perrings, C., Mäler, K.-G., Folke, C., Holling, C.S. and Jansson, B.-O. (eds). *Biodiversity loss: economic and ecological issues.* Cambridge: Cambridge University Press, pp. 44–83.

Kahn, J.R. 1998. *The economic approach to environmental and natural resources.* 2nd edn. Orlando: The Dryden Press.

Kooten, G.C. van and Bulte, E.H. 2000. *The economics of nature: managing biological assets.* Malden, MA and Oxford, UK: Blackwell Publishers.

Krutilla, J.V. and Fisher, A.C. 1975. *The economics of natural environments; studies in the valuation of commodity and amenity resources.* Washington, DC: The Johns Hopkins University Press.

Levin, S.A. 1999. *Fragile dominion: complexity and the commons.* Cambridge, MA: Perseus Publishing.

Loomis, J.B. and White, D.S. 1996. Economic benefits of rare and endangered species: summary and meta-analysis. *Ecological Economics.* 18: 197–206.

Moran, D. and Pearce, D. 1997. The economics of biodiversity. In: Folmer, H. and Tietenberg, T. (eds). *The international yearbook of environmental and resource economics 1997/1998: a survey of current issues.* Cheltenham, UK and Lyme, USA: Edward Elgar, pp. 82–113.

Moran, D., Pearce, D. and Wendelaar, A. 1996. Global biodiversity priorities; a cost-effectiveness index for investments. *Global Environmental Change.* 6 (2): 103–19.

Moran, D., Pearce, D. and Wendelaar, A. 1997. Investing in biodiversity: an economic perspective on global priority setting. *Biodiversity and Conservation.* 6 (9): 1219–43.

Munasinghe, M. 1992. Biodiversity protection policy: environmental valuation and distribution issues. *Ambio.* 21 (3): 227–36.

Nijkamp, P. (ed). 1976. *Environmental economics*. Leiden: Martinus Nijhoff Social Sciences Division.

Norton, B.G. and Toman, M.A. 1997. Sustainability: ecological and economic perspectives. *Land Economics*. 73 (4): 553–68.

Nunes, P.A.L.D. and van den Bergh, J.C.J.M. 2001. Economic valuation of biodiversity: sense or nonsense? *Ecological Economics*. 39: 203–22.

Nunes, P.A.L.D., van den Bergh, J.C.J.M. and Nijkamp, P. 2000. *Ecological-economic analysis and valuation of biodiversity*. Tinbergen Institute Discussion Paper – 00–100/3. Amsterdam.

Odum, H.T. 1989. Self-organization, transformity, and information. *Science*. 242: 1132–9.

OECD. 1999. *Handbook of incentive measures for biodiversity; design and implementation*. Paris: OECD.

Pearce, D.W. and Turner, R.K. 1990. *Economics of natural resources and the environment*. London: Harvester Wheatsheaf.

Perman, R., Ma, Y. and McGilvray, J. 1996. *Natural resource and environmental economics*. London and New York: Longman.

Perrings, C. 1995. The economic value of biodiversity. In: Heywood, V.H. (ed). *Global biodiversity assessment*. Cambridge: Cambridge University Press, pp. 823–914.

Perrings, C., Folke, C.F. and Mäler, K.-G. 1992. The ecology and economics of biodiversity loss: the research agenda. *Ambio*. 21 (3): 201–11.

Polis, G.A. 1998. Stability is woven by complex webs. *Nature*. 395: 744–5.

Porter, R.C. 1982. The new approach to wilderness preservation through benefit–cost analysis. *Journal of Environmental Economics and Management*. 9 (1): 59–80.

Primack, R.B. 1998. *Essentials of conservation biology*. 2nd edn. Sunderland, MA: Sinauer Associates.

Randall, A. 1988. What mainstream economists have to say about the value of biodiversity. In: Wilson, E.O. (ed). *Biodiversity*. Washington, DC: National Academy Press, pp. 217–23.

Randall, A. and Farmer, M.C. 1995. Benefits, costs, and the safe minimum standard of conservation. In: Bromley, D.W. (ed). *Handbook of environmental economics*. Oxford and Cambridge: Basil Blackwell Ltd, pp. 26–44.

Scholten, H.J. and Stillwell, J.C.H. 1990. *Geographical information systems for urban and regional planning*. Dordrecht: Kluwer Academic Publishers.

Shechter, M. 1999. Valuing the environment. In: Folmer, H. and Gabel, H.L. (eds). *Principles of environmental and resource economics*. 2nd edn. Cheltenham: Edward Elgar. Chapter 3.

Spash, C.L. 1999. The development of environmental thinking in economics. *Environmental Values*. 8 (4): 413–35.

Strijker, D., Sijtsma, F.J. and Wiersma, D. 2000. Evaluation of nature conservation. *Environmental and Resource Economics*. 16 (4): 363–78.

Swanson, T.M. 1992. Economics of a biodiversity convention. *Ambio*. 21 (3): 250–57.

Swanson, T., 1995. The international regulation of biodiversity decline: optimal policy and evolutionary product. In: Perrings, C., Mäler, K.-G., Folke, C., Holling, C.S. and Jansson, B.-O. (eds). *Biodiversity loss: economic and ecological issues*. Cambridge: Cambridge University Press, pp. 225–59.

Tisdell, C.A. 1991. *Economics of environmental conservation: economics for environmental and ecological management*. Amsterdam, London, New York and Tokyo: Elsevier Science Publishers BV.

Turner, M.G. 1998. Landscape ecology: living in a mosaic. In: Dodson, S.I., Allen, T.F.H., Carpenter, S.R., Ives, A.R., Jeanne, R.L., Kitchell, J.F., Langston, N.E. and Turner, M.G. *Ecology*. New York and Oxford: Oxford University Press, pp. 77–122.

Turner, R.K., van den Bergh, J.C.J.M., Söderqvist, T., Barendregt, A., van der Straaten, J., Maltby, E. and van Ierland, E.C. 2000. Ecological-economic analysis of wetlands: scientific integration for management and policy. *Ecological Economics*. 35: 7–23.

Turner, R.K., Button, K. and Nijkamp, P. 1999. Introduction. In: Turner, R.K., Button, K. and Nijkamp, P. (eds). *Ecosystems and nature; economics, science and policy*. Cheltenham, UK and Northampton, USA: Edward Elgar, pp. xvii–xxxvii.

Turner, R.K., Pearce, D. and Bateman, I. 1994. *Environmental economics: an elementary introduction*. New York: Harvester Wheatsheaf.

Turner, R.K., Perrings, C. and Folke, C. 1997. Ecological economics: paradigm or perspective. In: van den Bergh, J.C.J.M. and van der Straaten, J. (eds). *Economy and ecosystems in change*. Cheltenham, UK and Lyme, USA: Edward Elgar, pp. 25–49.

van den Bergh, J.C.J.M., Barendregt, A., Gilbert, A.J., van Herwijnen, M., van Horssen, P., Kandelaars, P.A.A.H. and Lorenz, C. 2001. Spatial economic-hydro-ecological modelling and evaluation of land use impacts in the Vecht wetlands area. *Environmental Modeling and Assessment*. 6: 87–100.

van der Heide, C.M., van den Bergh, J.C.J.M. and van Ierland, E.C. 2002a. Economic analysis of biodiversity: solving Weitzman's paradox. Free University Amsterdam, mimeo.

van der Heide, C.M., van Ierland, E.C. and van den Bergh, J.C.J.M. 2002b. An economic-ecological analysis of nature development scenarios for the Veluwe. (In Dutch). Free University Amsterdam, mimeo.

Verbruggen, H. 1994. Environmental policy failures and environmental policy levels. In: Opschoor, J.B. and Turner, R.K. (eds). *Economic incentives and environmental policies*. Dordrecht: Kluwer Academic Publishers, pp. 41–54.

Weitzman, M.L. 1998. The Noah's ark problem. *Econometrica*. 66 (6): 1279–98.

Wells, M. 1992. Biodiversity conservation, affluence and poverty: mismatched costs and benefits and efforts to remedy them. *Ambio*. 21 (3): 237–43.

Wills, A. 1997. *Economics and the environment: a signalling and incentives approach*. St. Leonards, NSW: Allen & Unwin.

Witting, L., Tomiuk, J. and Loeschcke, V. 2000. Modelling the optimal conservation of interacting species. *Ecological Modelling*. 125: 123–43.

Woodward, R.T. and Wui, Y.-S. 2001. The economic value of wetland services: a meta-analysis. *Ecological Economics*. 37: 257–70.

10. Modelling stochastic technological change in economy and environment using the Kalman filter

David I. Stern   US, Botswana

This chapter reports on empirical work (Perrings and Stern 2000; Stern 1994) that uses the Kalman filter to estimate stochastic trends in the context of resource use models. This modelling approach treats changes in the environment and changes in the production possibilities of the economy as similar processes, which in both cases can be seen as changes in either capital stocks or changes in technology. The two case studies are a model of production and technological change in the US macroeconomy in the post-war period, and a model of rangeland utilization and degradation in Botswana in the 30 years to the mid-1990s.

Perrings (1987) presents a vision of a dynamic, evolving economy that receives inputs from its environment and returns surplus outputs to its environment. These surplus outputs substantively change the nature of the resource base on which the economy depends and the changing nature of the resource structure precipitates technological change within the controlled economy itself. Technological change and controlled capital accumulation within the economy forces uncontrolled capital accumulation and technological change in the environment (O'Connor 1993). Perrings modelled this system using a von Neumann-type technology and the mass balance principle as key features. This vision was extended and refined by O'Connor (1991) to include energy flows and thermodynamic considerations regarding energy.

The framework presented in this chapter is nowhere near as complete or encompassing. However, it does incorporate some aspects of such a system. Its primary advantage is that it is an empirical approach utilizing advanced econometric techniques to describe the state and evolution of technology. Unlike the Perrings and O'Connor models, the models in this chapter utilize neoclassical principles of optimization. Additionally, the US model embodies a neoclassical production function that allows continuous substitution of factor inputs within a given state of technology. The technology in the rangeland model consists of a group of logistic growth functions.

Conventional econometric modelling of agricultural and industrial production technologies (for example Capalbo 1988; Berndt and Khaled 1979) has assumed that such systems can be approximated by deterministic production technologies that are inherently linear in the parameters. The stochastic components of these models are stationary random variables due to optimization errors by producers. There are two reasons why this approach is inappropriate as a model of joint economy-environment systems. The first is that they are probably inappropriate as a model of industrial systems. Technological change is now widely seen as a non-stationary stochastic process (Slade 1989; Solow 1994). Second, the natural environment is an additional source of stochastic variation, uncertainty, unpredictability, and evolutionary and sometimes 'surprising' behaviour (O'Connor 1993; Perrings 1987).

Cointegration modelling and Kalman filtering are two approaches to the econometric modelling of non-stationary systems that have been rapidly introduced to all areas of applied econometrics (Cuthbertson et al. 1992). Cointegration modelling (Engle and Granger 1987) assumes that a linear combination of random variables is stationary.[1] Kalman filtering (Kalman 1960; Kalman and Bucy 1961) can be used to model explicitly non-stationary random variables. It has been used in this context to model technological change as a stochastic trend (Harvey and Marshall 1991; Slade 1989; Stern 1994). Extremely complex and non-linear models may be amenable to econometric estimation using the Kalman filter. Both studies in this chapter use Kalman filter techniques. Cointegration modelling only enters explicitly to the extent that the equations in the Botswana model incorporate a form of error correction mechanism. Implicitly, we test all equations for stationary residuals and hence for the presence of cointegration.[2]

Changes in the quality of environmental resources such as rangelands in sub-Saharan Africa can be visualized as a process of uncontrolled technological change in the environment. As such they can be modelled in a similar way to technological change in controlled economic systems. In this chapter, we use the Kalman filter to model factor-augmenting technological change trends in the US macroeconomy in the post-war period. Standard linear regression techniques are of no use in estimating this type of model where the trend variables are stochastic rather then simple deterministic trends. This model is a fairly standard econometric model of technological change in the economy though we know of no other study that actually estimates multiple stochastic technical change trends. The main substantive point of interest for ecological economists and environmental management scholars is the estimated trend in autonomous energy efficiency.[3]

We also use the Kalman filter to model the current and climax state of rangeland in Botswana in a 30-year period up to the mid-1990s within an optimal control model of pastoralists' behaviour. Both state variables are unobserved by the econometrician and represent the state of natural technology in livestock production or dually the level of natural capital present. Of particular interest is the distinction between short-run, reversible rangeland degradation, represented by declines in the current state of the rangeland, and long-run and irreversible rangeland degradation, represented by declines in the climax state of the rangeland. We interpret the latter to be the result of the loss of resilience in the agro-ecosystem.

The advantage of this modelling approach is that we do not need to be able to directly measure the availability of natural capital stocks in order to integrate a simple model of the ecology of the system into a behavioural model of the economic system. This generalized technological change approach may have many other integrative applications in ecological economics.

The remainder of the chapter is divided into three main parts. The next part covers the theory of generalized technological change and state space models and the Kalman filter. The third part presents the empirical examples and the fourth provides some conclusions.

THEORY

Generalized Technological Change

Let us examine in more detail the relationship between the conventional definition of technology and the broader definition proposed here. In a general production system any aggregate indicator of the state of technology is a composite of the state of the natural resource base and the state of technology in the usual sense (Cleveland and Stern 1993; Stern 1999a). More specifically, assume that technology is given by the following transformation frontier:

$$Q = f(A_1X_1, \ldots, A_nX_n, B_1R_1, \ldots, B_mR_m, N) \qquad (10.1)$$

R is a vector of resource inputs (for example the area of agricultural land, stock of petroleum in a reservoir) and N is a vector of additional environmental variables such as rainfall and temperature. The X_i are other factors of production controlled by the extractor (such as capital, labour, energy and materials), and the A_i and B_i are augmentation factors associated with the respective factors of production. Factor augmentation is a (fairly weak) restriction on the possible nature of technological change. It specifies that technical change increases or decreases the effective quantity of each factor of production available per crude unit of the input used.[4] Taking the derivative of lnQ with respect to time yields:

$$\dot{Q} = \sum_i \sigma_i \dot{A}_i + \sum_j \rho_j \dot{B}_j + \sum_i \sigma_i \dot{X}_i + \sum_j \rho_j \dot{R}_j + v\dot{N} \qquad (10.2)$$

where the σ_i, ρ_j, and v are the output elasticities of the various inputs. A dot on a variable indicates the derivative of the logarithm with respect to time. Four measures of resource productivity or resource scarcity in a cost of production sense (Cleveland and Stern, 1993; Stern, 1999a) can be derived from (10.2). The crudest indicator is resource productivity (Q/R):

$$\dot{Q} - \dot{R} = \sum_i \sigma_i \dot{A}_i + \sum_j \rho_j \dot{B}_j + \sum_i \sigma_i \dot{X}_i + v\dot{N} \qquad (10.3)$$

where R is an aggregate of the resource inputs. Examples of this indicator are energy-intensity (E/GDP) and crop yields. This indicator is not very informative about likely long-run developments in resource availability because it is likely to be dominated in the short run at least by changes in the quantities of other inputs X.

Multifactor productivity (MFP) is a measure of the quantity of produced inputs required to extract a unit of resource commodity and is thus an indirect measure of the combined state of technology and state of nature and the availability of resources (see Stern, 1999a). This measure is a generalization of the unit cost indicator of resource scarcity introduced by Barnett and Morse (1963). An advantage of this indicator is that we do not need any data about the state of the resource stock, R. The change in *lnMFP* is given by:

$$\dot{MFP} = \dot{Q} - \sum_i \sigma_i \dot{X}_i = \sum_i \sigma_i \dot{A}_i + \sum_j \rho_j \dot{B}_j + \sum_j \rho_j \dot{R}_j + v\dot{N} \qquad (10.4)$$

Thus moves in this indicator are the sum of the four terms on the *RHS* of (10.4), respectively:

1. Technical change
2. Resource depletion or augmentation
3. Change in the dimension of the resource stock, for example area farmed
4   Change in environmental variables such as rainfall and temperature in agriculture

The sum of terms 1, 2, and 4 are what energy analysts call resource quality (Gever et al. 1986). This definition of resource quality allows changes in the state of technology to compensate for a decline in the physical quality of the resource. MFP is not affected by the prices and availability of those other inputs that can obscure the long-term trends in resource quality and availability.[5]

When we have data available on the extent of the resource base, we can compute total factor productivity (TFP), which expresses the productivity of the joint system:

$$\dot{TFP} = \dot{Q} - \sum_i \sigma_i \dot{X}_i - \sum_j \rho_j \dot{R}_j = \sum_i \sigma_i \dot{A}_i + \sum_j \rho_j \dot{B}_j + v\dot{N} \qquad (10.5)$$

This indicator is identical with the resource quality concept mentioned above. We can obtain even more information by breaking the right-hand side of (10.5) into its components – the factor augmentation trends. The augmentation trends tell us about the contribution of the relevant inputs to productivity holding the quantities and effectivities of all the other inputs constant. In the US growth model example, one of the augmentation trends estimated is the autonomous energy efficiency. In the Botswana case study, the main indicator is the carrying capacity of the rangeland or the 'state of the rangeland'. The former trend is mainly due to changes in technology that allow consumers to use energy more or less effectively. The latter trend is more in the nature of a change in the natural capital stock, but it can be treated as if it was a change in technology.

Recent research on technological change has emphasized that to a large extent technological change is endogenous – rather than changes arriving as exogenous 'manna from heaven' they may occur as a result of the economic process and agents may invest in research and development. In the US example we assume that technological change is exogenous. This does not mean that technological change occurs at a constant rate or that it is unaffected by economic factors. Quite to the contrary, we assume that the rate of technological change varies over time as it follows a stochastic time path. Economic events and variables may indeed affect the course of this path; however, the econometric model does not specify the ways in which this happens. Technology is exogenous in the sense that economic agents are not free to choose the technology with which they produce. However, following standard neoclassical assumptions they are free to choose the technique that they use from among those afforded by the technology. Therefore, optimization processes are constructed for the purposes of econometric estimation assuming that [at least some] prices, technology and uncontrolled inputs are given, but agents are free to choose quantities of controlled inputs.

On the other hand, in the Botswana case study changes in the state of the rangeland are partly endogenous – grazing by cattle affects the state of the rangeland – and partly exogenous – the effects of rainfall and random shocks. However, we assume that pastoralists do not take the state of the rangeland into account in their decision-making. Their impact on the rangeland is treated as an external cost.

State Space Models and Kalman Filter

The Kalman filter is an algorithm for estimating unobserved time-varying variables and has numerous applications in modern time series econometrics. In our application we use the filter to estimate unobserved stochastic trends.[6] The first step in applying the Kalman filter to an estimation problem is to reformulate the model in question in terms of a state space model. A non-linear generalization of the linear state space model is given by (De Jong, 1991a, 1991b; Harvey, 1989):

$$y_t = z(a_t) + E(a_t) u_t \qquad t = 1, \ldots, T \qquad (10.6)$$

$$a_{t+1} = r(a_t) + H(a_t) u_t \qquad t = 1, \ldots, T \qquad (10.7)$$

where equations (10.6) are the measurement equations and equations (10.7) are the transition equations; y_t is the vector of 'dependent' variables, the observations; a_t is a vector of unobserved stochastic state variables; u_t is a vector of normally distributed disturbances with zero mean and covariance $\sigma_u^2 I$ (and is assumed to be serially uncorrelated and uncorrelated with $a()$; $z()$, $r()$, $E()$, and $H()$ are possibly non-linear functions of the state vector. In the Botswana case study, $E()$ and $H()$ are constant matrices. Additionally in the US study, $r()$ is a linear function.

As the state variables are unobserved and the current state depends on previous unobserved states, the Kalman filter must be used to estimate the current state vector. The filter is also used to compute the prediction error decomposition of the likelihood function. We use the Davidon–Fletcher–Powell quasi-Newton algorithm (Greene 1990) to maximize this likelihood function with respect to the fixed hyperparameters that define the functions in (10.6) and (10.7). The derivatives are calculated by the finite difference method. Given maximum likelihood estimates of the hyperparameters, the Kalman filter produces maximum likelihood estimates of the state variables using only data for previous periods. Given these estimates, a smoother algorithm (De Jong 1991a, 1991b) is used to calculate values for the unobserved state variables utilizing the entire data set. We use the extended Kalman filter suitable for such non-linear state space models. Details of the use of the Kalman filter in this context are given by De Jong (1991a, 1991b), Harvey (1989), Harvey and Marshall (1991), Slade (1989), and Stern (1994).

APPLICATIONS

Energy and Growth

There has been extensive debate concerning the trend in energy efficiency in the developed economies, especially since the two oil price shocks of the 1970s. Taking the example of the US economy, energy consumption hardly changed in the period 1973 to 1990 (Figure 10.1). This was despite a significant increase in GDP. These facts are indisputable. What has been the subject

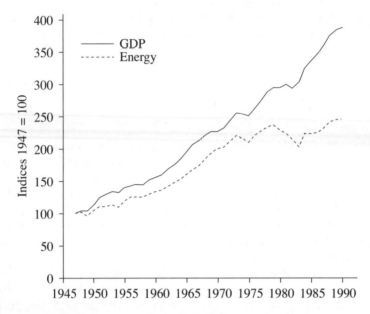

Figure 10.1   US gross energy use and GDP

of argument is what were the reasons for the break in the trend. It is commonly asserted that there has been a decoupling of economic output and resources, which implies that the limits to growth are no longer as restricting as in the past (for example Bohi 1989; IBRD 1992). There are four main explanations of decoupling:

1. Decoupling may be due to shifts from lower-quality fuels such as coal to higher quality fuels such as electricity, which are more productive (Kaufmann 1992; US Congress 1990). Figure 10.2 shows that when we adjust energy use for shifts in energy quality, much less decoupling is evident.
2. Decoupling could be due to substitution of other inputs for energy.
3. Shifts in the output mix might result in decoupling if economies dematerialize as the share of the service sector in economic activity grows over the course of economic development.
4. Finally, a fourth possible cause of decoupling is growing autonomous energy efficiency.

Jorgensen and Wilcoxen (1993) estimated that autonomous energy efficiency is declining. Berndt et al. (1993) use a model in which this index is

Figure 10.2   USA: quality-weighted final energy use and GDP

assumed to change at a constant rate. They estimate that in the US manufacturing industry between 1965 and 1987, the energy augmentation index was
increasing at between 1.75 per cent and 13.09 per cent per annum depending
on the assumptions made.

Perhaps these rather inconsistent and wide-ranging estimates are due to the
inappropriate assumption that the trend is deterministic. We can use the
Kalman filter to estimate an autonomous energy efficiency trend that is
stochastic rather than deterministic. The trend is estimated as a factor-
augmenting technical change trend alongside those for capital and labour by
using a group of equations derived from a macroeconomic production function.

We use a similar method to Harvey and Marshall (1991) with the following
modifications. Like Slade (1989) and Darby and Wren-Lewis (1992), we
assume that the trends follow a local linear trend (Harvey 1989), rather than a
random walk with drift. We do not assume constant returns to scale (but do
assume homotheticity) and use a production function rather than a cost function.[7] Also, we estimate the model in the time domain rather than the
frequency domain and do not make the assumption of statistical homogeneity.

Similarly to Harvey and Marshall (1991), we assume that factor markets
are competitive. It is not assumed that output markets are competitive. We also

assume that a translog function can provide a reasonable approximation to the underlying production technology. We assume that there is weak separability between the two groups capital–labour energy (KLE), and materials, which allows us to omit materials from models of the marginal product of the other factors (Lakshmanan et al. 1984). This is the only assumption required to estimate the factor share equations (see below) with the omission of materials. However, in order to estimate an output equation excluding a materials variable, we have to assume also that non-energy materials are strictly complementary to aggregate KLE input and therefore have a zero marginal product. Any increase in output due to an increase in materials use with constant KLE input is credited to technical change. This is a strong assumption. While it could be argued that these are reasonable approximations in a manufacturing industry, they are clearly unreasonable approximations in an industry such as agriculture where fertilizers, pesticides, water and so on can be used in varying proportions and clearly do have a marginal product.

In accordance with Harvey and Marshall (1991), it is assumed that technical change is both of the factor-augmenting type represented by three stochastic trend variables, A_K, A_L, and A_E, and also of a factor neutral type represented by a stochastic trend A_0. However, such a trend is unidentifiable in the model developed here and therefore it was dropped.[8] The translog production function for period t, imposing symmetry restrictions (see Berndt and Christensen 1973) on the cross-product coefficients π_{ij}, is:

$$\ln Q_t = \pi_0 + \sum_i \pi_i \ln(X_{it} A_{it}) + \tfrac{1}{2} \sum_i \sum_j \pi_{ij} \ln(X_{it} A_{it}) \ln(X_{jt} A_{jt}) \qquad (10.8)$$

where Q is output and the X are the various factor inputs. Following Kim (1992), and given the above assumptions, we derive inverse factor demand functions from the production function that determine the price of each of the three factors of production. These demand functions yield after various manipulations, the cost share equations:

$$S_{it} = (\partial C_t / \partial Q_t) \, [\pi_i + \sum_j \pi_{ij} \ln A_{jt} + \sum_j \pi_{ij} \ln X_{jt} + \varepsilon_{it}] \qquad (10.9)$$

where C is total cost and the S_i the shares of each factor in costs. We assume that the production function is homogeneous, but do not impose constant returns to scale. As the cost shares sum to a constant in every period, the covariance matrix of their disturbances is singular, that is $\sum_i \varepsilon_i = 0$ and it is not possible to obtain a maximum likelihood estimate of all three equations jointly (Barten 1969). We chose to drop the energy share equation.

In order to estimate all three augmentation trends, at least three equations are required. The obvious third equation is the production function. However, the production function itself involves multiples of the unobserved augmentation variables, which cannot then be estimated using the diffuse Kalman filter.[9] For this reason the output equation is not the production function (10.8) but is instead based on integrating (10.2) under the assumption of factor market equilibrium and substituting into (10.8):

$$\ln Q_t = \pi_0 + (\partial C_t/\partial Q_t)^{-1}[\sum_j S_{it} \ln A_{jt} + \sum_j S_{it} \ln X_{jt} + \varepsilon_{Qt}] \quad (10.10)$$

The local linear trend model follows a random walk with a time-varying drift that itself follows a random walk:

$$\ln A_{it} = \ln A_{it-1} + \gamma_{it-1} + \eta_{Ait} \quad (10.11)$$

$$\gamma_{it} = \gamma_{it-1} + \eta_{\gamma it} \quad (10.12)$$

All the error terms η are assumed to be uncorrelated. The elements of a_t in (10.7) are therefore:

$$a_t = [\ln A_{Kt}, \ln A_{Lt}, \ln A_{Et}, \gamma_{Kt}, \gamma_{Lt}, \gamma_{Et}]' \quad (10.13)$$

where γ_{Kt}, γ_{Lt}, and γ_{Et} are the stochastic trend terms and the transition matrix in (10.7) is:

$$R = \begin{bmatrix} I_3 & I_3 \\ 0_3 & I_3 \end{bmatrix} \quad (10.14)$$

The initial state of A is set to zero with zero variance, while γ has a diffuse prior distribution. This indexes the augmentation trends to one in the first year. The observed variables are also indexed to one.

To summarize – two of equations (10.9) are estimated for labour and capital together with (10.10). We use De Jong's (1991a, 1991b) diffuse Kalman filter algorithm. In total there are six parameters of the production function that must be estimated by maximum likelihood: π_0, π_K, π_L, π_E, π_{KK}, π_{KL}, and π_{LL}, which form the parameters of $z()$ in (10.6) as well as five in the constant covariance matrix E and six in H. An estimate of the error variance of the first equation σ^2_u that is concentrated out of the likelihood function is also produced. Maximum likelihood is performed iteratively using the Broyden, Fletcher, Goldfarb and Shanno approximation of the Hessian matrix and finite difference derivatives.

Full details of the data employed are provided in Stern (2000). Labour is measured in hours worked by full- and part-time employees in domestic industries. Capital is measured by a Divisia index aggregating producer's private capital. Energy is measured by a Divisia index aggregating a variety of fuel types (shown in Figure 10.2). Output is gross output calculated using a Divisia index as the real value of GDP and energy.[10] Due to this high level of aggregation, it is possible that the estimate of autonomous energy efficiency will incorporate the effects of some aspects of structural change on the output side of the economy (Solow 1987). The time period employed is 1948–1990.

The estimates of the hyperparameters, their standard errors and the estimate of σ^2_u are presented in Table 10.1. Most of the parameters are highly significant. Some of the error variances are insignificant as is π_{LL}. The main features of the results concern the estimated production function parameters and the stochastic properties of the technical change trends. The production technology is characterized by increasing returns to scale. The degree of returns to scale is 1.146. This compares to Kim's (1992) estimate for US

Table 10.1   Maximum likelihood estimates of hyperparameters in the US macro model

Parameter	Estimate (standard error in parentheses)	Parameter	Estimate (standard error in parentheses)
π_K	0.4819 (0.0312)	$E_{3,2}$	−0.3787 (0.1323)
π_L	0.5739 (0.0388)	$E_{3,3}$	5.4255e−04 (0.5884)
π_E	0.0902 (7.4482E–03)	$H_{1,4}$	5.5423e−04 (0.8351)
π_{KK}	−0.2660 (0.0842)	$H_{2,5}$	3.5193e−04 (0.4324)
π_{KL}	0.2263 (0.0594)	$H_{3,6}$	4.8293 (1.7930)
π_{LL}	−0.2861 (0.3215)	$H_{4,7}$	1.7571 (0.9496)
π_0	4.3584E–03 (6.5663e–03)	$H_{5,8}$	0.7041 (0.2686)
$E_{2,1}$	−0.8166 (0.1039)	$H_{6,9}$	3.3614 (1.8105)
$E_{2,2}$	0.1925 (0.0882)	σ^2_u	4.28478e−05
$E_{3,1}$	1.5075 (0.2540)		

Table 10.2   Residual diagnostics: US macro model

	Equation			
	S_K	S_L	S_E	$\ln Q$
DW	1.7885	2.0268	2.1195	1.8892
Q(18)	23.2226	16.1559	17.0336	19.3560
	(0.1822)	(0.5817)	(0.5208)	(0.3702)
LM(1)	1.0211	2.0867	1.5877	1.6054
	(0.3122)	(0.1486)	(0.2077)	(0.2051)
t(43)	0.1950E–01	–0.2191E–01	0.1564E–02	0.2092E–01
	(0.9845)	(0.9826)	(0.9988)	(0.9834)

Notes: significance levels in parentheses. Tests are as follows:
DW   = Durbin–Watson test for first order serial correlation;
Q(18) = Box–Pierce *Q* test for general serial correlation/non-stationarity;
LM(1) = Breusch–Pagan Lagrange Multiplier Heteroskedasticity Test H1: $e_t^2 = f(t)$;
t(43)   = *t* test on residual sample mean H0: $E(e_t) = 0$.

manufacturing of 1.15 for a homogeneous function and 1.28 for a non-homothetic function, and Capalbo's (1988) estimate of 0.77 for the US agricultural sector. The parameters of the production function have the expected relationships. Increasing application of any factor leads, *ceteris paribus*, to diminishing and eventually decreasing returns. Also the second derivatives of the function are all positive within some range of input values. Increasing the use of other factors raises the marginal product of a factor of production. Table 10.2 presents the results of diagnostic tests on the residuals of each equation. The results show that the model is an adequate representation of the data for all the equations.

As seen from the estimates of the variances of the relevant disturbances (*H*), the labour and capital trends are integrated random walks as the variance of η_{Ai} is insignificantly different from zero. The energy trend is a local linear trend where both the disturbances have significant variances. Figure 10.3 presents the time paths of the technical change trends. Capital would be expected to have little trend, as the quantity of capital is theoretically the capitalized sum of capital services. This should hold as long as the government statisticians succeed in dividing changes in the nominal stock of capital between volume and inflationary components. However, as explained above in this model, there is also a factor-neutral technical change trend that has not been estimated. Therefore, we should assume that the general downward trend in the capital augmentation factor is due to a similar upward trend in the factor-neutral technical change trend. As a result of the high estimated degree of returns to scale, estimated overall technical change has been fairly

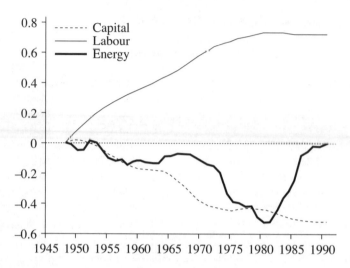

Figure 10.3   USA: factor augmentation trends

modest with around a 50 per cent increase in effectiveness over the period.
The fluctuations in the trend would be partly due to changes in the capacity
utilization of capital.

Relative to this overall trend, the efficiency of labour use has increased
substantially over time. The rise in labour efficiency is expected given the high
share of labour in costs, which would induce labour-saving technical change
and higher levels of human capital accumulation over time.

Relative to the overall upward trend, energy shows large fluctuations. Until
the mid-1960s autonomous energy efficiency is increasing and then it starts a
sharp decline. However, the results show that the first oil shock in 1973 does
not disrupt the overall downward trend in energy efficiency. Only after the
second oil shock does the trend reverse and energy efficiency increase. Finally
in the late 1980s the rate of improvement in autonomous energy efficiency
slows as the price of oil again falls.

These results show that when the overall TFP trend is broken down into its
component parts, technical change is shown to be a much more fragile and
erratic process than is often assumed in the literature (for example Barnett and
Morse 1963). The augmentation indices for different inputs may be moving in
opposite directions and even change direction as in the case of energy here. At
different points in time various of the alternative theories of the coupling and
decoupling of energy use and GDP discussed above appear to explain the
trend. The impression is of initial gains in energy efficiency that eventually
'run out of steam' due to the effects of rising personal energy consumption and
lower marginal productivities of new energy applications as the price of

energy fell in the first three decades after World War II. The first oil shock was not significant enough to totally reverse that trend and even after the trend reversed it was not sustainable.

Rangelands in Botswana

Ecosystem stability and resilience are critical in the generation and maintenance of economic welfare. Current human activity, although aimed at increasing the productivity and stability of production of natural systems, may adversely affect the resilience of those systems and render them more susceptible to systemic shocks and stress. Declining resilience may mean that current human activity is unsustainable into the future.

Though some theoretical issues have been explored (for example Barbier 1993; Perrings et al. 1995), little progress has been made on empirical measurement. Naturally, the lack of data on environmental and biological variables is as much a constraint here as in any other area of natural resource economics (Conrad and Clark 1987). The generalized technological change approach could be valuable here as it can be used to estimate unobserved changes in the states of environmental variables that affect economic productivity. This approach is illustrated using a study of rangeland productivity in Botswana. The reader can find a description of the background to the case study and the rationale for the way the model is constructed in the paper we have already published on this topic (Perrings and Stern 2000). In this chapter, we therefore focus on describing the model and explaining the results.

It is assumed that the economy is made up of identical price-taking livestock farmers who enjoy open access to the range, and who maximize the utility derived from the profits, Π, from livestock production. The property rights regime is assumed to be essentially open-access, implying that there are no economic or social incentives for farmers to take the external costs of natural resource degradation into account in their stocking strategies. Although the introduction of boreholes is now introducing some private control over access to the range, the assumption is not unreasonable for the period being evaluated. Individual livestock farmers are, therefore, assumed to neglect the effect of their actions on the state of the range. Hence, the private decision problem is to maximize the utility of the net benefits of livestock production subject to the dynamics of the farmer's own herd. The short- and long-run dynamics of the range are assumed to be irrelevant to the private decisions of farmers. The only livestock to enter the farmers' profit function is cattle. Sheep and goats are excluded from the model, although they are very important in reality. They are assumed to be risk-averse. Risk-neutral models were tested, but performed extremely poorly. The general form of the model is given by the optimization problem that follows. Pastoralists maximize the net present value of their welfare W over time:

$$Max_{Uit} \ W_{it} = \sum_{t=0}^{\infty} \rho^t W(\Pi_{it}) \qquad (10.15)$$

subject to the following growth equation for their cattle herd:

$$\Delta X_{it+1} = X_{it} [\alpha_1 (1 - X_t/K_t) + \alpha_2 (s_t - 1)] - U_{it} + \varepsilon_{Xit} \qquad (10.16)$$

where:

U_t is herd offtake,
X_t is the aggregate stock on the rangeland,
X_{it} is the farmer's own herd,
K_t is the state of the range,
s_t is rainfall,
ρ is the discount factor,
ε_X, η_t are random error terms.

The period interval is a year starting in September. The animal stock variable is measured at the beginning of each time period, whereas the flow variables are measured for the duration of the time period. Peak rainfall occurs in summer (southern hemisphere). Animal growth depends on the state of K at the beginning of the time period, the rainfall within the period and offtake. Recent theories of rangeland dynamics argue that herd dynamics are most influenced by rainfall in years of exceptionally high or low rainfall and most influenced by stocking density in years of average rainfall (Arntzen 1994; Perrings 1994). Unlike Perrings (1994), we assume that rainfall only interacts with X_{it} and not with $X_{it} X_t/K_t$. This is because the functional form in Perrings (1994) implies that increases in rainfall reduce the growth of livestock when cattle exceed the current carrying capacity, which is counter-intuitive.

We assume that profits are given by:

$$\Pi_{it} = p_{Ut} \ U_{it} - C(X_{it}, Y_t, s_t) \qquad (10.17)$$

where p_{Ut} is the price of cattle offtake. The net cost function, C_0, may be either positive or negative, since it admits the possibility that there may be stock benefits to livestock holdings. The function has the following form:

$$C(X_{it}, Y_t, s_t) = (\kappa_0 + \kappa_X X_{it} + \kappa_Y Y_t + \kappa_s s_t) X_{it} \qquad (10.18)$$

where X_{it} is the cattle stock of herder i, Y_t is a measure of the non-farm costs or benefits of agriculture, and s_t is a measure of rainfall deficit (rainfall relative to the mean over the sample period). The cost of holding livestock, κ_x, includes labour and material intermediate inputs. Labour costs of herding each additional animal are thought to decline initially with increasing herd size, but eventually to increase. The stock benefits of livestock are the sum of benefits derived from draft power, non-meat products, insurance against adverse climatic conditions and so on (Perrings 1996).

In the estimated cost function, Y_t is proxied by GDP per capita. This reflects two things. First, subsidies to agriculture are highly correlated with per capita GDP. Second, increased wealth increases demand for livestock – styled a 'sink for savings' by Collier and Lal (1984) – and raises the benefits of livestock holding. Rainfall is expected to reduce the cost of production through its impact on demand for supplementary feed, water and the like. This will vary with the size of the herd.

Utility of farmer i at time t, W_{it}, is given by the Box–Cox transformation utility function:

$$W_{it} = ((\Pi_{it})^\delta - 1)/\delta \qquad (10.19)$$

which allows us to estimate the degree of risk aversion reflected in the value of the parameter δ. For a risk averse farmer $\delta < 1$.

The growth of cattle herds is assumed to be a function of rainfall, a time trend, the average availability of graze and the area grazed. The latter is a function of the increase in the number of boreholes (tubewells) sunk over this period (Braat and Opschoor 1990). We therefore model the annual increase in grazing area as a function of the number of boreholes. There are two equations of motion describing range dynamics. The first (10.20) describes the dynamics of the current carrying capacity, K_t. The second (10.21) describes the dynamics of the long-run maximum carrying capacity or climax state, M_t.

$$\Delta K_{t+1} = K_t [\beta_1 (1 - K_t/M_t) + \beta_2 (s_t - 1)] - \mu \hat{X}_{t+1} + K_t \eta_t/M_t \qquad (10.20)$$

$$\Delta M_{t+1} = \frac{g_1 M_t/\hat{K}_{t+1}}{1 + \exp(g_2(1 + g_3 M_t/\hat{K}_{t+1}))} + \eta_t \qquad (10.21)$$

where:

$$\hat{K}_{t+1} = K_t [\beta_1 (1 - K_t/M_t) + \beta_2 (s_t - 1)] - \mu \hat{X}_{t+1} \qquad (10.22)$$

$$\hat{X}_{t+1} = X_{it} [\alpha_1 (1 - X_t/K_t) + \alpha_2 (s_t - 1)] - U_{it} \qquad (10.23)$$

and η is a random error term. The first of these equations is the more familiar, although it has some distinctive features. It assumes that the growth of graze and browse in any given period – and hence carrying capacity – follows a logistic path, in which the natural rate of regeneration varies with rainfall. The growth of graze and browse is also assumed to vary with consumption during the period. Since this includes consumption by calves and stock added during the period, it is described by the term μX_{t+1}.

The second equation of motion is less familiar. It does not derive from existing range ecology models, although it is intended to capture the sense of the informal state and transition models. Equation (10.21) describes the evolution of the long-run or potential carrying capacity of the range. M can be reduced when the current carrying capacity is less than a minimum proportion of the equilibrium value M. This use of the threshold level of $M_t/\hat{K}_{t+1}$ below which M is unchanged expresses the idea of a loss of resilience. The system is less resilient the further K is from M. The functional form used to transmit changes in K to changes in M is a smooth transition regression model (STR) (Granger and Teräsvirta 1993). $\Gamma = 1/(1 + \exp(\gamma_2 (1 + \gamma_3 M_t/\hat{K}_{t+1})))$ switches between 0 and 1 along a logistic curve as $M_t/\hat{K}_{t+1})$ increases. The error term η_t means that in the absence of such loss of resilience changes in M (and therefore K) are possible. These changes may reflect permanent expansion of grazing into new areas by the expansion of the number of waterholes but also temporary variations in the area grazed each year.

Perrings and Stern (2000) solve the optimal control problem to show that the privately optimal rate of offtake U_{it}^* is given by:

$$U_{it}^* = \frac{C_{it} + \left(\dfrac{\lambda_t}{P_{Ut}(1 + \alpha_1(1 - X_t/K_t) + \alpha_2(s_t - 1)) - \dfrac{\partial C}{\partial X_{it}}} \right)^{\frac{1}{\delta - 1}}}{P_{Ut}} \quad (10.24)$$

We treat λ_{it} as an additional state variable estimated using the Kalman filter. It evolves deterministically according to:

$$\lambda_{it+1} = \left(\frac{1 + r}{1 + \alpha_1(1 - X_t/K_t) + \alpha_2(s_t - 1)} \right) \frac{\partial C}{\partial X_{it}} \Pi_{it}^{\delta-1} + \lambda_{it} \quad (10.25)$$

Equation (10.24) gives the privately optimal offtake for a single herd. Aggregating and adding a random error term, ε_{Ut}, we have

$$U_t^* = n_t \, U_{it}^* + \varepsilon_{Ut} \qquad (10.26)$$

where n is the number of herds.

This completes specification of the whole model. It consists of the two state space measurement equations (10.16) and (10.26); and the two transition equations (10.20), and (10.21).[11]

We estimate the initial state (K_1, M_1, λ_1) assuming that X and K are in a steady state and λ is at its (privately) optimal value. The first observation is not, however, used in the calculation of the likelihood function, which means that it is treated as a diffuse prior. The initial state covariance matrix is given by HH' where H is a 3×1 matrix, with $H_{11} = K_1 H_{21}/M_1$, $H_{31} = 0$, and H_{21} is estimated. The initial states are derived from (10.16), (10.20), and (10.21):

$$K_1 = -\alpha_1 \, X_1^2/(U_1 - \alpha_1 X_1) \qquad (10.27)$$

$$M_1 = -\beta_1 \, K_1^2/(\mu X_1 - \beta_1 \, K_1) \qquad (10.28)$$

$$\lambda_1 = (1 + r) \, p_{U1} \, (p_{U1} \, U_{i1} - C_{i1})^{\delta - 1} \qquad (10.29)$$

In order to identify K we set $\alpha_1 = 0.3$. This value is the same as in Perrings (1994) and is close to that (0.265) estimated in a linear regression of (10.16) assuming that K is constant. Because (10.16), (10.26) is a recursive system an additional identification restriction is required. We set the correlation between the error terms of the two measurement equations ε_{xt} and ε_{Ut} to zero. $\sigma\varepsilon_x$ is concentrated out of the likelihood function so that E_{11} is set to 1. This leaves 15 parameters to be estimated. Full details of the data employed are provided in Perrings and Stern (2000). In that paper we also conducted a number of policy experiments with the model that are omitted here.

Residual diagnostics for the measurement equations are given in Table 10.3. Both equations fit the data reasonably well. The residual diagnostic statistics are also encouraging.[12] The maximum likelihood estimates of the hyperparameters are given in Table 10.4. The standard errors are estimated using the Berndt et al. (1974) algorithm. Around half the estimated parameters have t-statistics greater than one. This implies that a more parametrically parsimonious model might be developed or optimally a longer time series is required to obtain more accurate parameter estimates. σ^2_u is the estimate of the standard error of the residuals in the cattle stock equation (10.16), which was concentrated out of the likelihood function. The other error variances involve this term so that for example the standard deviation of the residuals in the offtake equation (10.26) is $\sigma_u E_{2,2} = 0.001038$.

Figure 10.4 presents estimates of the variables that drive private stocking and offtake decisions: the price of offtake, the net cost of livestock holdings and the

Table 10.3   Residual diagnostics: Botswana model

	Equation	
	U_t	X_{t+1}
R^2	0.77721	0.99376
DW	1.426290	2.584818
$Q(7)$	13.778183	11.538466
	(0.05527020)	(0.11679514)
ADF	−4.18073	−4.06454
$B–P$	2.627091	6.947954
	(0.26886503)	(0.03099352)

Notes: significance levels in parentheses. Tests are as follows:
DW = Durbin–Watson test for first order serial correlation;
$Q(7)$ = Box–Pierce Q test for general serial correlation/non-stationarity;
ADF = Augmented Dickey–Fuller test for residual stationarity;
$B–P$ = Breusch–Pagan test for coefficient variation.

Table 10.4   Maximum likelihood estimates of hyperparameters: Botswana model

Parameter	Estimate	Parameter	Estimate
α_2	0.13859	r	0.16501
	(0.05495)		(0.04824)
β_1	1.19394	κ_0	−0.04793
	(1.02271)		(0.08279)
β_2	0.61842	κ_X	0.0001514
	(0.48354)		(0.0006198)
μ	0.65206	κ_Y	0.01544
	(0.71201)		(0.00984)
γ_1	397.52479	κ_s	−0.01689
	(773.14788)		(0.00877)
γ_2	−181.89518	$E_{2,2}$	0.62907
	(369.21253)		(0.25000)
γ_3	−1.25890	$H_{2,3}$	13.96006
	(12.04458)		(8.38597)
δ	−0.48003	σ_u	0.00165
	(0.83499)		

Note: Figures in parentheses are standard errors.

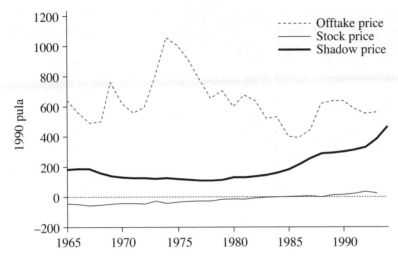

Figure 10.4   Livestock prices

private user cost of herd growth. The net cost of livestock holdings is initially negative, implying that there were net private benefits to holding cattle stocks (draft power, non-meat products, tax advantages and so on dominated the cost of herd maintenance). The relative value of the private benefits of offtake and live-stock holdings is summarized in Figure 10.5. In the late 1960s and early 1970s, the net benefits of livestock holdings were about equal to offtake benefits. This

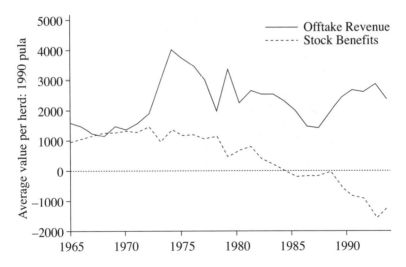

Figure 10.5   Livestock cost and offtake revenue (average herd)

might be expected from the literature on cattle herding in sub-Saharan Africa. But from the mid-1970s on, stock benefits declined as the opportunity cost of agricultural labour rose, becoming negative in the mid-1980s.

The parameter estimates for the cattle stock equation imply that, given the state of the range, rainfall in the current year has only moderate effects on the herd. The estimated parameter of 0.1389 is close to the OLS estimate of 0.125. The parameter estimates for the range transition equation imply that the intrinsic growth rate is 1.19394. The growth of the carrying capacity of the range fluctuates strongly with current rainfall. The grazing coefficient is 0.65206. All these coefficients are higher than we previously supposed (Perrings 1993, 1994). The estimated initial values for K and M are 2.29 million and 3.48 million, respectively, implying that X was at 59 per cent of K and K at 66 per cent of M. That is, initial stocking rates were above the maximum sustainable yield (given water availability in 1964/65).

The parameters of the cost function show evidence of decreasing returns to scale. There are net benefits for small herds when national income is low. At the average GDP per capita for the period, net stock benefits peak for a herd of 22 animals, while stock costs exceed stock benefits for herds of greater than 44 animals. At 1965 income levels net stock benefits peaked at a herd size of 120. It would thus appear that economic development has reduced the net benefits from stockholdings. This may be because it has raised the opportunity cost of labour used in herding or because use of cattle for non-consumption purposes such as draft power has fallen.

Figure 10.6 shows the evolution of the state variables over time. These

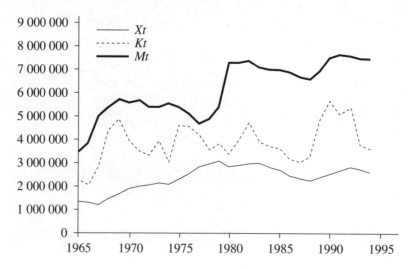

Figure 10.6   State variables

include both the two unobserved variables estimated by the Kalman filter, and the cattle stock. The stocks are the relevant quantities at the beginning of the years shown: that is X_{1994} is the cattle stock at the end of 1993. The trend in the time series for M is a function of the spread of boreholes. That is, the maximum carrying capacity of the range increased with the supply of water for livestock. Our results show that this expansion is not uniform. There are substantial increases in M during periods when the cattle herd approached current carrying capacity and some consolidation in the intervening period. But we cannot tell if the decline in M in those periods is due to change in the area grazed or due to a slow degradation of the rangeland that is not associated with loss of resilience. The current carrying capacity K shows large fluctuations as would be expected from the high estimates we obtained for the parameters in its equation of motion. The cattle stock never actually exceeds the estimated carrying capacity.

Figure 10.7 decomposes the changes in M into random fluctuations and the contribution of the parametric loss of resilience function. The changes are in terms of $\bullet M_{t+1}$ so that the changes occurring in the years indicated result in the increase or decrease in M in the following year. The results indicate one potential loss of resilience event in 1985–1986 (contributing an 8 per cent reduction in M going into 1986/87). However, as the parameters γ_1, γ_2, and γ_3 are statistically insignificant, we are unable to confirm a loss of resilience. M itself declines by only 3.7 per cent between 1985/86 and 1986/87. This may have been due to expansion into new grazing areas occurring simultaneously with

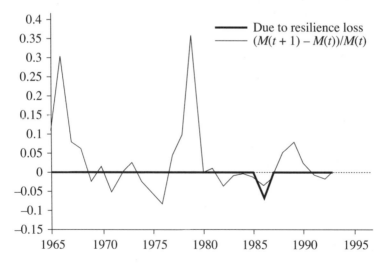

Figure 10.7   Decomposition of climax state M into random fluctuations and loss of resilience function

the loss of resilience in some areas of the rangeland. These kind of potential responses make determining whether a loss of resilience has occurred from aggregate data of the sort we use here particularly difficult.

These episodes are a response to rainfall deficit shocks, and occur when the system is stressed due to high grazing pressure. 1985/86 was the fifth year of a major drought. Rainfall was actually slightly higher than in the previous year, but the cumulative effects of drought worked to lower current carrying capacity relative to the size of the herd. X/K is at a maximum for the entire sample in 1985/86. They also work to reduce K_{t+1}/M_t, the variable that actually controls the loss of resilience switch in our model. This is at a minimum in 1985/86. The large coefficients for the transition equation for M imply that the resilience threshold is very sharp.

We are interested in whether it is possible to detect change in the capacity of the system to absorb exogenous shocks (the measure of resilience *sensu* Holling 1986). The changing sensitivity of the system to rainfall shocks is illustrated in Figure 10.8. This shows the threshold level of rainfall that we estimate to have been sufficient to induce a loss of resilience compared to actual rainfall. This was derived using a one-step ahead simulation – that is lagged values of variables are actual observations not simulations and the error terms from the econometric model are treated as exogenous variables. Changes in rainfall affect M by affecting the optimal offtake, the growth of the herd and the growth of the range. The optimal offtake impacts on $\hat{X}_{t+1}$ in addition to the direct rainfall affect on $\hat{X}_{t+1}$ which then affects $\hat{\kappa}_{t+1}$ in addition to the direct rainfall affect

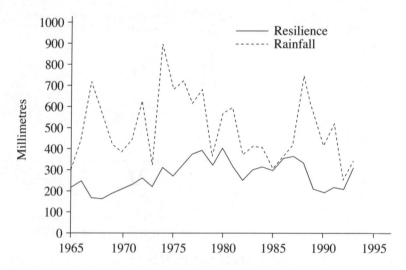

Figure 10.8   Resilience with respect to rainfall

on $\hat{K}_{t+1}$. $\hat{K}_{t+1}$ alone then enters the loss of resilience function. We then perturb actual rainfall until $\Gamma = 1/(1 + \exp(\gamma_2 (1 + \gamma_3 M_t/\hat{K}_{t+1}))) = 0.5$, that is halfway switched on. This rainfall figure is the reported 'resilience' in Figure 10.5. The dating is the same as in Figure 10.4 so that rainfall would have to be 360 millimetres and below in 1986 to cause a loss of resilience that would result in M declining from that year to 1987. The link between change in the resilience of the range and herd size is complicated by the fact that there was extensive growth of the livestock sector in the period. More range was brought into use. As a result, resilience is not a monotonically decreasing function of herd size. Nevertheless, it does turn out that the system came closest to losing resilience in 1979, when the size of the national herd was at its highest.

The implications of this for the speed of return to equilibrium are illustrated in Figures 10.9 and 10.10. These report a sequence of impulse responses of K and X to a change in rainfall. The responses are measured in LSUK/millimetre of rainfall (thousand livestock units per millimetre of rainfall). The graphs show the one-, three-, five- and ten-year responses to a change in rainfall in the year on the X axis. The impulse response function is not shown in other years for simplicity. As this is a non-linear model the impulse response function is different for a perturbation in each of the years in the sample. Range vegetation is inherently more responsive to rainfall fluctuations than livestock, as is to be expected. This is partly because of the grazing term. Growth of the vegetative cover of rangeland slows as cattle stocks build up in wet periods. The higher the figure the larger the movement for a given shock and the more 'unstable' or responsive is the system.

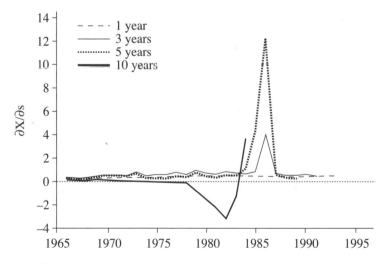

Figure 10.9   Response of cattle stock to rainfall

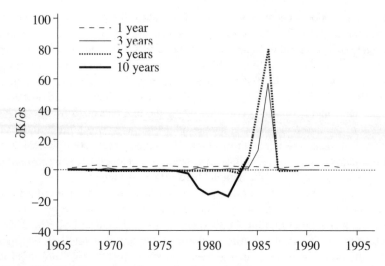

Figure 10.10   Response of rangeland to rainfall

The one period impulse responses of the two variables are generally opposite; that is the responsiveness of K increases as that of X decreases. X is strongly influenced by the effect of rainfall on offtake. Higher rainfall reduces offtake, spurring the growth of X, and vice versa. As grazing pressure rises in droughts, the growth rate of X slows down for any given level of rainfall. Overall, though, the one period responsiveness of both livestock and vegetation to variations in rainfall rises over the period. That is, the reduction in resilience of the system implies an increase in its volatility. It takes a progressively smaller change in rainfall to induce the same response in both vegetation and livestock. In general, K is more responsive to rainfall shocks than X, but the nature of the response varies over the period. Up until the late 1970s, the immediate rangeland response to rainfall is typically substantial, but dies out fast. The return time to the previous equilibrium involves a period of between three and five years. By contrast, the cattle stock initially responds slowly. The effects of a shock build up over three to five years and the return time to equilibrium takes a much longer period – typically exceeding 10 years. From the late 1970s on, however, the pattern changes. The return time for rangeland increases until it, too, exceeds 10 years. In the mid-1980s, drought, the loss of resilience in K is reflected in a very sharp increase in the impulse response over all but the very short period. By the late 1980s, the response to rainfall shocks is again a decreasing one as the system converges on a new equilibrium.[13] The general pattern of the impulse responses of X is similar. In the mid-1970s, during a period of high rainfall, the maximum response of cattle stocks to rainfall shocks occurs in one year. By the early 1980s, however, the position is reversed. The 10-year response is equivalent to four times the one-year response; while in 1985 the ratio rises to about seven to one. That is, consistent with a loss of resilience, the effect of a rainfall shock in those years is explosive, rather than damped.

CONCLUSIONS

In this chapter we have argued that an alternative tractable way of estimating changes in environmental and natural capital stocks is to treat the impact of those changes on the economic system in the same way as econometricians have traditionally modelled the effects of unobserved changes in technology on economic output. This idea is derived from Perrings (1987) and O'Connor's (1993) conception of change in the economy-environment system as a process of uncontrolled technological change.

The US case study illustrates what it is possible to do with sophisticated time series techniques in the arena of the conventional modelling of technological change. In particular, a time-varying estimate of the unobserved autonomous energy efficiency trend was extracted from the US macro data using a simple optimization model of economic behaviour and a simple structural time series model of technological change estimated with the Kalman filter.

The Botswana study is both interdisciplinary and integrated. Insights from ecology are combined with economic intertemporal optimization theory in a form relevant to the particular institutional conditions of Botswana. The Kalman filter is again used to estimate a model that jointly includes parameters of the economic system such as risk aversion and the discount rate and the unobserved state variables of the natural system – the current and equilibrium states of the rangeland. These estimates are extracted from the data containing minimal information about the natural system – the number of cattle and level of rainfall each year and the number of tubewells as a proxy for the area grazed.

It seems that many such similar integrative ecological-economic applications could be developed to model integrated systems for which we have limited measurements of the relevant natural capital variables. The technique might also be extended to investigate pure natural science problems. A step in this direction is provided by Stern and Kaufmann (2000) in a model of global climate change. Further development of such a model could include modelling unobserved time series such as stored ocean heat, which plays a similar role in the climate system that renewable natural capital stocks do in ecological-economic systems.

NOTES

1. A stationary variable has constant mean and variance. Classical regression methods and inference are only applicable to stationary variables. If the variables are non-stationary, standard regression results may indicate that there is a significant relation between the variables when in fact none exists – a so-called spurious regression (Granger and Newbold 1974). But in some cases the non-stationary components of a number of time series are shared so that a linear combination of the series is stationary. This phenomenon is called cointegration. When the variables cointegrate, valid inference is possible in regression models.
2. Stern (2000) examines the US macro data using cointegration modelling. The implication of the latter results is that a linear combination of the stochastic trends estimated in the model in this chapter cointegrate – in other words, the linear aggregate is a stationary variable.
3. Simple measures of energy efficiency divide GDP by energy used and hence require no econometric estimation. Autonomous energy efficiency refers to changes in the effectiveness with which energy is used holding the effective units of the other inputs constant. Only econometrics can provide estimates of this trend at the macroeconomic level. At the micro-level engineering based studies can also be used.
4. Equation (10.1) can be obviously generalized to multiple outputs. A useful simplifying assumption is that the production function exhibits constant returns to scale in all inputs including the resource inputs. This implies that there are decreasing returns when more inputs are applied to a given resource stock R. Again, generalizations can be made. If N is measured in terms of rainfall, temperature and so on, rather than water, heat and so on, the relevant constant returns relates to the expansion of X and R but not N.
5. Stern (1999b), in an empirical study of US agriculture, shows how non-comprehensive measures of MFP – that is the traditional Barnett and Morse unit cost and energy cost are strongly affected by changes in the prices of other inputs in a way that obscures the long run trend in resource quality and availability. See also Cleveland and Stern (1993) for a discussion of alternative indicators in US forestry. Mattey (1990) shows that stumpage prices are an ineffective indicator of resource scarcity in forestry.
6. The simplest type of stochastic trend is a random walk. The current value of a random walk is equal to the previous value plus a random shock and perhaps a constant or drift term. This means that the stochastic trend has a different value in every time period. If we attempted to estimate this model using classical linear regression, we would have more parameters to estimate than observations to estimate them with. Therefore, the model cannot be estimated using regression methods. But using the Kalman filter only the variance of the shocks and the value of the drift constant – two parameters – need to be estimated using maximum likelihood methods. Given these estimated hyperparameters, the Kalman filter algorithm computes the value of the stochastic trend in each period given the observed data. In the US model the stochastic trends are modelled using a local linear trend model, which is a random walk where the drift term is itself a random walk. The Botswana model has more complex non-linear stochastic trends.
7. We can assume that in the macroeconomy, the quantities of factor inputs are exogenous at least in the short run, but that factor prices are endogenous. This obviously is not strictly true, especially for energy prices. However, it is a more reasonable assumption for the macroeconomy than for a single industry or firm. Also, we should expect the production technology at the macroeconomic level to be non-monotonic. This is because the assumption of free disposal may no longer hold (Stern 1994).
8. This means that the estimate of autonomous energy efficiency is not absolute but relative to overall technical progress.
9. De Jong's diffuse Kalman filter algorithm avoids the need to specify initial conditions for non-stationary stochastic trends but it can only handle models that are linear in the state variables. This is also the reason why homogeneity of the production function is assumed.
10. This approach was used by Berndt et al. (1993).
11. Note that although the cattle stock is a state variable in the private decision problem, it is an observation in the Kalman filter estimation.

12. Neither Durbin–Watson statistic shows definite evidence of first order serial correlation. The Box–Pierce Q statistics present a similar picture. There are no tabulated significance levels for the augmented Dickey–Fuller statistic in a non-linear model of this type but these statistics would indicate reasonable residual stationarity if these were linear regressions. The Breusch–Pagan test for coefficient variation shows that the Kalman filter model is picking up most of the coefficient variation that is present, although the statistic for the $Xt + 1$ equation is significant at the 5 per cent level but not at the 1 per cent level.
13. Note that the effects of the 1992 loss of resilience do not show up in Figure 10.6 as there are only two periods remaining in the sample.

ACKNOWLEDGEMENTS

The work described in this chapter has its origins in David Stern's dissertation research at Boston University carried out under a Doctoral Dissertation Fellowship from the Institute for the Study of World Politics and continued later at the University of York, Boston University and the Australian National University. The Botswana model was developed in collaboration with Charles Perrings.

BIBLIOGRAPHY

Arntzen, J.W. 1994. *Reevaluation of communal rangelands: the Southern African experience*. Paper presented at the 3rd Biennial Conference of the International Society for Ecological Economics, San José, Costa Rica, October.

Barbier, E.B. (ed). 1993. *Economics and ecology: new frontiers and sustainable development*. London: Chapman & Hall.

Barnett, H.J. and Morse, C. 1963. *Scarcity and growth: the economics of natural resource availability*. Baltimore: The Johns Hopkins University Press.

Barten, A.P. 1969. Maximum likelihood estimation of a complete system of demand equations. *European Economic Review*. 1. 7–73.

Berndt E.R. and Christensen, L.R. 1973. The translog function and the substitution of equipment, structures, and labor in U.S. manufacturing. *Journal of Econometrics*. 1: 81–113.

Berndt E.R., Hall, B., Hall, R. and Hausman, J. 1974. Estimation and inference in nonlinear structural models. *Annals of Economic and Social Measurement*. 3–4: 653–65.

Berndt E.R. and Khaled, M.S. 1979. Parametric productivity measurement and choice among flexible functional forms. *Journal of Political Economy*. 87: 1220–45.

Berndt E.R., Kolstad, C. and Lee, J.-K. 1993. Measuring the energy efficiency and productivity impacts of embodied technical change. *Energy Journal*. 14: 33–55.

Bohi, D. 1989. *Energy price shocks and macroeconomic performance*. Washington, DC: Resources for the Future.

Braat, L.C. and Opschoor, J.B. 1990. Risks in the Botswana range-cattle system. In: Dixon J.A., James, D.E. and Sherman, P.B. (eds). *Dryland management: economic case studies*. London: Earthscan, pp. 153–74.

Capalbo, S.M. 1988. Measuring the components of aggregate productivity growth in U.S. agriculture. *Western Journal of Agricultural Economics.* 13 (1): 53–62.

Cleveland, C.J. and Stern, D.I. 1993. Productive and exchange scarcity: an empirical analysis of the U.S. forest products industry. *Canadian Journal of Forest Research.* 23: 1537–49.

Collier, P. and Lal, D. 1984. Why poor people get rich: Kenya 1960–79. *World Development.* 12: 1007–18.

Conrad, J.M. and Clark, C.W. 1987. *Natural resource economics: notes and problems.* Cambridge: Cambridge University Press.

Cuthbertson, K., Hall, S.G. and Taylor, M.P. 1992. *Applied econometric techniques.* Ann Arbor, MI: University of Michigan Press.

Darby, J. and Wren-Lewis, S. 1992. Changing trends in international manufacturing. *Scandinavian Journal of Economics.* 94: 457–77.

De Jong, P. 1991a. Stable algorithms for the state space model. *Journal of Time Series Analysis.* 12 (2): 143–57.

De Jong, P. 1991b. The diffuse Kalman filter. *Annals of Statistics.* 19: 1073–83.

Engle R.F. and Granger, C.W.J. 1987. Co-integration and error correction: representation, estimation and testing. *Econometrica.* 55: 251–76.

Gever, J., Kaufmann, R.K., Skole, D. and Vörösmarty, C. 1986. *Beyond oil: the threat to food and fuel in the coming decades.* Cambridge, MA: Ballinger.

Granger, C.W.J. and Newbold, P. 1974. Spurious regressions in econometrics. *Journal of Econometrics.* 2: 111–20.

Granger, C.W.J. and Teräsvirta, T. 1993. *Modelling nonlinear economic relationships.* New York: Oxford University Press.

Greene, W.H. 1990. *Econometric analysis.* New York: Macmillan.

Harvey, A.C. 1989. *Forecasting, structural time series models, and the Kalman filter.* Cambridge: Cambridge University Press.

Harvey, A.C. and Marshall, P. 1991. Inter-fuel substitution, technical change and the demand for energy in the UK economy. *Applied Economics.* 23: 1077–86.

Holling, C.S. 1986. Resilience of ecosystems: local surprise and global change. In: Clarke, W.C. and Munn, R.E. (eds). *Sustainable Development of the Biosphere.* Cambridge: Cambridge University Press, pp. 292–317.

IBRD. 1992. *World development report 1992.* New Work: Oxford University Press.

Jorgensen, D.W. and Wilcoxen, P.J. 1993. Reducing US carbon emissions: an econometric general equilibrium assessment. *Resource and Energy Economics.* 15: 7–25.

Kalman, R.E. 1960. A new approach to linear filtering and prediction problems. *Transactions ASME Journal of Basic Engineering.* 82: 35–45.

Kalman, R.E. and Bucy, R.S. 1961. New results in linear filtering and prediction theory. *Transactions ASME Journal of Basic Engineering.* 83: 95–103.

Kaufmann, R.K. 1992. A biophysical analysis of the energy/real GDP ratio: implications for substitution and technical change. *Ecological Economics.* 6: 35–56.

Kim, H.Y. 1992. The translog production function and variable returns to scale. *Review of Economics and Statistics.* 74: 546–52.

Lakshmanan, T.R., Anderson, W. and Jourbachi, M. 1984. Regional dimensions of factor and fuel substitution in U.S. manufacturing. *Regional Science and Urban Economics.* 14: 381–98.

Mattey, J.P. 1990. *The timber bubble that burst: government policy and the bailout of 1984.* New York: Oxford University Press.

O'Connor, M.P. 1991. Time and environment. Ph.D. thesis, Department of Eocnomics, University of Auckland, Auckland.

O'Connor, M.P. 1993. Entropic irreversibility and uncontrolled technological change in the economy and environment. *Journal of Evolutionary Economics*. 3: 285–315.

Perrings, C.A. 1987. *Economy and environment: a theoretical essay on the interdependence of economic and environmental systems*. Cambridge: Cambridge University Press.

Perrings, C.A. 1993. *Pastoral strategies in sub-Saharan Africa: the economic and ecological sustainability of dryland range management*. Environment Working Paper 57. Washington, DC: World Bank Environment Department.

Perrings, C.A. 1994. *Ecological resilience and the sustainability of economic development*. Discussion Papers in Environmental Economics and Environmental Management 9405. Work: EEEM, University of York.

Perrings, C.A. 1996. *Sustainable development and poverty alleviation in sub-Saharan Africa: the case of Botswana*. London: Macmillan.

Perrings, C.A., Mäler, K.-G., Folke, C., Holling, C.S. and Jansson, B.-O. (eds). 1995. *Biodiversity loss: ecological and economic issues*. Cambridge: Cambridge University Press.

Perrings C.A. and Stern, D.I. 2000. Modelling loss of resilience in agroecosystems: to rangelands degradation in Botswana. *Environmental and Resource Economics*. 16: 185–210.

Slade, M.E. 1989. Modeling stochastic and cyclical components of technical change: an application of the Kalman filter. *Journal of Econometrics*. 41: 363–83.

Solow, J.L. 1987. The capital-energy complementarity debate revisited. *American Economic Review*. 77: 605–14.

Solow, R.M. 1994. Perspectives on growth theory. *Journal of Economic Perspectives*. 8: 45–54.

Stern, D.I. 1994. Natural resources as factors of production: three empirical studies. Ph.D. dissertation, Boston University, Boston, MA.

Stern, D.I. 1999a. Use value, exchange value, and resource scarcity. *Energy Policy*. 27: 469–76.

Stern, D.I. 1999b. Is energy cost an accurate indicator of natural resource quality? *Ecological Economics*. 31: 381–94.

Stern, D.I. 2000. A multivariate cointegration analysis of the role of energy in the U.S. macroeconomy. *Energy Economics*. 22: 267–83.

Stern, D.I. and Kaufmann, R.K. 2000. Detecting a global warming signal in hemispheric temperature series: a structural time series analysis. *Climatic Change*. 47: 411–38.

US Congress, Office of Technology Assessment. 1990. *Energy use and the U.S. economy*. OTA-BP-E-57, U.S. Washington, DC: Government Printing Office.

11. Effective policy interventions in environmental systems using material budgets

Robert J. Wasson

Policies and actions, designed to solve natural resource and environmental problems, interact with the natural world, produce biophysical responses that in turn often produce either an adjustment or abandonment of polices and actions. These interactions constitute a complex system, in the sense of Waldrop (1992) where there are many components and actors (or agents) that interact in a great many ways producing spontaneous self-organization, and in which adaptive behaviour is common among the biological components including people. It has long been argued that such a system can only be adequately analysed by examining the whole. This is because the interactions between the parts produce behaviour and properties that cannot be understood solely by examining the components, and interactions in a complex system will produce unintended and often disastrous consequences if the whole system is not understood (for example Sterman 2000; Thomas 1974).

Effective policy interventions are those that solve environmental problems at minimum cost while meeting social and cultural goals. Solving problems requires identification not only of the problem but also the high leverage points in a system, so that maximum remediation and/or conservation can be achieved while expenditure and foregone income are minimized. Identifying high leverage points demands an understanding of the whole system. Monitoring of both the behaviour of such a system and its response to intervention also needs to be based on an understanding of the whole, so that the points can be identified in the system where maximum information can be obtained.

An analytical framework is therefore required that encompasses whole system properties, ideally to be applied to a great many natural resource and environmental problems, and facilitates both biophysical and economic co-analysis. A material budget is such an analytical framework, as part of a dynamic systems perspective (Sterman 2000; Vellinga et al. 1998).

This idea is not new, but in the face of long-standing and continuing calls for the integration of natural sciences and economics (for example Hall et al. 2001; Leontieff 1982; Wilen 1973), it is desirable to keep repeating it. The first proposal to use material budgets as a framework for interpretation of natural science and economics came from Kneese et al. (1970), and has been most recently developed for many sectors of the economy by Vellinga et al. (1998).

Kneese et al. (1970) applied the approach to economic production largely in the industrial sphere. But the material budget concept has more of a pedigree in environmental science when applied to rural landscapes and agricultural production. Geomorphologists have used sediment budgets since Trimble (1983), and biogeochemists have examined fluxes and storage of nutrients, carbon and metals from global to local scales starting with Vernadsky in 1889 (see Smil 1997).

One of the major purposes of Kneese et al. (1970) was to demonstrate that waste is an inevitable consequence of economic development, and that this class of externalities is a normal part of consumption and production activities; not an '. . . isolated and somewhat freakish aberration . . .'. Georgescu-Roegen (1971) makes the same argument, from the perspective of thermodynamics.

The internalization of externalities in economic analyses and models is underway, aided by environmental accounting, alternatives to gross domestic product (GDP) such as the General Progress Index, rights markets and emission trading and by attempts to monetize environmental services. In analyses of the economic costs of pollution by the agricultural, industrial and domestic sectors of the economy, material budgets have at least two major functions:

1. By means of a whole-system perspective, they provide quantification of the major sources and sinks (stores) of pollution, thereby providing economists with a basis for costing remediation and identifying changes to production systems that will reduce waste.
2. With sufficient examples, budgets can be used to classify system types so that the results of economic analyses of a few cases can be applied widely with confidence.

Both functions are illustrated in this chapter, but first a formal account of material budgets is provided, with some discussion of disciplinary applications.

BUDGETS: MATERIALS, INFORMATION AND SOCIAL CAPITAL

The central concepts in dynamic systems theory are stocks, flows, feedbacks and delays (Sterman 2000), and these are discussed in turn below.

Stocks and Flows

Stocks are accumulations or inventories. The state of a river catchment, for example, is best described in terms of stocks because they modulate the behaviour of the catchment by accumulating the difference between inflow and outflow. By this means stocks create delays because outflows do not occur simultaneously with inflow to a stock. Disequilibrium is therefore caused by stocks, by decoupling rates of flow into and out of stocks.

Flows are the rates of increase or decrease in stocks. The net flow into a stock is the rate of change of the stock. This statement has a precise meaning, and can be represented by

$$Stock\ (t) = \int_{t_o}^{t} [Inflow\ (s) - Outflow\ (s)]\ ds + Stock\ (t_o)$$

where inflow (s) is the quantity of the inflow at any time between the initial time (t_o) and the current time (t).

In differential form, the net change of a stock is the inflow minus the outflow:

$$d\ (Stock)/dt = Inflow\ (t) - Outflow\ (t)$$

Obviously, if both inflows and outflows are known then change in the stock is easily calculated. If, however, only the stock is known, then inflow and outflow are indeterminate because there is a very large range of variation in inflows and outflows that can produce a particular stock size and behaviour. Stocks are measured as amounts (for example 1 kg of sediment or numbers of species), or in the case of 'social capital' as an index consisting of rankings of, for example, membership of labour-sharing groups, ways of dealing with crop disease or natural disasters, trust, solidarity and reciprocity (Krishna 2001). Social capital is defined by Putnam (1995) as 'features of social organization such as networks, norms and social trust that facilitate coordination and compensation for mutual benefit'. This is similar to the concept of 'human capital' that is constructed by investing in education, training, medical care and so on (Becker 1993). When applied to environmental and natural resource management, or economic development, and compiled as an index, social (or human) capital can be thought of as a stock, changes in which are flows measured as amounts per time (for example index value/year). Flows in the non-human world are measured as mass/time, number/time or as some energy value.

The concepts of stock and flow are applicable to many phenomena; physical, biological and human. Many academic disciplines recognize stocks and flows, and their differences (Sterman, 2000) (Table 11.1). The fundamental

Table 11.1.   Stocks and flows as recognized in different academic disciplines

Discipline	Stocks	Flows
Mathematics, physics, engineering	Integrals, states, state variables, stocks	Derivates, rates of change, flows
Chemistry	Reactants and reaction products	Reaction rates
Biogeochemistry	Reservoirs, reactants and reactant products, compartments	Fluxes, flows, reaction rates
Geomorphology	Stores, stocks	Fluxes, flows
Ecology	Stocks of energy and nutrients	Flows
Manufacturing	Buffers, inventories	Throughput
Economics	Levels	Rates
Environmental economics	Stocks	Flows
Accounting	Stocks, balance sheet items	Flows, cash flow or income statement items
Biology, physiology	Compartments	Diffusion rates, flows
Medicine, epidemiology	Prevalence, reservoirs	Incidence, infection, morbidity and mortality rates
Social science	Human capital stocks	Flows of human capital
Demography	Stocks	Flows

Source: Adapted and extended from Sterman 2000.

difference between stocks and flows is that stocks are accumulations and are states of the system. Flows are the rates at which these states change. Sterman (2000) imagines a system frozen in time. In this condition, stocks are those things that can be counted or measured, including human characteristics of the kind mentioned earlier when discussing human capital. The rates are no longer quantifiable, such as the flow of water into and out of a reservoir, but the stock of water in the reservoir can be measured. It is important in interdisciplinary research, where different phenomena are being included in a stock and flow analytical framework, to use the two concepts unambiguously.

Feedbacks

Feedbacks are either positive or negative. A negative feedback is self-correcting while a positive feedback is self-reinforcing. These concepts apply to all

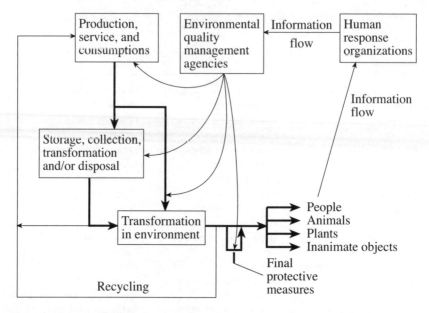

Source: Adapted from Kneese et al. (1970).

Figure 11.1 A waste (residuals) management system

of the phenomena treated by the academic disciplines listed in Table 11.1. To illustrate these concepts, ideas from Kneese et al. (1970) are used. Their Chart 13 depicts a residual (waste) management system in an economy, and is reproduced here as Figure 11.1.

Residuals resulting from production, services and/or consumption can be stored, collected, transformed in the economy or disposed of into the environment. Some residuals reach the environment more directly, where transformation occurs. The products of the transformation, as pollutants, reach various receptors (people, animals, plants, and inanimate objects such as rocks and the atmosphere). But some pollutants are judged so dangerous that 'final protective measures' are installed such as tertiary sewage treatment so that only harmless by-products reach the receptors. Along these pathways, some residuals are recycled either deliberately or 'naturally'; this constitutes the first type of feedback. The second type of feedback occurs when people, as receptors, respond to a load of pollutants and cause environmental quality management agencies to alter their regulations, change their practices and/or mount educational programmes to alter production, service and consumption types and amounts, storage, collection, transportation and disposal practices and magnitudes, and perhaps even intervene in the ways in which transformation occurs in the environment.

The feedback produced by recycling is generally negative because, as recycling increases, the quantities of primary materials required in production can be reduced and so reduce the residual stream per unit of production. Feedbacks in the information flow system are also usually negative, in that high pollution loads produce regulatory and/or incentive regimes that reduce residuals streams and enhance effective transformation in the environment. However, if 'final protective measures' are end-of-pipe solutions that are generally regarded as solving the problem, then feedback can be positive in the information system. In this case, people believe that the problem is solved, and so regulation can be relaxed and production increased. This situation can boost economic development with either minimal environmental damage, the so-called 'win-win' case, or with increased damage if the solutions are not effective.

The recycling feedback and informational feedback are conceptually identical but may have different elements. For example, information is not a psychologically neutral phenomenon, while the reduction in a residual stream is readily measured and more likely to be psychologically neutral. Many psychological experiments have shown how people only see what they expect to see.

Feedbacks are common in many fields, not least in scholarship. In natural science Kuhn (1962) argued that a paradigm suppresses the perception of inconsistent data, so that the paradigm persists longer than it should. This is a case of positive feedback: the stronger the paradigm becomes, the more likely it is to become stronger and so persist. The same analysis might be applied to general equilibrium models in economics, which depend on negative feedback to dampen excursions from equilibrium, despite evidence for positive feedbacks. Positive feedback in the economy is what Arthur (1987, 1990) called 'increasing returns' or, as Waldrop (1992) puts it: 'them that has gets'. This is simply the observation that sales of particular products, the growth of firms and the attractions of places for economic development tend to grow once they have a small edge on their competitors.

The 'small edge' can, and often is, the result of historical contingency (see Jervis 1997; Waldrop 1992). In economic development, this is particularly so in knowledge-based industries, as pointed out by David (1995) and Arthur (1990). Arthur also observes that diminishing (marginal) returns, or negative feedback, is common in resource-based parts of the economy such as agriculture and mining. Where positive feedback occurs, however, there can be considerable instability in the early stages of the development of industry, but a particular path is locked in by either a chance event or quality of product. This is known as path dependence, and is illustrated by Jervis (1997) by the familiar saying 'Nothing succeeds like success'. The path-dependant aspect of positive feedback is a reason for historical analysis of system dynamics, a topic to be returned to below. Of course, if a system is dominated by negative feedback, or is assumed to be so dominated, then equilibrium in the long-term average is assumed and history is irrelevant.

Feedback is a fundamental property of all interconnected phenomena; and social and political systems are not immune. Jervis (1997) uses the concept of feedbacks, and delays (see below), to analyse international politics. Among the many cases discussed by Jervis, one will be sufficient to illustrate feedback, where the build-up of arms in one country leads to a build-up in its principal adversary. Where such a build-up leads to the adversary becoming militarily weaker, negative feedback has occurred. Of course, positive feedback cannot last forever, and eventually a ceiling is reached where, in the case of armament, the stability of the state is threatened because there is little money for other parts of society such as education and health care. Negative feedback then takes over so that the arms race slows as the expenditure on arms continues to increase but the state falters, because of decreasing human capital, and is unable to effectively deploy the weapons.

Positive and negative feedbacks are often coupled end to end, so that, for example, the growth of either the length or volume of a gully can be described by an S-shaped curve. After initiation, a gully will grow rapidly by headward cutting because the amount of runoff relative to the size of the gully is large. The curve of length or volume grows exponentially in positive feedback. As the gully grows headward, the area of catchment, and so the amount of runoff, contributed to the headcut reduces. The rate of headward migration slows as negative feedback occurs. The curve of length or volume flattens and approaches the upper asymptote where the gully stops growing because it has reached as far into the catchment as runoff will allow. The S-shaped growth type applies to food supplies, the number of people susceptible to viral infection and to the potential market for new products (Sterman 2000), among others.

It is usual to link stock and flow analyses with an understanding of feedbacks. While this is common in natural science and many economic applications, Jervis (1997) does not use stocks and flows. It is possible that the idea of 'human capital', configured as a stock, which 'flows' by gain or loss to the stock, could be used in a conventional stock and flow analysis as suggested earlier. The link to feedback in social and political systems could be achieved if human capital is indexed by variables that can be represented in analyses of feedbacks. This appears to be an underexplored field of research, although it was clearly set out by Becker (1993).

Stocks and flows, and feedbacks, are important concepts for practical analyses in the field of natural resource and environmental analysis, among many others (Table 11.1). But they are also appearing in different language in abstract theorizing about human-environment relationships. One recent and prominent example is Panarchy (Gunderson and Holling 2002; Holling 2001). This is essentially an account of human-environment relationship as an adaptive cycle. Both ecosystems and human societies exploit 'new territories' by means of colonizing species and new economic development. Conservation occurs by means of slow accumulation of energy and biomass in an arena of contest competition. Entrepreneurial markets occur during the exploitation phase, followed by regulated and more bureaucratic systems during the conservation phase. This phase is tightly bound and susceptible to chance triggering events such as a large fire or a vagary of the stock market. This is the release phase during which the tight bonds are broken. A phase of reorganization follows, during which soil processes minimize nutrient loss allowing another phase of exploitation. Reorganization in society occurs by the destruction of old institutions and practices, providing space for innovation. These processes constitute both positive and negative feedback.

Delays

Accumulations in stocks produce delays, another fundamental property of connected systems. Outputs and inputs to stocks are always at different times. Material delays are familiar in catchment processes and economic production. The sediment released by erosion in a catchment does not immediately appear at the outlet as yield. The sediment takes time to be transported, and can be temporarily stored in channels and on floodplains, to be re-released by another erosion event. The economic production process can be delayed because of slow delivery of key material, labour and capital. Information delays are also important. The gradual adjustment of perceptions or beliefs, and changes to value systems, create such delays (Sterman 2000).

Both of these kinds of delays appear in Figure 11.1. Material delays occur in the residual waste stream, and in the recycling feedback. Information delays occur in the information flow feedbacks.

USES OF MATERIAL BUDGETS

In the account just given of the components of budgets, a wide range of applications within various academic disciplines has been given. It therefore can be concluded that this conceptual framework has a wide application, not only in natural resource and environmental analysis and management, but also in many other fields. There is therefore the potential for connections between many disciplines using this approach, not only between natural science and economics: although this is a natural intersection. There also appears to be the potential for application of the framework to aspects of society and humanity that have not been extensively included within its ambit. Social capital is an example, and information may also be included. This is therefore a rich area for research.

For the discussion of uses of budgets, attention is now given to material budgets alone. There are four clear-cut uses: for setting remediation and control targets; for calculating the costs of remediation; for effective monitoring; and for the design of appropriate economic instruments.

Targets for Remediation and Control

Control of flows of troublesome materials such as sediment and nutrients in river catchments requires information about the material budget: source stocks, depositional stocks, rates of flow, delays and feedbacks. Remediation of source stocks, enhancement of both depositional stocks and negative (stabilizing) feedbacks can then be properly targeted.

The construction of material budgets for each catchment that requires management is an onerous task, although some progress using simple models has recently been made in Australia (National Land and Water Resources Audit 2001). However, these model-based estimates have only been used to calculate flows and some depositional stocks. Feedback and delays are neglected. Documenting all of the key concepts of catchment dynamics may ultimately be possible by system modelling, but at the moment must rely upon classification of system types in the hope that sufficient is known about unmonitored catchments to place them into a particular class.

Wasson and Sidorchuk (2000) have advanced a two end-member classification of catchment sediment system types. In most agricultural landscapes, at the extremes, the source of sediment is dominated by either sheet and rill erosion of hillslopes, or by gully and stream bank erosion. There are obviously intermediate cases. Figure 11.2 is reproduced from Wasson and Sidorchuk (2000), and depicts the temporal dynamics of key depositional stocks and flows for the end-members.

Type A is dominated by sheet and rill erosion. The erosion rate (flows from source stocks) reaches a quasi-equilibrium with erosive land uses (ELU), provided that climatic conditions are constant or their changes are unimportant. A lag between ELU and erosion rate can occur if soil condition takes time to deteriorate, after land-cover/land-use change, before erosion increases or decreases substantially. Once deterioration has occurred, particularly of soil structure decline and loss of organic matter, ELU and erosion rate approximately parallel each other until the soil is completely eroded. Sedimentation in valley floors (depositional stocks) absorbs most of the material eroded from hillslopes, and the rate of sedimentation peaks after the erosion rate has become nearly constant. Yield from the catchment is a small fraction of the

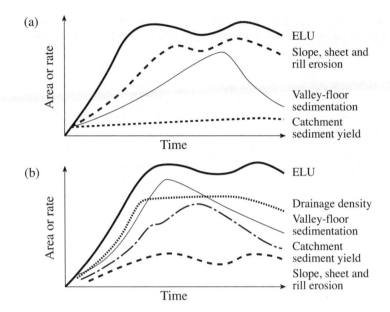

Figure 11.2   Summary diagrams of system types (a) and (b) showing the
erosive land use (ELU) and catchment response for the simple
case of erosive land use arising after settlement/clearing to a
near constant value. In both, the horizontal axis represents
approximately 200 years

erosion rate, because of sedimentation, but increases as the valley-floor depositional stocks saturate. Here is a negative feedback, that is, a process that
increases the elevation of the floodplain beyond the reach of many floods with
a consequent reduction in sedimentation in the valley-floor stock.

   Type B is dominated by gully and channel erosion. The stream channel
network grows by gullying then becomes constant where each fingertip of the
network reaches its limit set by runoff rate, as described earlier. Sedimentation
rate in valley-floor stocks peaks early, and negative feedback is caused as
deposition on floodplains decreases the rate. That is, sedimentation on floodplains raises them above the level of floods until they are no longer inundated
and sedimentation ceases. The sediment that would have been stored on the
floodplain stock now flows downstream, some of which is stored in channel
stocks (as bars or on the channel bed), while the rest contributes to catchment
yield. Sediment yield is a much higher proportion of total erosion than is the
case in Type A, and peaks twice: once as drainage density (length of chan-
nels/unit area of catchment) rapidly increases but before valley-floor sedimentation peaks; and second at or soon after drainage density reaches a

maximum. Yield then declines as channels stabilize, and some small channels are infilled by sediment eroded from adjacent hillslopes. Sheet and rill erosion behaves as in Type Λ.

Depending on which of these types occurs in a particular catchment, or part of a catchment, control and remediation strategies should differ. In the case of the catchment of Lake Burley Griffin, in Australia, catchment management authorities assumed that the catchment is of Type A. Management was therefore targeted at reducing hillslope sheet and rill erosion by constructing adsorption banks and promoting improved pastures and low stocking rates. Wasson et al. (1998) demonstrated that the catchment is of Type B, and that most of the management effort had been wasted given the aim of reducing sediment yield to the lake. The management effort had improved farm management, and probably productivity, although this has not been quantified; nor was it the aim of the managers.

Wasson and Sidorchuk (2000) concluded that Types A and B, and the intergrades, should be more fully documented, to discover where and how commonly they occur. This is essential if the classification is to be used for catchments where monitoring has not occurred.

A second example involves phosphorus (P), a crucial nutrient in agriculture and a major causative agent of eutrophication. Phosphorus budgets have been used for many years to guide catchment management aimed at controlling eutrophication and simultaneously reducing the input costs of fertilizers on farms. The study by Bennett et al. (1999) of the Lake Mendota catchment in the USA is a good example of this type of study. Figure 11.3 summarizes the results, showing that fertilizer dominates inputs, yield is a small fraction of the inputs and almost as much P is stored in the catchment as is exported in agricultural products. It has to be assumed that all components of the budget have been accounted for and that there is no erosion of non-fertilizer P (so-called 'native P') from subsoils exposed by gullies and channels. There appears to be no sewage source, although the authors describe increasing urbanization.

If this catchment were managed so that fertilizer P application each year equalled the quantity of P exported in agricultural produce, assuming that this would not reduce productivity, then the current stock of fertilizer P would be removed in more than 260 years. This is a significant delay.

The P sequestered in soil is a 'chemical time bomb', according to Bennett et al. (1999), because it could be released by extreme erosion or by acid precipitation. Certainly as P concentration increases in surface soils, the same magnitude erosion event repeated over time will move more and more P.

The example is instructive because it provides both insights into the behaviour of P in this catchment, and clear understanding on which to base policy and management decisions. But if at least the outline of this budget was used in a different catchment type, major components of the budget would be missing

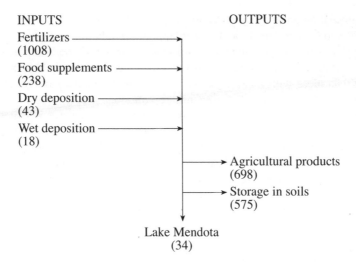

INPUTS   OUTPUTS

Fertilizers
(1008)

Food supplements
(238)

Dry deposition
(43)

Wet deposition
(18)

→ Agricultural products
(698)

→ Storage in soils
(575)

Lake Mendota
(34)

Note: Quantities in brackets are X 10³kg P/yr.

Source: Derived from data in Bennett et al. (1999)

Figure 11.3   Phosphorus budget for Lake Mendota catchment

and management would be poorly guided. This is equivalent to using insights gained from a Type A sediment system to manage a Type B catchment.

Wallbrink et al. (1996) and Caitcheon et al. (1995) show that in the Murrumbidgee River catchment of southern Australia, the majority of P in the river is natural ('native P'). About 90 per cent of the suspended sediment in the Lower River comes from channel banks and gully walls, and is subsoil material. Because most of the P in the river is particulate and is mobilized by erosion, most of it comes from the same source as the fine sediment. Particulate P concentrations in the river sediments are consistent with those observed in the fine fractions of catchments soils, supporting the idea that most of the P is natural. Point source input from sewage treatment works is quantitatively unimportant. This example demonstrates the need for material budgets, and classifications of budget types like those presented by Wasson and Sidorchuk (2000). If the implications of the Lake Mendota results were applied to the Murrumbidgee catchment, serious errors would result.

Calculating the Cost of Remediation and Control

It is a simple logical step to conclude that material budgets should guide policy and management in the cases just described, and that calculations of the costs of remediation and control also should be based on budgets. Van der Veeren (1998) shows how this logic has been applied to reduce non-point source or dissipative nutrient emissions in European catchments. He demonstrated how sources that have the lowest remediation (abatement) costs should be reduced more than those with relatively high costs, so as to achieve reduced nutrient emissions at least cost. Reducing nitrate emissions where sources include sewage, agriculture, waste water treatment plants, and construction sites and urban runoff, it is concluded that because abatement costs for construction site and urban runoff are very high, their emissions will be reduced only a little. On farms, the highest priority should be given to reducing nitrate emissions from arable sands. The risk to water pollution of fertilizer application to sandy soils is reduced at least cost compared to other soil types, and sewage treatment.

A similar but more straightforward case from Western Australia is reported by Young and Evans (1997). Nitrate and phosphorus concentrations in Geographe Bay, 100 km south of Perth, were unacceptably high. A proposal to dispose of effluent, from the Busselton Waste Water Treatment Plant, by irrigating a woodlot to produce timber, would cost A\$4.5 million over five years. Running costs would be A\$0.5 million each year. This was an attractive option, comparable to policies adopted in the Murray–Darling catchment in eastern Australia where the management of eutrophication was first tackled by removing sewage treatment plant disposal from rivers. However, a material budget for the catchment of Geographe Bay showed that the proposed woodlot would have reduced the phosphorus inputs to the Bay by ~3 per cent, and nitrate inputs by ~1 per cent. Reduction of non-point emissions from farms is essential to have any impact on the Bay.

Effective Monitoring

> Erosion and sediment yield in any stream basin are rarely in a steady state. For monitoring environmental change, it is thus necessary to construct a sediment budget that accounts for storage fluxes within the basin during any time period (Trimble 1999).

If the purpose of monitoring the flow of material in a river is to determine the effectiveness of catchment management, the dynamics of the material budget must be understood before monitoring data can be interpreted. This is a plausible interpretation of the quote from Trimble. Monitoring of the effectiveness of riparian reafforestation and improvements in agricultural land management in the $360km^2$ catchment of Coon Creek (USA) by measuring sediment flow at its outlet would be a waste of time. Trimble (1999) shows that yield has been between 36 and 38×10^3 Mg/year between 1853 and 1993; a remarkably constant rate, despite large changes in erosional sources, erosion

Table 11.2   Elements of the Coon Creek catchment budget (derived from data in Trimble 1999)

Years	Erosional stock losses	Depositional stock accumulations	Yield
1853–1938	441	405	38
1938–1975	240	204	36
1975–1993	117	80	37

Note: Flows and accumulation rates are 10^3Mg/yr.

Source: After Trimble (1999).

stock losses and depositional stock accumulation rates (Table 11.2). Between the first and second periods, source flows decreased by 46 per cent, and between the second and third periods by a further 51 per cent. Deposition in stocks decreased by 30 per cent and 61 per cent during the same two time periods. Deposition therefore compensated for decreased erosion, and so yield was unchanged. Monitoring of yield alone would have led to the conclusion that better land management had achieved nothing. Evidence from the budget indicates that erosion has been reduced and flood flows are less severe because of better land management.

Designing Appropriate Economic Instruments

Only recently has the design of economic instruments for non-point pollution control become a priority for environmental protection (Shortle and Horan 2001). Charges, subsidies, trading, contracts and emission proxies have all been considered in a literature, which Shortle and Horan describe as largely theoretical and aimed at finding instruments that have economically appealing properties. These authors emphasize the 'challenging informational issues inherent in the problem', particularly when compared to the control of point sources. The information challenge derives from the difficulty of monitoring huge numbers of non-point source flows, the stochastic nature of the flows, the difficulty of directly and unambiguously relating land management process, pollutant emissions and human decision-making. Shortle and Horan also identify major research gaps, particularly on monitoring and enforcement mechanisms, behaviour of people where collective penalty or reward mechanisms are used and where multiple instruments are applied. Furthermore, they conclude that the greatest advances will be made by empirical research designed to illuminate and test theory.

The review by Shortle and Horan demonstrates that much of the theoretical work on economic instruments is sophisticated to the point of being well ahead of other empirical studies of both instruments and natural science. It is likely that by using budget as a guide to both the location within a catchment and the types of source stocks that dominate the budget, it will be possible to inform the choice of emission proxies.

The design of taxes and standards for emissions by Griffin and Bromley (1982) assumes that the proxies for emissions (for example land uses, climate, production and pollution control practices) are a perfect substitute for measured emissions and that the emissions are not stochastic (Shortle and Horan 2001). These assumptions are unnecessarily restrictive because the statistical relationship between proxies and average annual emissions is likely to be all that is available in most catchments, and stochastic behaviour cannot be assumed away. A factor of safety approach, like that applied in engineering, may be a way of including the rare high magnitude concentration such as an intense summer rainstorm on a fallow field beside a stream. The factor of safety would be calculated from the few well-studied sites in a region or country, and applied to other catchments.

Approaches of this kind, while mathematically inelegant, are most likely to be practical. The need from empirical research called for by Shortle and Horan is clear, using budgets to guide the construction of practical economic instruments.

CONCLUDING REMARKS

Budgets of material, information and even human capital have wide application, both actual and potential. The large number of academic disciplines that already use budgets, specifically adopting the stock and flow concept, indicate that a conceptual framework already exists for many fruitful interdisciplinary interactions. Quantification of stocks and flows, and identification of feedbacks and delays, are all well advanced in the natural sciences and economics for the purposes of natural resource and environmental analysis and management. Much remains to be done to include ideas like social capital, particularly with regard to feedbacks.

While conceptual development is advanced, and applications widespread, use for management purposes is still limited. Leaving aside the contested idea that whole-of-system thinking is not natural to humans, the other reason for poor uptake may be narrow technical training of managers and insufficient time and/or resources to carry out the necessary data collection and analysis. The best way forward is likely to be for academics, policy-makers, and managers to work together to use budgets for joint analyses of environmental, economic and social issues; to both analyse existing conditions and identify better futures.

BIBLIOGRAPHY

Arthur, W.B. 1987. *Self-reinforcing mechanisms in economics.* Reading, MA: Addison-Wesley. Santa Fe Institute Studies in Complexity.

Arthur, W.B. 1990. Positive feedback in the economy. *Scientific American.* February: 92–9.

Becker, G.S. 1993. *Human capital.* Chicago: University of Chicago Press.

Bennett, E.M., Read-Anderson, T., Houser, J.N., Gabriel, J.R. and Carpenter, S.R. 1999. A phosphorus budget for the Lake Mendota Watershed. *Ecosystems.* 2: 69–75.

Caitcheon, G., Donnelly, T., Olive, L., Olley, J., Murray, A., Short, D., Wallbrink, P. and Wasson, R.J. 1995. *Sources of suspended sediment and phosphorus to the Murrumbidgee River.* CSIRO Division of Water Resources, Consultancy Report 95–32. Canberra: CSIRO.

David, P. 1995. *Technical choice, innovation and economic growth.* New York: Cambridge University Press.

Georgescu-Roegen, N. 1971. *The entropy law and the economic process.* Cambridge, MA: Harvard University Press.

Griffin, R.C. and Bromley, D.W. 1982. Agricultural runoff as a nonpoint externality: a theoretical development. *American Journal of Agricultural Economics.* 64: 547–52.

Gunderson, L.H. and Holling, C.S. (eds). 2002. *Panarchy: understanding transformation in human and natural systems.* Washington, DC: Island Press.

Hall, C., Lindenmayer, D., Kummel, R., Kroger, T. and Eichhorn, W. 2001. The need to reintegrate the natural sciences with economics. *BioScience.* 51: 663–73.

Holling, C.S. 2001. Understanding the complexity of economic, ecological and social systems. *Ecosystems.* 4: 390–405.

Jervis, R. 1997. *System effects: complexity in political and social life.* New Jersey: Princeton University Press.

Kneese, A.V., Ayers, R.V. and D'Arge, R.C. 1970. *Economics and the environment: a material balance approach.* Baltimore: Resources for the Future, The Johns Hopkins Press.

Krishna, A. 2001. Moving from the stock of social capital to the flow of benefits: the role of agency. *World Development.* 29: 925–43.

Kuhn, T.S. 1962. *The structure of scientific revolutions.* Chicago: University of Chicago Press.

Leontieff, W. 1982. Academic economics. *Science.* 217: 104–7.

National Land and Water Resources Audit. 2001. *Australia agriculture assessment.* Vol. 2. Canberra: Commonwealth of Australia.

Putnam, R.D. 1995. Bowling alone: America's declining social capital. *Journal of Democracy.* 6: 65–78.

Shortle, J.S. and Horan, R.D. 2001. The economics of nonpoint pollution control. *Journal of Economic Surveys.* 15: 255–89.

Smil, V. 1997. *Cycles of life: civilization and the biosphere.* New York: Scientific American Library.

Sterman, J.D. 2000. *Business dynamics: systems thinking and modelling for a complex world.* Boston: Irwin McGraw-Hill.

Thomas, L. 1974. *The lives of a cell: notes of a biology watcher*. New York: Viking Press.

Trimble, S.W. 1983. A sediment budget for Coon Creek basin in the Driftless area, Wisconsin, 1853–1977. *American Journal of Science*. 283: 454–74.

Trimble, S.W. 1999. Decreased rates of alluvial sediment storage in the Coon Creek Basin, Wisconsin 1975–93. *Science*. 285: 1244–6.

van der Veeren, R. 1998. Dissipative emissions: manageable or inevitable? In: Vellinga, P., Berkhout, F. and Gupta, J. (eds). *Managing a material world: perspectives in industrial ecology*. Dordrecht: Kluwer, pp. 217–28.

Vellinga, P., Berkhout, F. and Gupta, J. (eds). 1998. *Managing a material world: perspectives in industrial ecology*. Dordrecht: Kluwer.

Waldrop, M.M. 1992. *Complexity*. London: Penguin.

Wallbrink, P.J., Olley, J.M., Murray, S. and Olive L.J. 1996. The contribution of channel banks and gully walls to total phosphorus loads in the Murrumbidgee River. *Proceedings: First National Conference on Stream Management in Australia, Merrijig*, pp. 1–6.

Wasson, R.J., Mazari, R.K., Starr, B. and Clifton, G. 1998. The recent history of erosion and sedimentation on the Southern Tablelands of southeastern Australia: sediment flux dominated by channel incision. *Geomorphology*. 24: 291–308.

Wasson, R.J. and Sidorchuk, A.Y. 2000. History for soil conservation and catchment management. In: Dovers, S. (ed). *Environmental history and policy: still settling Australia*. Melbourne: Oxford, pp. 97–117.

Wilen, J.W. 1973. A model of economic system-ecosystem interaction. *Environment and Planning*. 5: 409–20.

Young, M.D. and Evans, R. 1997. *Right opportunity: using rights markets to manage diffuse groundwater pollution*. Occasional Paper Land & Water Resources Research and Development Corporation, Occasional Paper 1997/27. Canberra: LWRRDC.

12. Expanding the concept of flows and developing frameworks for linking social, economic and environmental accounting systems: two approaches for integration

Sasha Courville

Conventional approaches within international trade policy and research have failed to address how social and ecological sustainability could be integrated into analysis and practice. Two main reasons account for this. First, research and policy have traditionally divided a very complex and multifaceted international trade system into discrete components and levels of analysis. As most social and ecological costs lie across various production and consumption activities, a wider unit of analysis is needed: the entire production-to-consumption system. Furthermore, there is a lack of integrative and interdisciplinary approaches to bring together social, economic, ecological and organizational dimensions of production, trade and consumption across local to global spatial scales. The first section of this chapter discusses why an integrative approach is needed in the study of international trade and sustainability.

The second section outlines two possible approaches for research and policy development into sustainable trade. The first is an integrative report card based on elements of life-cycle analysis, sustainability indicators, social and environmental auditing, accounting and reporting. The second approach is an expansion of the concept of flows analysis. Material and energy flows, monetary flows and information flows are each examined individually through the production-to-consumption system before exploring the dynamics between them. In illustrating these approaches, production-to-consumption examples of coffee are used.

The last section summarizes how the two approaches examined can overcome the problems highlighted here facing traditional disciplinary research and policy on international trade and how they help to provide new frameworks in which social justice and ecological protection concerns can be integrated into international trade analysis.

WHY IS AN INTEGRATIVE APPROACH NEEDED?

For researchers and policy-makers, the relationship between international trade, environmental protection and social justice is a difficult one. In an increasingly interdependent world, activity in international trade is one of the most important factors in determining a country's prospects for development (Brack 1995: 498–499; Grossman and Helpman 1995: 238; Repetto 1994; Wallace 1996: 84; World Bank 1997: 97). However, international trade is also seen as a major threat to social justice and equity issues in global development (Arden-Clarke 1992: 125; George 1990; Khor 1993). There are theoretical arguments and evidence in practice to demonstrate that international trade can be both damaging and beneficial for environmental and social justice objectives. Making sense of these complex and divergent perspectives requires new research frameworks capable of integrating different kinds of disciplinary learning across a number of scales of analysis.

While there is a strong imperative to ensure that international trade moves towards more socially and ecologically sustainable outcomes, governments, industry and communities have had great difficulty in making any substantive systemic progress in this arena. This is due to a fundamental mismatch between the traditional focus of analysis and practice and the broader context in which the social and environmental implications of trade policies are played out.

From International Trade to Production-to-consumption Systems

Conventional approaches within international trade policy and research have failed to address how social and ecological sustainability could be integrated into analysis and practice. One main reason for this is that political and economic theories of trade have traditionally divided a very complex and multifaceted international trade system into discrete components and levels of analysis. For example, while macroeconomic theory analyses national level dynamics and microeconomic theory focuses on the firm level, international trade theory has emphasized market transactions. Trade theory has generally paid limited attention to consumption processes, emphasizing instead production activities at an aggregate level. As most social and ecological costs lie in concrete production-related processes and in consumption as well as in the trade sphere, a wider lens or unit of analysis is needed across a number of spatial levels: the entire production-to-consumption system and other social and environmental systems that it interacts with. This, however, requires new research frameworks and methodologies that expand the research unit to the entire production-to-consumption system including the producer of raw materials through to processing and packaging, wholesale and retail sales as well as final consumption and disposal by the end-consumer.

One of the reasons for the narrow determination of boundaries in trade research to date is the influence of the political and legal institutions that regulate production, trade and consumption activities. While certain national governments have begun to move environmental and industry policy in this direction for production-to-consumption systems that lie entirely within their jurisdiction, a production-to-consumption focus across international trade challenges a number of current concepts embedded in international trade law.

Article I of GATT contains the Most Favoured Nation (MFN) clause stating that any trade advantage granted by any contracting party to any product either for import or export must also be applied to any like product originating from any other contracting party (GATT 1947 Art. I(1)). In other words, there can be no discrimination between any like products from any member state. In Article III of GATT, the National Treatment clause states that the treatment of like products, whether domestic or imported, must be equal with respect to internal taxes and regulations (GATT 1947 Art. III (1)).

One of the most contentious issues in the trade and environment debate hinges on the definition of the word 'like product' used in both of these articles. The definition of a 'like product' implies 'similar in characteristics and uses' (Berg 1996). As the definition is open to interpretation, World Trade Organization (WTO) dispute settlement panels have generally interpreted the definition of a like product to include product-related 'production and process methods' (PPMs) but not non-product-related process methods (OECD 1995: 7–8; Ward 1997: 141). Therefore, if people can physically detect a difference between two products then they are not like products. For example, paper that is 75 per cent recycled and paper that is made with 100 per cent virgin fibre are not like products. However, timber that has been sustainably managed and timber cut by unsustainable logging practices causing widespread deforestation and biodiversity loss cannot be distinguished in international law as they are like products.

The issue of PPMs raises tremendous questions about the compatibility of the environment and trade dimensions. Does a country have a right to control its own environmental and social impacts of consumption? If so, then production and process methods must be taken into account. If not, then in an arena of increased international trade with Most Favoured Nation and National Treatment requirements, governments and domestic industries that address environmental and social justice production and process methods issues in domestic policy and legislation will be 'under continual siege from those concerned with international competitiveness' (Ekins et al. 1994). Without clarification on the issue of PPMs in international trade, internalization of environmental and social costs cannot occur (see Arden-Clarke 1998).

The greatest criticism in recent years in the PPM debate has come from developing countries, with the concern that the ability to discriminate between the PPMs would in effect amount to eco-imperialism where the North imposes its own environmental standards on others (Bhagwati 1993). A central concern is that incorporating PPMs into international trade would result in destroying the basis for comparative advantage as it ignores the fact that countries have unique socio-economic and ecological conditions that underlie production cost structures (Brack 1995: 505–506). Environmental impacts and their severity also vary across countries and regions. Trade can reduce the total impact by allocating damaging activities to where they cause the least damage. It is also true that people in different countries in different life situations hold different value systems with respect to the environment. On a practical level, a further concern is that actually taking PPMs into account in international trade would result in high information and complex evaluation costs (Esty and Geradin 1998: 29).

These concerns must be addressed while, at the same time, there is an urgent need to consider the full impact of international trade from production to consumption (Arden-Clarke 1998). How to take into account these concerns and still address the issue of PPMs is extremely complex. Integrative and appropriate research and policy tools that start with the entire production-to-consumption system as the unit of analysis are urgently needed.

Tools Needed for Integrative and Interdisciplinary Approaches

A second main reason for the failure of conventional approaches to integrate social and ecological sustainability into international trade analysis and practice is the lack of integrative and interdisciplinary approaches to bring together social, economic, ecological and organizational dimensions of production, trade and consumption across local to global spatial scales.

The 'real' world, made up of structures, systems and actors that we study, is not compartmentalized by disciplines. Academic institutions have created these logical divisions to make research manageable. However, no single discipline or area would be able to effectively and comprehensively address the complexities of the relationship between social justice, ecological protection and international trade. As such, disciplinary boundaries are less useful and new transdisciplinary research is needed. The following list outlines a number of fields and disciplines that examine some aspect of the dynamics between international trade, environment and development or social justice: geography, anthropology, management studies, international law, psychology, international relations, political economy, organizational theory, ecology, accounting, commerce, philosophy, engineering, development studies, trade theory, sociology, economics and human ecology, among others. Each of these would examine the relationship with a particular lens and theoretical understanding of the world.

We need to develop new research and policy frameworks that can draw on the learning gained from various disciplines in building more sophisticated analytical tools to examine such complex systems. Social, ecological, economic and institutional dimensions have each tended to be the focus of particular disciplines. While examining one of these dimensions on its own has value for particular research purposes, where the research or policy goal is to better integrate social and environmental concerns into international trade, the focus must be on examining the interactions between these different dimensions.

The question of scale is a further complication facing disciplinary research frameworks. International trade, in its expanded conceptualization, spans across local, national and global scales of analysis. While there are many local foci in a production-to-consumption system, from the producer in the field or the importer in the warehouse to the consumer in the supermarket, these constitute one level of analysis. There are also national regulatory frameworks that impact on the same production-to-consumption system ranging from minimum wage legislation to sanitary and phytosanitary requirements. A further global level of analysis includes the impacts of international trade law, or global environmental issues such as biodiversity protection and carbon sequestration on the production-to-consumption system. Traditional disciplinary policy and research frameworks examining international trade such as economics, trade theory and commerce, have tended to focus on one scale of analysis or another; however, given that each level has outcomes and implications for other levels, these need to be examined in an integrative way. Much can be learned by applying insight from disciplines with dynamic tools for spatial analysis such as geography to international trade research.

APPLICATIONS: TOOLS FOR INTEGRATION

This section presents two possible approaches for integrative research into sustainable trade. The first is an integrative report card while the second approach is an expansion of the concept of flows analysis to include material and energy flows, monetary flows and information flows applications to production-to-consumption systems. To illustrate these approaches, examples of their application to coffee production-to-consumption systems are presented.

Integrative Report Card

Tools to identify, measure and communicate various aspects of the interactions between human and environmental systems, both in terms of impacts and in terms of changes over time, have recently proliferated. These include environmental and social auditing and reporting techniques, life-cycle assessment and sustainability indicator sets. As the integrative report card draws from elements of each of these approaches, they are briefly presented here.

Environmental auditing and reporting techniques have developed from the disciplines of accounting, finance and economics, to address the environmental impacts of specific economic activities. While environmental auditing is seen as an internal management tool used by a company to assess and improve its environmental performance, environmental reporting is essentially a vehicle for external communication of the same issues to various stakeholders.

Where environmental auditing and reporting techniques have developed over the past decade, social auditing and reporting have been conspicuously absent until recently (Owen 1996). The practical application of social auditing and reporting tools has been limited to date by difficulties associated with the measurement of social dimensions, as well as the perception that addressing social justice issues could have far-reaching consequences for a company's activities. Like environmental auditing and reporting tools, their social counterparts are either applied as company-specific or site-specific tools.

Life cycle assessment (LCA) is an analytical tool originating from global modelling studies and energy audits of the late 1960s and early 1970s (World Resource Foundation 1995). Instead of a company focus, LCA is product-focused. The goal of the LCA is to describe and quantify all the environmental impacts along a given product chain, thus allowing for comparisons regarding the impacts of other products with the same or similar function. LCA widens environmental analysis beyond the environmental management system and site-specific production approaches as these can easily hide environmental impacts occurring up or down the supply chain. However, LCA is necessarily complex; if no boundaries are placed on the analysis, it becomes impossible to carry out. Difficulties with LCA include the high costs involved in gathering information, difficulties in evaluating impacts of disposal and decomposition, difficulties in comparing different environmental impacts and the lack of application to social and economic impacts (Schaltegger and Burritt 2000: 201–203; von Moltke et al. 1998: 29; Welford 1998: 144–146).

Sustainability indicator sets represent another measurement and communication tool, usually used in developing auditing and reporting frameworks. With the rise of sustainability as a key issue for policy-makers, a great deal of information is needed to guide policies and decisions to reduce negative impacts. Indicators can provide this information and can function as a measuring stick, by which we can evaluate how well we are accomplishing explicit goals.

Sustainability indicators are situated within a framework that crosses social, ecological and economic realms. The institutional realm is addressed in the literature as a separate category or as a part of the social or economic realms. While sustainability indicators have developed from a number of different disciplines, the natural sciences and economics feature most prominently. These sets have evolved from economic and environmental indicator approaches. As such, the types of indicators used and the values for measurement are generally restricted to numerical values, ruling out the possibility of qualitative indicators (Gallopin 1997: 17; OECD 1993; World Bank 1995). For social systems, a key dimension of sustainability, quantitative data presents problems. Indicators to ensure that social aspects are not ignored within the sustainability framework are essential. Yet, social concepts have been noted to be 'ultimately unmeasurable' or at least ' not adequately evaluated in monetary terms' (MacGillivray 1997; McKinley 1997).

The concepts of space and time impact on sustainability indicators. While auditing and reporting tools are focused on a particular corporation and while LCA is product-focused, most sustainability indicators are developed and applied for specific geographic spaces such as a particular region or country. Many indicator sets are designed to be applied at a number of levels from the community to the global level, creating tension between simplicity in analysis and ensuring that all critical factors and levels are covered (Dahl 1997: 72). With regard to time, indicator sets address two different types of information: information about the state of a given system and information about the position of these systems with respect to targets or goals (Bossel 1999: 11).

A range of frameworks have been developed for sustainability indicators including, among others, the Wuppertal model and subsequent variations such as the Compass stakeholder methodology as well as the Well-being of Nations (WON) system assessment model and the Barometer of Sustainability, both from the International Union for the Conservation of Nature (IUCN) (Kuhndt et al. 2002; Prescott-Allen 1999; Wuppertal Institute for Climate, Environment, Energy 1998). While each framework is undoubtedly useful for a particular industry sector or geographic region, it is hard to see how these systems could be applied across different spatial levels of analysis, through an entire production-to-consumption system. Given this, an integrative report card framework was specifically developed as a tool to evaluate the social, environmental and economic impacts of trade across a given production-to-consumption system.

The integrative report card is intended to show where social and ecological impacts lie within the production-to-consumption system and where changes have been made to move towards more sustainable practices. An explicit normative direction towards sustainability underlies the report card within which current status and practice can be situated. The integrative report card is developed based on a core set of principles.

First, the report card is presented within a framework of human systems embedded in ecological systems. It includes a number of sustainability indicators that can be understood to belong to social, environmental or economic dimensions, or a combination of these. The specific indicators chosen will vary depending on the production-to-consumption system examined, be it timber furniture, coffee or toys, but should in all cases include indicators representing a range of dimensions.

Second, given that the report card is intended to examine complete production-to-consumption systems, the indicators chosen should cover the main social, environmental and economic impacts along the supply chain. In this way, the report card draws from LCA concepts. However, each actor or specific location in the production-to-consumption system is evaluated independently using the report card. Some of the indicators may be relevant to many of the companies in the production-to-consumption system including indicators such as participation of women, energy use or fair wages/returns. Other indicators will be relevant only to specific points within the production-to-consumption system; for example, chemical inputs and pest management is only relevant for the production component of an agricultural production-to-consumption system. Given this supply chain focus, the report card spans across a range of nested spatial scales including the local level (producer's farm or an importer's warehouse), to the watershed or community level (the ecosystem in which the producer's farm is based or the consumer's town), to the national level (the exporting and importing countries with their respective regulatory regimes) and the international level.

Third, by differentiating between specific actors and locations in the production-to-consumption system, the report card can provide two different kinds of information: information about the state of the system and information about a specific company's performance with regard to the indicator. Most of the indicators in the report card address situations where actors have the ability to change their performance with regard to a specific indicator. For example, farmers have the ability to change agricultural practices to improve soil conservation on the farm; however, a broader indicator such as landscape management depends not only on farmers or their organizations but the broader community. Similarly, while stability of land tenure is a critical issue for long-term sustainability, it is not within the power of producers to control but within the power of the government, actors external to the production-to-consumption system. For such issues, while it makes no sense to rate the actors in terms of performance, the background information is still important to understand the range of possibilities and constraints. The match or mismatch between where social and environmental impacts are located and where the power and responsibility to address the impacts lies is a key issue to examine.

Fourth, the explicit normative direction of the integrative report card is presented through a vector ranking. The objective of the report card is to provide information on how well the production-to-consumption system and specific actors within it are doing in moving toward sustainable systems. For each performance indicator, the relevant actor(s) in the supply chain is evaluated through the vector ranking below.

Towards unsustainable systems/practices	1 2 3 4	Towards sustainable systems/practices

The rankings can be absolute or relative. A number of companies with the same function across different production-to-consumption systems can be compared with each other or companies can be compared against best international practice for that particular indicator and sector. For each indicator, the parameters for sustainability and the criteria by which the actors are judged need to be specified. Sustainability is off the scale; a ranking of four represents 'best' practice or 'best' state of system health within the unit of the production-to-consumption. While the data used to measure the status and performance of the production-to-consumption system actors include a range of both qualitative and quantitative types, the four-point structure allows for a common format across social, environmental and economic dimensions for measuring the status and performance of all indicators. A ranking out of four avoids fence sitting on a neutral number. The following is an example of its application to a production-to-consumption system of coffee.

One of the key indicators in determining whether a coffee production-to-consumption system is moving towards sustainability is soil conservation. Soil conservation can be considered to be a performance indicator as farming techniques can help to conserve soils and improve fertility. However, it should be noted that there are absolute limits depending on the initial condition, type and quality of the soils. Soil conservation is only significant at the production site. The criteria used to evaluate six coffee-producing communities of three producer-owned cooperative organizations in Mexico are as follows: the presence or absence of shade, number of nitrogen-fixing species and the use of specific farming techniques including the application of organic compost, the use of live barriers and terraces (where useful), leaf litter all year and the use of ground cover species. For this indicator, the parameter for evaluation was best national (Mexican) practice in soil conservation for coffee production. The rankings are shown in Table 12.1.

The coffee production systems rated extremely well for the indicator of soil conservation. Two communities scored below the rest because of a lack of soil conservation techniques. This in turn was caused by a lack of technical assistance. The higher scoring producer groups are also organically certified.

Table 12.1   Integrative report card: soil conservation at coffee producer community level

Regional or community level of producer organizations	Sustainability rating
Community A, producer organization 1	1 2 3 4 (4)
Community B, producer organization 1	1 2 3 4 (3)
Community A, producer organization 2	1 2 3 4 (4)
Community B, producer organization 2	1 2 3 4 (4)
Community A, producer organization 3	1 2 3 4 (4)
Community B, producer organization 3	1 2 3 4 (3)

Expanding the Concept of Flows Analysis

A second integrative approach for analysing the interactions between social justice, environmental protection and international trade is an expanded concept of flows analysis. This approach involves examining not only material and energy flows and monetary flows within the production-to-consumption system but also information and learning flows. Multidimensional and interdisciplinary flows analysis allows the researcher and policy-maker to examine the dynamics between the different sets of flows across international trade.

The study of material and energy flows can be situated within ecological economics, environmental engineering, metabolism studies of human systems, industrial ecology and ecological modernization, all fields in which environmental and economic issues are integrated in planning and design. Material and energy flows analysis is based on the laws of thermodynamics (see Ayres and Kneese 1989; Pearce and Turner 1990: 41). While founded on the same basic principles, there are many approaches for examining material and energy flows from lifecycle analysis of products and services, metabolism approaches, accounting models using stocks and flows and quantifying inputs and outputs with particular processes (see Hannon 1991), Odum's embodied energy or Emergy model (Odum 1998: 45; Odum 1996) and the Material Inputs per unit of Service model (see Hinterberger et al. 1997).

A simple material and energy flows analysis approach is described here for the coffee production-to-consumption system. Material input–output diagrams, based on the approach taken by Bayliss-Smith (Bayliss-Smith 1982), are developed for each key phase in the production-to-consumption system: production on farm, wet processing, dry processing, import/roasting, consumption and transport. All processes are then added together to get a single composite diagram of total material and energy flows. The composite diagram shows all the material and energy inputs into the system, the outputs, where the outputs go and the environmental sinks from the process. With coffee, very few materials actually flow through the system, while energy makes up the vast majority of physical flows. Material stocks such as the land, wet and dry processing machinery, warehouses and transport infrastructure are identified but are not considered in the flows analysis given that the main objective in using this approach is to compare different production processes where the material stocks are relatively similar. While simple, the diagrams are useful for highlighting differences between production-to-consumption systems, such as between organically certified and intensive chemical input coffee systems. Figure 12.1 is an example of an organically certified coffee production-to-consumption system. The data shown are averages for 1 kg of coffee.

The study of monetary flows is well entrenched into the disciplines of finance, economics and accounting. Monetary flows are commonly discussed at a macro level, such as exploring the movement of capital into and out of particular regions of the world through trade, investment and aid (Guitian 1999). They can also be examined within a given firm or supply chain (see Rich 1999). In the context of a production-to-consumption system, monetary flows analysis involves an assessment of the movement of money in the

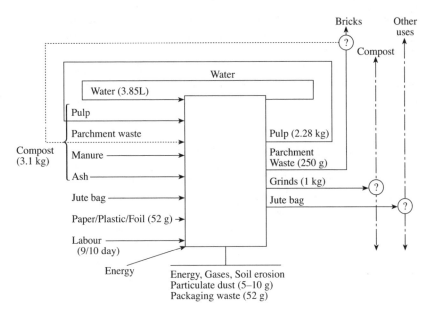

Figure 12.1   Organic production-to-consumption system composite

system, including credit, payment for inputs and outputs or for goods and services, operational costs and the distribution of profit between actors. It is used in this framework to compare the monetary flows both within and between production-to-consumption systems of the same product.

A monetary flows approach applied to production-to-consumption systems is a good tool to compare prices received for coffee and the value-adding of capital at every stage, both between different production-to-consumption case studies and between companies in each system. The methodology is simple though gaining access to data for the analysis may not be. Returning to the coffee production-to-consumption system example, for each actor in the supply chain, the prices received for one unit of coffee[1] (1 kg) are recorded. This would range from the producer's farm gate price to the exporter's sale price to the wholesale price received by the retailer and the final retail price paid by the consumer. Operating costs and profit margins are also considered. Other values can be examined to put the monetary flows in context including the total volume of product sold or traded and total sales of coffee per supply chain actor. Standard values for comparison purposes can be used such as a generalized price that producers receive in the region from intermediaries, average New York C market prices compared to the export–import contract price, and the average consumer prices for different quality bands of coffee.

A key result from this approach is the distribution of the monetary flows in a given production-to-consumption system, including the percentage of the final retail price that the producer receives. If production-to-consumption systems are compared, significant differences between national markets can be found including different levels of competition on the part of processors and retailers and large differences in consumer prices. Based on this approach, people could evaluate a number of issues including the impact of price fluctuations in the supply chain and examine impact of fair trade, organic and other market-based certification tools on monetary flows.

While the study of monetary flows is widely used and material and energy flows analysis is becoming more common in certain fields, expanding the concept to the metaphor of information flows is relatively new in examining the movement of processes towards sustainability. Information flows are increasingly the focus of business research, intrinsically linked to the study of management in the firm (see Ellis 2000; Park and Kim 1999; Verspagen 1999). Similarly, this is a growing area of research within economic geography (see French 2000; Hughes 2000; Morgan and Murdoch 2000) and in the context of agricultural research and extension work (see Roling 1990). Most research into information flows has adopted a mechanistic approach. In the field of communication research, communication is either conceptualized as a series of actions and interactions where information flows from one person to another, or it is conceptualized as a relationship, a situated and co-constructed accomplishment (Berger and Chaffee 1987; Fiske 1990; Schement and Ruben 1993; Stewart 1997). While these are usually considered to be mutually exclusive positions, there is something to learn from each approach and that the former provides a baseline on which more complex issues can be examined using the second approach. The information flows analysis presented here is mechanistic; however, it lays the foundation for more sophisticated analysis of the relationships between different production-to-consumption actors across international trade.

In this approach, the actors involved in communication through the production-to-consumption system, and the vehicles or structures through which information can flow, are identified. The nature and type of information flowing through the system is examined. Different production-to-consumption systems can be examined for similarities and differences in their organizational structures and feedback mechanisms and the interactions and relationships between the actors can be examined.

One possible way to synthesize and analyse information flow data is through visual representation. In Figure 12.2, information flows are presented through three layers of analysis. The first is an organizational perspective, examining the size and structures of the networks including the core production-to-consumption system actors (producers, processors, exporters, importers, retailers, consumers) and other influential organizations. These are represented as clear square or rectangular boxes.

The second layer of analysis is an examination of the channels or modes of

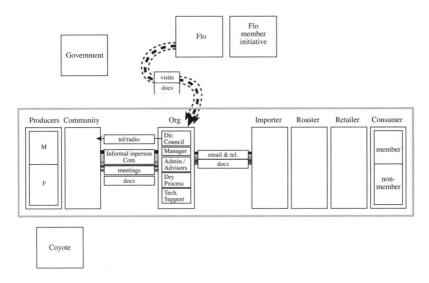

Figure 12.2   Information flows techniques

communication such as meetings, telephone, fax and email communication, written documents and third party inspections, including addressing issues such as capacity and multiplexity (number of relations between actors through the modes) of the channels. These are represented diagrammatically as small horizontal rectangles with the type of mode written on the box.

The third layer of analysis is a discussion of the information flows themselves, examining information flow symmetry, strength and intensity as well as different types of information flow such as financial information, environmental information, socio-economic information, technical information (agronomic), and so on. Depending on the particular sector, different types of information will flow through the production-to-consumption system. Different information types are allocated specific colours (or, as shown in Figure 12.2, different shades or patterns). The size of the information flows is a measure of the relative volume of information flowing through a particular mode of communication. Information flows can either move from one actor to another (indicated by directional arrows) or between actors (no arrows for simplicity). Where information flows are restricted, the flows are drawn as dotted lines. The figure illustrates one way in which information flows can be presented and analysed.

Once material and energy flows, monetary flows and information flows have each been developed for particular production-to-consumption systems, the analysis can be expanded to the dynamic interaction between these types of flows.

CONTRIBUTIONS OF INTEGRATIVE APPROACHES IN INTERNATIONAL TRADE POLICY AND RESEARCH

Two approaches have been presented here as possible tools to support integrative research and policy development into how to move towards more sustainable trade patterns. Both the integrative report card framework and the expanded flows analysis approach address two of the key challenges identified in this chapter facing disciplinary policy and research in examining the relationship between international trade, environment and development or social justice dimensions.

As discussed in the first section, a wider unit of analysis beyond discrete components and separate levels of analysis is necessary if we are to develop research and policy frameworks that support sustainable trade systems because most social and environmental impacts of trade lie beyond this narrow focus. As has been seen, sustainability report cards can be applied to the entire production-to-consumption system of any industry or sector with specific indicators chosen to examine key impacts at every stage in the supply chain and at different levels of analysis, from the local to the global. This also helps to clarify who has the power to make changes and allows each production-to-consumption system actor to focus on those activities that they can change. However, a focus on production-to-consumption system actors does not mean that other actors who impact on this system should not be evaluated as well. The role of governments and non-governmental regulatory actors such as private certification systems also need to be considered.

The report card is an integrative approach that addresses many of the difficulties facing disciplinary research. It provides a common normative framework within which indicators covering social, environmental, economic and organizational dimensions can be examined side by side. The criteria used to evaluate performance against the indicators can include a range of data types and the indicators themselves can be applied to a range of geographic spaces along the production-to-consumption system. They can also be applied to examine different levels of impact of the production-to-consumption system of any given commodity, from the local to the national or global level.

An expanded conceptualization of flows analysis is the second integrative approach presented. Given the nature of flows analysis, material and energy, monetary and information flows are well suited to the study of production-to-consumption systems, from producers through to the end consumers. In this way, the research and policy learning is expanded beyond the boundaries of international trade and is linked with production and consumption activities.

The flows concept and metaphor is a useful integrative framework to link three very different types of data from different disciplines in a meaningful way. While the application of each type of flows analysis to a given production-to-consumption system alone will yield important outcomes, the strength of the approach lies in the possibility of examining the interactions between material and energy flows, monetary flows and information flows. Examples of dynamic interaction leading to improved sustainability outcomes that can be analysed through integrated flows analysis are the following: improved product quality resulting in economic and environmental improvements due to improved feedback mechanisms; environmental improvements caused by a strengthening of technical assistance provided to farmers advocating recycling of nutrients and closing the production-to-consumption systems; improved access to time-sensitive capital by different actors in the production-to-consumption system leading to increased materials flow (coffee) and increased income to producers; premium prices received by producers based on increased and credible information flows through certification between producers and consumers about the social and environmental benefits of particular production systems.

While the report card and the expanded flows analysis are useful tools to expand the traditional focus of research and policy on international trade and to provide common frameworks for social, economic and ecological dimensions of research, these should be seen as two possible approaches that could complement disciplinary or other transdisciplinary research and policy development in the area of international trade and sustainability. Further research is needed to examine how these approaches can be applied to a diverse range of production-to-consumption systems and how to simplify the frameworks to reduce the amount of data needed or to improve supply chain management of that data.

NOTE

1. This needs to be adjusted for the differences in mass that take place during coffee processing from parchment to green and from green to roasted.

REFERENCES

Arden-Clarke, C. 1992. South–North terms of trade: environmental protection and sustainable development. *International Environmental Affairs.* 4: 122–37.

Arden-Clarke, C. 1998. Process and production methods. In: Brack, D. (ed). *Trade and environment: conflict or compatibility?* London: Earthscan, pp. 72–8.

Ayres, R. and Kneese, A. 1989. Externalities: economics and thermodynamics. In: Archibugi, F. and Nijkamp, P. (eds). *Economy and ecology: towards sustainable development.* Dordrecht: Kluwer Academic Publishers, pp. 89–118.

Bayliss-Smith, T.P. 1982. *The ecology of agricultural systems.* Cambridge: Cambridge University Press.

Berg, G.C. 1996. An economic interpretation of 'like product'. *Journal of World Trade.* 30: 195–209.

Berger, C.R. and Chaffee, S.H. (eds.). 1987. *Handbook of communication science.* Newbury Park: Sage Publications.

Bhagwati, J. 1993. The case for free trade. *Scientific American.* November: 18–23.

Bossel, H. 1999. *Indicators for sustainable development: theory, method and applications. A report to the Balaton Group.* Winnipeg: International Institute for Sustainable Development.

Brack, D. 1995. Balancing trade and the environment. *International Affairs.* 71: 497–512.

Dahl, A.L. 1997. The big picture: comprehensive approaches. Part one: introduction. In: Moldan, B., Billharz, S. and Matravers, R. (eds). *Sustainability indicators: a report on the project on indicators of sustainable development.* Chichester: John Wiley and Sons, pp. 69–83.

Ekins, P., Folke, C. and Costanza, R. 1994. Trade, environment and development: the issues in perspective. *Ecological Economics.* 9: 1–12.

Ellis, K.M. 2000. Strategic contexts, knowledge flows, and the competitiveness of MNCs: a procedural justice approach. *Competitiveness Review.* 10: 9–24.

Esty, D. and Geradin, D. 1998. Environmental protection and international competitiveness: a conceptual framework. *Journal of World Trade.* 32: 5–46.

Fiske, J. (ed). 1990. *Introduction to communication studies*. London: Routledge.
French, S. 2000. Re-scaling the economic geography of knowledge and information: constructing life assurance markets. *Geoforum*. 31: 101–19.
Gallopin, G.C. 1997. Indicators and their use: information for decision-making. In: Moldan, B., Billharz, Sj. and Matravers, R. (eds). *Sustainability indicators: a report on the project of indicators of sustainable development*. Chichester: John Wiley and sons, pp. 13–27.
GATT. 1947. General Agreement on Tariffs and Trade. Geneva.
George, S. 1990. *A fate worse than debt*. London: Penguin Books.
Grossman, G. and Helpman, E. 1995. *Innovation and growth in the global economy*. Cambridge: The MIT Press.
Guitian, M. 1999. Economic policy implications of global financial flows. *Finance and Development*. 36: 26–9.
Hannon, B. 1991. Accounting in ecological systems. In: Costanza, R. (ed). *Ecological economics: the science and management of sustainability*. New York: Columbia University Press, pp. 234–51.
Hinterberger, F., Luks, F. and Schmidt-Bleek, F. 1997. Material flows vs. 'natural capital'. What makes an economy sustainable? *Ecological Economics*. 22: 1–14.
Hughes, A. 2000. Retailers, knowledges and changing commodity networks: the case of the cut flower trade. *Geoforum*. 31: 175–90.
Khor, M. 1993. Free trade and the Third World. In: Nader, R. et al. (eds). *The case against free trade: GATT, NAFTA, and the globalization of corporate power*. San Francisco: Earth Island Press, pp. 97–107.
Kuhndt, M., von Geibler, J. and Eckermann, A. 2002. Developing a sectoral sustainability indicator set taking a stakeholder approach. In: *10th International Greening of Industry Network Conference*. Goteborg, Sweden.
MacGillivray, A. 1997. Social development indicators. In: Moldan, B., Billharz, S. and Matravers, R. (eds). *Sustainability indicators: a report on the project on indicators of sustainable development*. Chichester: John Wiley and Sons. pp. 257–63.
McKinley, T. 1997. Linking sustainability to human deprivation. In: Moldan, B., Billharz, S. and Matravers, R. (eds). *Sustainability indicators: a report on the project on indicators of sustainable development*: John Wiley and Sons, pp. 253–5.
Morgan, K. and Murdoch, J. 2000. Organic vs. conventional agriculture: knowledge, power and innovation in the food chain. *Geoforum*. 31: 159–73.
Odum, E. 1998. *Ecological vignettes: ecological approaches to dealing with human predicaments*. Amsterdam: Harwood Academic Publishers.
Odum, H.T. 1996. *Environmental accounting: EMERGY and environmental decision-making*. New York: Wiley.
OECD. 1993. *Organization for Economic Co-operation and Development core set of indicators for environmental performance reviews: a synthesis report by the Group on the State of the Environment*. Paris: OECD.
OECD. 1995. Report on trade and environment to the OECD Council at Ministerial Level. Paris: OECD.
Owen, D.L. 1996. A critical perspective on the development of European corporate environmental accounting and reporting. In: Institute of Environmental Studies. University of New South Wales. (ed). *Tracking progress: linking environment and economy through indicators and accounting systems*. Sydney: Australian Academy of Science Fenner Conference on the Environment, Institute of Environmental Studies.
Park, Y.T. and Kim, M.-S. 1999. A taxonomy of industries based on knowledge flow structure. *Technology Analysis and Strategic Management*. 11: 541–9.

Pearce, D. and Turner, R.-K. 1990. *Economics of natural resources and the environment*. New York: Harvester Wheatsheaf.

Prescott-Allen, R. 1999. The Wellbeing of Nations (WON) system assessment method. PADATA and The World Conservation Union.

Repetto, R. 1994. *Trade and sustainable development*. Geneva: UNEP.

Rich, N. 1999. Supply-chain management: the measurement 'wall'. *Logistics Focus*. 7: 26–31.

Roling, N. 1990. The agricultural research-technology transfer interface: a knowledge systems perspective. In: Kaimowitz, D. (ed). *Making the link: agricultural research and technology transfer in developing countries*. Boulder: Westview Press, pp. 1–42.

Schaltegger, S. and Burritt, R.L. 2000. *Contemporary environmental accounting: issues, concepts and practice*. Sheffield: Greenleaf Publishing.

Schement, J.R. and Ruben, B.D. (eds). 1993. *Between communication and information*. New Brunswick: Transaction Publishers.

Stewart, J. 1997. Developing communication theories. In: Philipsen, G. and Albrecht, T.L. (eds). *Developing communication theories*. Albany: State University of New York Press, pp. 157–92.

Verspagen, B. 1999. Large firms and knowledge flows in the Dutch RandD system: a case study of Philips Electronics. *Technology Analysis and Strategic Management*. 11: 211–33.

von Moltke, K., Kuik, O., van Der Grijp, N., Salazar, C., Banuri, T., Mupimpila, C., Inman, C., Mesa, N., Oleas, R. and de los Santos, J.J. 1998. *Global product chains: northern consumers, southern producers and sustainability*. Geneva: UNEP.

Wallace, D. 1996. *Sustainable industrialization*. London: Earthscan.

Ward, H. 1997. Trade and environment issues in voluntary eco-labelling and life cycle analysis. *Review of EC and International Environmental Law*. 6: 139–47.

Welford, R. (ed). 1998. *Corporate environmental management 1: systems and strategies*. London: Earthscan.

World Bank. 1995. *Monitoring environmental progress*. Washington, DC: World Bank.

World Bank. 1997. *Global economic prospects and the developing countries*. Washington, DC: World Bank.

World Resource Foundation. 1995. *Life cycle analysis and assessment*. Tonbridge: World Resource Foundation.

Wuppertal Institute for Climate, Environment, Energy. 1998. *Annual Report 1997/1998*. Wuppertal: Wuppertal Institute, p. 118.

Index

additive approach to research 39–40
Agenda 21 53
aggregation of data, and values 30–31
Apthorne, R. 57, 58
Arrow, K.J. 82, 129
Arthur, W.B. 181
assets, natural see natural assets

Bailes, K. 59
Becker, E. 56, 104, 105
Becker, G.S. 182
behavioural economics
    and environmental valuation 77–85
    see also economic psychology
Benartzi, S. 84
Bennett, E.M. 186
Bennett, J. 55
Bentham van den Bergh, G. van 57, 58
Bergh, J.C.J.M. van den 134
Berndt, E.R. 152–3
biodiversity
    protection priorities 131–2
    value of 31–2
Blaikie, P. 62
Bookchin, M. 59, 63–4
boreholes, effect on cattle stocking 167
Botswana rangelands, modelling 147–8,
    159–71
Boyden, S. 59, 61
Bromley, D.W. 190
Brookfield, H. 62
Bryant, R. 62

Caitcheon, G. 187
Capalbo, S.M. 157
capital–labour–energy trends 153–9
cattle stocking, Botswana rangelands
    163–71
CBA (cost–benefit analysis) and nature
    policy 127–8
certification and green products 97
charitable giving 94
Clark, J. 63

coevolution of values 32–3
coffee production-to-consumption
    system 201–6
cointegration modelling 147
Collier, P. 161
Collingwood, R. 55
Coming Anarchy, The 67
Common, M. 60
consumers, green motivation 96–8
context dependence of economic values
    78–84
contingent valuation method, natural
    assets 138
control costs, use of material budgets
    187–8
control targets, use of material budgets
    184–7
Coon Creek, catchment management
    188–9
Costanza, R. 2, 132
cost–benefit analysis, nature policy
    127–8
Crotty, M. 37
CVM (contingent valuation method),
    natural assets 138

Dahlberg, K. 55
Dalby, S. 67
Daly, H. 24, 28
Darby, J. 153
Dasgupta, P. 82
David, P. 181
De Jong, P. 155
decoupling of economic output and
    resources 152
delays in dynamic systems 183
developing countries, natural resource
    protection 136–7
development studies and sustainability
    57–9
Diamond, J. 59
Diamond, P.A. 84
disciplinary research 39

211